15 ̄mB

Bardot

also by Glenys Roberts

Metropolitan Myths

Bardot

A Personal Biography

by

GLENYS ROBERTS

SIDGWICK & JACKSON
LONDON

For my mother

First published in Great Britain in 1984
by Sidgwick & Jackson Limited

Copyright © 1984 by Glenys Roberts

Picture research by Annie Horton
Picture sections designed by Sue Hadden

ISBN 0-283-99103-8

Phototypeset by Falcon Graphic Art Ltd
Wallington, Surrey
Printed in Great Britain by
R.J. Acford, Industrial Estate, Chichester, Sussex
for Sidgwick & Jackson Limited
1 Tavistock Chambers, Bloomsbury Way
London WC1A 2SG

Contents

Preface

Jean Anouilh, the French playwright who was responsible for Brigitte Bardot's only stage performance, said that writers don't write about the past, they write about the future.

Life can imitate art in a bizarre fashion. Actors are especially victimized by this. Scenes which at the time appear to have no relevance to their personal lives are suddenly acted out years later perhaps, sometimes with tragic consequences. Natalie Wood bought herself a boat which she called *Splendour in the Grass* after the 1961 Kazan film in which she played a girl who tries to drown herself. Twenty years later Natalie, who had a healthy wariness of water, drowned off *Splendour in the Grass*. Julie Christie acted in a fine Nic Roeg film called *Don't Look Now* in which the pivotal opening scene shows a child drowning in Miss Christie's country pond. Some time later a friend's child did exactly this.

In just this way Bardot's life has been dogged by her plots, for good and for bad. To highlight this I have used the titles of her films as chapter headings. They are not always in the order of their making but, as Anouilh said, they don't have to be. Each film is also discussed in the text and there is a filmography at the end of the book which lists them chronologically. Most translations from the French throughout the story are my own.

So many people have been fascinated by Bardot over the last thirty years, and have theorized about every aspect of her, that it is possible I have overlooked the origins of some observations for which I am grateful all the same. My starting points were Louis Malle's witty and sympathetic truths about the nature of actresses over tea in New York, Roger Vadim's 'diabolical' lucidity on the subject of his ex-wife in his memoirs and face to face, and Alain Bougrain-Dubourg's charming television film about her. I appreciate Tony Crawley's sterling job in collecting together all the critical reactions to her films.

My thanks are particularly due to Peter Evans, Bardot's very first biographer, for his interest and encouragement all through my project; to Russell T. Grant for his astrological insights; to all my friends and acquaintances in the acting profession, many of whom are mentioned in the book itself, who shed light on their particular world; and to my colleagues in Paris. I must also thank John Byrne for his attention at the proof-reading stage, my daughter and her friends in class *quatrième quatre* for their French reading list and my friend Adrian George for his conversation; and Brigitte Bardot herself for providing ample inspiration.

Introduction

For most of the evening Brigitte Bardot sat on Gunther Sachs's knee. It was, after all, their wedding night. They had been married, and remarried for the cameras in Las Vegas and then flown by private Lear jet to Hollywood. Danny Kaye had been at the controls and now he was cooking them a Chinese dinner in the twin woks in his lean-to kitchen in Beverly Hills. There was a handful of other guests. I was one of them.

There scarcely seems to have been a time when Brigitte Bardot was merely a cinema star. She has always seemed like an event that happened to the world. When it was fashionable to be young, she was young, she married at the age young girls yearn to be wed. With liberation in the air she was liberated. She was informal at the right time, she lived in sin when sin was in. Professor Higgins would have been delighted with her – she showed a woman could be (almost) like a man. When women's lib became monotonous she discovered animal lib and now the frontiers of old age have receded, she has discovered that it is possible to be, at least in spirit, eternally young. And all these notions of hers were doubly, trebly beguiling because they came wrapped up in a physical package which no one could ignore.

Why her? Why should a suburban French girl with unorthodox looks and annoying views command such attention? It is a question she has often asked herself. What does it mean to be 'someone', her own description of fame? She asked it when she was a reluctant screen debutante, the freckled hope of France. She asks it now she has retired from public view to lead the life virtually of an 'open' prisoner in any one of several properties acquired with her considerable wealth. Why should people want to breach her privacy? What exactly is star quality?

No one is exempt from hero-worship, including the stars themselves, indeed none are more star-struck than they are and later in this book Bardot tells us about her own heroes. But there are heroes and heroes and only a very few are common to everyone. We usually know why we admire people, what skills they share with us and where we can learn from them. Once in a while, however, someone comes along who seems to have no particularly useful gifts. They may even seem to be the antithesis of acceptable fashion. At certain periods of history they might have been ostracized, stoned to death or burned at a stake. They are after all the visionaries, plugged into the roots of the psychology men share with the animals and with which most humans seem to have lost touch, but we hear them, for like the Pied Piper they play a magic tune which all of us follow. Their tune has not been learned like a role in a play, which is how most of us acquire our public identities, it comes from deep within their soul. Theirs are the needs and desires which we have obscured in ourselves and their resurrection of them is not a performance but an act of being. These people are then famous for being famous, in those famous modern words which are always uttered with more than a hint of contempt. There seems to be no hard work attached to such fame. It is all a colossal piece of luck – bad as well as good, a constellation of things unseen, a piece of timing.

We are all obsessed with this phenomenon in our century but it is hard to believe that it did not exist formerly. Nowadays of course news travels faster and wider, offering everyone the carrot of being famous for five minutes. Ben Hecht, the brilliant American screenwriter of *Front Page* and *Wuthering Heights*, the highest paid scenarist in the world while the child Bardot was growing up, recognized this phenomenon way before Andy Warhol exploited it in the sixties (Hecht died in 1964). He wrote in his biography *A Child of the Century*:

There is also a new sort of fame in our day . . . seemingly invented out of whole cloth, needing only a press agent to keep it alive. People become famous who are no more than advertisements. They are famous for stopping in hotels, for holding hands in public, for speaking to each other, for having babies, for getting invited to parties. This is true not only of movie stars but of statesmen and mountain climbers.

A depersonalized citizenry avid for identity has invented this new type of fame. The lonely city dwellers elect representatives to live for them. Our new type of famous ones rumba for us, answer erudite questions on the television for us, cohabit for us, marry and divorce for us, and even lie in hospitals battling diseases for us . . . such a one is Bardot.

When Hecht wrote those words Bardot was at the height of her scandalous fame, juggling nudity, suicide attempts, sunworshipping, divorces, child neglect and the odd film part in some three-ringed circus of neuroses. The parts got the least attention for the critics were always so surprised that she could actually stand upright, they rarely paid any attention to her acting. It is not easy for people to know how to deal with superstars. Do you stand open-mouthed at their overwhelming charisma, like press agents in public, or do you take a bitchy swipe at them to show your sophisticated judgement, like the same press agents behind their backs? Indefinable star quality often seems both a personal affront to intelligent members of the human race and a huge source of animal excitement. Everyone must decide whether he is a courtier or above the issue. If you last in the limelight in these circumstances for thirty years for no particular reason as Bardot has, it must be attributed to a fabulous confluence of forces, which says a lot about the times in which we live. Other people have been sexy, blonde, childlike, witty, profligate, and anti-social but very few have survived the heavy destiny of multiple scrutiny. You may baulk at the idea that Brigitte Bardot has something in common with everyone alive today, but you cannot dispute the fact that the Western world has undergone a sexual revolution which has affected everyone, and so strongly that we are now embarking on a moral backlash, which indicates that it is exactly the right time to put into perspective the Bardot years in a way which could never have been done before.

Everyone has a Bardot story from the permissive years, often a funny, innocent one. Thousands of girls, even millions, dyed their hair, blacked their eyebrows and practised their pouts in front of the mirror at home. The results failed on the whole to drive the opposite sex crazy, only the parent generation who could never get inside the bathroom door. A fashion grew up among teenage and much older girls of wearing braces in the mouth to distort the upper lip a whole twenty-five years after Brigitte admitted she had actually needed them for her teeth as a child. It didn't matter whether you lived in France, England, America or on the other side of the world. In Australia one girl who was at boarding school when the first Bardot films were being shown, remembers making a pact with all the girls in the dorm not to break into a smile for six months because Bardot had decreed that the way to look sexy was to be languid and sullen and never to react to anything. In America I lived my own Bardot story when I spent the evening of her third wedding with her.

That night everyone treated Bardot and Sachs like prize specimens. They were rich, young, foreign, famous, and in love. It was an evening for voyeurs. All day people had behaved like courtiers at a medieval wedding. The knot was tied and now, on behalf of the whole world, the privileged few who were left behind expected to see the blood on the sheets. Except that there would be no blood on the sheets. These newly-weds had something much more immediately interesting to the public than a future. They had a past.

I knew that Brigitte, since the age of fourteen, had driven men mad. Every working man had a picture of the pouting sex kitten in his private cubbyhole. Every schoolboy fulfilled his first sexual fantasies to her image in a glossy magazine. Every schoolgirl wished she knew how this sort of power was won. Feminist intellectuals like Simone de Beauvoir debated the baby doll syndrome in print. Interest in Brigitte was not confined to her image on the screen – her private life was just as provocative. She could hardly wait for the age of consent before she married Roger Vadim. How exotic he seemed at the time because of his Russian ancestry, and how menacing too – the ultimate manipulator, upwardly, internationally, artistically, sexually mobile. A Svengali not only of the cinema but also of public taste. He endorsed Brigitte's change from a brunette to a blonde and created a fashion which would be a language for more than twenty years. People who had never met either of them adopted the long-haired, wayward look. He re-created Brigitte in countless look-alike successors, starting with Annette Stroyberg, mother of his first child. He could even mould for a while a strong personality like Jane Fonda, whom he had married the year before.

For it was Brigitte who left Vadim. She left him for Jean-Louis Trintignant, a byword for sex appeal in his time, who played her lover in *And God Created Woman*. Vadim directed his bride in a film about adultery and watched Trintignant act out the script in the actual marital bed. *And God Created Woman* was the film which turned America on to Bardot. Her amorous reputation finished the job. Trintignant was one of many co-stars Brigitte could not resist. They included Sacha Distel and Jacques Charrier, whom she married after Vadim and to whom she bore her only child, a son, though she scarcely ever seemed more than a child herself.

All this had made her a little insecure. By the time she reached California that night of her third marriage she had scandalized France by abandoning the baby Nicolas to his father. When asked whether she liked children she gave a distinctly negative impression. When asked why her parents did not take control of their grandchild she suggested she didn't much like them either. What she did like was men. One after the other till she got bored. Then she tried to commit suicide. She had very little sympathy from the French people, who bombarded her with letters while she was in hospital recovering from the overdose. The women felt particularly bitter. One tried to stab her, others jeered at her in the streets, all because they thought she would take away their men. But no one thought the remedy was to ignore her. Telescopic lenses peered into her boudoir and practically on to the obstetrician's couch. They were glad every time she came to rest, grounded as it were by the overt womanhood she flaunted.

Though this evening in Beverly Hills was ostensibly a time of rejoicing, you could also hear the sighs of relief. Bardot was safely married to one of her own kind, a heart-breaker whose track record round the European pleasure resorts seemed to indicate that he knew the value of nothing, though he could afford it all. In one way of course the whole thing was doomed from the start, which was another source of considerable pleasure. For, looked at in another vein, the two had nothing in common. It was a Franco-German alliance and everyone knew how treacherous *they* were. It was the fancy of an industrialist for a bohemian, of an aristocrat for a *petite bourgeoise*, of a man whose survival depended on the establishment with a woman whose survival depended on making waves. Sometimes she nearly drowned in them. It was the folly of a playboy for a fickle *femme fatale*. The battle would no doubt be bloody and brief but the consummation on that night was a piece of history.

Danny Kaye, exhibiting Bardot and Sachs like freaks in a town which is more than used to this sort of thing, wanted this fascinating, ultimate liaison to happen on his premises. He gave the impression that he derived vitality from their mutual lust. All through dinner he urged them upstairs. He succeeded. He was the first person to understand the frisson of the evening. But for this European-loving American the couple might never have been in Hollywood in the first place. For though Brigitte was a celluloid success in America, she was a very tender successor in men's hearts at the time to the recently dead Marilyn Monroe.

Danny was a sort of father-figure to Bardot, who bridged the gap of the Atlantic, though he gave the impression with his youthful, dancing gait that he could easily have been much more. He seemed steeped in France. One of his first hits was the song 'Anatole of Paris', written by his wife Sylvia Fine from whom he was currently separated. He could do a French accent better than Maurice Chevalier himself. And he often did during that evening, pouting his lips up to Bardot as if he was her mirror image. He could take off anybody, even the French superstar, and render them coy. He could do the same to her brand-new husband. Kaye had first made his name in Kurt Weill's *Lady in the Dark* as the man who could pronounce more Russian composers in quick succession in the song 'Tchaikovsky' than you thought had existed. His German accent was no worse than his Russian or his French. He didn't speak any of those languages but he gave the illusion that he did which was the important thing in Hollywood. It was a sort of skat singing he had perfected which meant nothing at all, but it didn't stop him posing as the perfect Prussian and taking off Gunther Sachs as well as his wife.

Danny had flirted with Europe for a long time, in fact as well as fiction, and with its crowned heads as well as its audiences, though he had once been very much a little kid from the wrong side of the Brooklyn tracks. His was a typical American success story. He swapped the gutters of New York for the swimming pools of LA and still thought he longed for Kiev. He ran away from home at fourteen and when he was hailed a star at the London Palladium about a decade later, it was confidently rumoured that one of his first ardent fans was the young stage-struck Princess Margaret. In his forties Vadim had sought him as a co-star for the projected American debut of the baby Brigitte. Now he was fifty-three and he had become a sort of patron of youth without noticing where the time had gone. His interest in UNICEF (United Nations Children's Fund) was only the outward manifestation of a much deeper involvement. People like the young Mia Farrow, wondering whether to marry the older Frank Sinatra, were always guests at his home. Where contemporaries put him on his guard, young people brought out the entertainer in him. He was entertaining now, a girl young enough to be his daughter, and a man handsome enough for any father to wish for a son-in-law. A son-in-law, moreover, who could pay the bills. The other guests were mostly Sachs's European coterie brought along for the ride. He moved with a retinue which protected him but seemed to suffocate Bardot. The new bride didn't care much for any of them. That was the guest list apart from me, but why was I there?

Hans Christian Andersen, the film in which Danny Kaye played the children's storyteller, was the first film I ever saw as a child. In fact I got into bad trouble for seeing it twice, once on the way home from school, which guaranteed him a fan in me for life. I became addicted to the world of the imagination, which the cinema stimulated in my generation more than any other influence. It was the reason I eventually gravitated to Hollywood to see for myself the connection between the fantasies which had reared us and the hard facts.

Coincidentally Danny was one of the first people I met. Later I got to know his daughter Dina. Both generations were fascinating to me. Danny, who could get President Nixon on the phone as easily as his housekeeper Estelle, was the same age as my parents. His reputation and that of his showbiz friends had moulded me just as surely as my family had. They had moulded Brigitte too, who was in turn a figurehead to me. Though my family, like hers, knew scarcely anyone in the public eye, they had heroes and heroines in common with those who did. The chain of influence was far-reaching and binding in a very subtle way. The younger generation, effortlessly rebellious, post-war, post-establishment, anti the media as I appreciated it, were what I feared to become. I did not want the fantasy bubble pricked. Neither did Bardot. Children who had been through the war even without noticing it at the time were different from those who came later.

I was astounded to learn that the connection between fantasy and fact which, due to the immense power of the screen I had imagined one and the same thing, was much less than I had anticipated. I simply did not know that a force which stood for good in the High Streets of gloomy post-war Europe – the cinema – stemmed from a town full of ignorance and commercial greed. I knew nothing of the animal morality of the casting couch or that the fortunes amassed beneath the arc lights were usually squandered on the most banal status symbols. I did not know that the

fame we adored as audiences made victims of our stars, sapping
them of their vital responses to life off-screen. Or that it made
audiences themselves into less than human idiots in the grip of
easy hero-worship under the impression that there were magical
quick bucks to be made.

I learned in Hollywood, however, acting in one of the soap
operas of the time, *The Wackiest Ship in the Army*, that the actors
had to be exceptionally professional just to survive in this town
which played for the highest stakes. They were proud of their
trooping and called non showbiz people 'civilians'. You had to
join up if only briefly in a place like that. Yet, though Hollywood
was my romance, I was wedded to the typewriter given to me by
my father. It was Brigitte's father who arranged her marriage with
the camera. We were both fickle brides at first, mistrusting our
condition even as we went down the aisle, because we knew that
as dutiful daughters we had not played around. Sometimes I
flirted with Hollywood and sometimes I hated it. I blamed the
town for the deaths by disillusion of Nathanael West and Fitzgerald. I blamed it later for the corruption of Mailer, for daring
him to take voyeurism right into Gary Gilmore's execution cell.
The bloodlust of the camera is a feature of our times and Brigitte's
lascivious courtship of it played a part in numbing all our
sensibilities.

And yet I loved Hollywood too. I loved its geography, so
similar to the geography Brigitte loves in the South of France, a
spot which is just as dominated by its myths. I loved the sea, the
mountain ranges, the tropical colours of the flowers. This sort of
scenery is some of the easiest on the eye and the spirit in the world,
which, combined with the climate and the light, is why artists
troubled in themselves gravitate towards it.

There was another thing I loved about Hollywood too. I met
not only bravado born of ignorance but also some of the quickest-
witted, most cultured and experienced people ever. This is an
insight you do not readily get in the European suburbs which had
been my habitat and Bardot's. The history of the great Hollywood
families – the Mankiewiczes, Fondas, Haywards, and Bridges –
touches more than the town itself. I met people who had seen the
turn of the last century and the San Francisco earthquake, who had
known the twenties in Paris and the thirties in Berlin. I met people
who had known Hitler personally, had been offered pacts by him,
seen them broken and had fled his devastation. I met people who

had shaken the hand of Picasso and could afford to collect him and the first editions I admired. Yet all of them still enjoyed life first hand. These people, whose best love was to prove themselves against other people, were lusty. They were not afraid. They screamed, they gambled, they suffered and I do believe they loved. But their best love was to create and manipulate their own empire, one of the very few left in a world becoming stunned by sameness.

The evening of Brigitte Bardot's third wedding brought many things in all our lives into focus. She was a child bride that night, even in her thirties and at her third wedding. We were still in the midst of the youth movement which she had heralded with such confidence. Though people started to pronounce on the cult with the Beatles, her generation had shown us the way. France was a symbol of sexual emancipation to Anglo-Saxon youth before Sinatra and Elvis turned the tables. The country had been trampled on and raped in war and she had also sold herself for a pair of nylons and a Hershey bar over and over again. America was seduced *en masse* by Europe in the sixties, where only the privileged traveller had loved it between the wars. We were at the same time to see natural impulses, ecology, and ethnic rights gain quite as much popularity as the most stunning technological advances. In fact we would see these things lead to a decline in the power of the cinema, the waning power of which had drawn us all together that night. Now here was the contradiction. Brigitte did not attempt to act for it like a previous generation. Vadim instead taught her to be herself. She, of all people, introduced that informality into acting which was to make my generation confused about the distinction between fiction and fact. The broad lines of the great Victorian theatrical tradition were now forgotten. Bardot made an art out of apparent spontaneity, which perfectly suited the proletarian times which were to come. She took the sex-goddess image which Marilyn Monroe projected before her and turned the deity into a slut. She brought to the fore the wayward woman inside rather than imposing the elegance and artificiality which had been a spur to previous generations. Actresses who came after her could openly take lovers and have children or not. They could despise the world, which had given them their opportunities, and refuse to court its audiences. They could make themselves thoroughly plain, tortuously intellectual, blatantly unerotic, maddeningly political, stupefyingly sane,

19

frank, healthy, and well adjusted. In short so boringly worthy that they would end up as flat, grey and insignificant as a blank screen awaiting the projectionist. Bardot would be the ultimate star, the one who shed the last veil.

After her, as they say in Paris, there could be nothing but pornography.

Glenys Roberts,
London, 1984

1. Image of her Father

Brigitte Bardot recently dined at the Colombe d'Or in the South of France, the fashionable hotel on the hillside at St-Paul de Vence full of middle-aged tourists and bartered Picassos. The night was rich with the sound of cicadas, the scent of rosemary and the twisted shadows of the olive trees. It was a typical evening in Provence. Bardot too was spending a typical evening.

In her fiftieth year she was surrounded by young men. She was wearing a lot of untidy blonde hair and few, rather cheap cotton clothes. 'She looked dirty to me,' said a woman at the next table who obviously expected better at those prices. She was a woman of about the same age as Bardot, dressed in a designer gown, who lived in a nearby luxury estate. She was happy, as only a woman could be, that time spares no one. 'They all looked dirty to me,' she said by way of revenge on life. 'It is not difficult to be admired by young men if you are a certain age in France.'

It was a great compliment to Bardot, though the speaker certainly did not mean it to be. The rich residents of the Côte d'Azur, where Bardot lives most of the time, want life to be absolutely predictable. They flit from the three-star Moulin de Mougins to the outrageously priced Bonne Auberge. They take drinks on the terrace of the Carlton in Cannes and the Voile d'Or outside Nice. They move in a pack from Cardin to Yves St-Laurent to buy their clothes, deciding on the telephone with each other before dinner that they will not all turn up wearing the same purple-shot taffeta plunge neckline trimmed with hot pink. They drive large Citroëns, Mercedes, and Rolls-Royces with the same popular music on the stereo system. They have access to the gossip aboard large yachts like Adnan Khashoggi's *Nabila*. They keep Superaquarama speedboats in Cannes or Antibes. Their idea of slumming it is to put on the Gucci sneakers without socks, take a picnic basket and do a little waterskiing within ridiculing distance of the nudist colony between the two islands. They swim, they drink and they have their liver complaints in unison.

Those residents who don't have money are even more stuck in their ways. They are in bed by ten, up preparing the *potage* with the dawn and the rustle of net curtains is as loud as in any English suburb. Though the popular image of the French across the Channel and the Atlantic may be a very worldly one indeed, things are quite different on their home ground. The Anglo-Saxon wet dream of the sophisticated land where you must sow your wild oats because the streets are lined with tarts is unrecognizable to the majority of the country's inhabitants. At any moment a free spirit in France is likely to clash with one of their many guardians of public morality.

Brigitte Bardot has had her clashes and still has them. She has earned a lot of money in her life but she refuses to spend it on other people's status symbols. 'I absolutely loathe luxury,' she says. 'It is the one thing I cannot stand.' She drives a Minimoke and sits on the floor. She hangs out with people half her age and stays up half the night. She also hangs out with people twice her age – or thereabouts. She is very fond of certain old people. In such things she is completely irreproachable, though she attracts very little approval. Bardot's life is not her own and though there is nothing new in that for cinema stars, hers is a very particular history.

It is the story of the fall from grace of the middle classes from which she sprang – the middle classes who were traditionally so virtuous and God-fearing and whose expectations for their daughters were chastity, charity and maternity. The middle classes have not forgiven her for exposing them as flesh and blood. Nor have they forgiven her for abandoning them by retiring from public life and apparently refusing to show them what happens after the liberation movement, which she unwittingly pioneered.

Whenever I see Bardot I am amazed at the extent to which she remains a typical *bonne bourgeoise*. Perhaps few people ever really get free of their origins. Yet to talk to her contemporaries who have also drawn attention to themselves is to talk to quite different kinds of women. You really couldn't think of Françoise Sagan as some sort of glorified concierge, as you can at times with Bardot. Françoise Sagan is always a classy eccentric – still the 'charming little monster' that François Mauriac called her at the time she wrote *Bonjour Tristesse* when she and Brigitte were teenagers.

Jeanne Moreau is a cunning animal, Leslie Caron a bewildered piece of porcelain china, Catherine Deneuve a shrewd little stockbroker. Sagan became Bardot's friend, Moreau acted with her, Caron nearly deprived her of her very first part, Deneuve had a son by her ex-husband. Their lives are all intertwined, yet they have less in common with her than has the woman in the street, which is why the woman in the street has always reacted to Bardot so violently.

The symbolic Bardot holds up a mirror to mid-twentieth-century woman with all her fears, her fantasies, and apparent freedom. Bardot, with her inelegant accent, her 'poufs' and her 'eh b'ens', her permanent rather sullen expectations of better things, could be a grocer's wife in the *banlieue*. Her speech seems so ordinary at times that one French observer who knows her background says it is hard to believe she did not deliberately acquire downward mobility along the way in anticipation of future idols from the middle classes like Mick Jagger or Bardot look-alike Marianne Faithfull. Everything about Bardot is completely ordinary except her physical presence. She hates the ordinary, vastly preferring any accusation of vulgarity, yet she is stuck with the attitude that comes out of her mouth and only her sense of humour saves her sometimes from utter banality.

This is not my opinion alone. You can hear it in many quarters from well-wishers and detractors alike. Eddy Barclay, a French record producer, has built a sumptuous palace in St-Tropez and knows Brigitte very well. He wrote a song 'Tu Es Venu Mon Amour', which she recorded twelve years ago at a time when the two of them were grimly locked on the threshold of middle age into a regular card game with two other locals. He 'brought out' her shy son Nicolas at his house-warming and has been trying to set him on the road to a musical career. In his more unguarded moments he has been known to confess complete contempt for Bardot's lifestyle which she simply will not change. 'She is a person who refuses to keep an open mind,' he tells friends by way of explaining their mutual disaffection. 'She has no curiosity and she will always be bored by life because she refuses to learn.'

Barclay's reputation is hardly that of the parish priest. Even self-avowed hedonists have been shocked by his idea of an interesting time. But it must be significant that even those Bardot-watchers among his worst critics have come to similar conclusions about Brigitte. 'Childlike', they call the same stubborn character traits, 'idealistic', and they find it either enduringly charming or surprisingly naïve.

Bardot's reputation rests on being slightly seamy, just off-key both on and off-screen. Though her beauty could be impeccable and sweet, she irritated people from her earliest years because there was a blatant aura of self-gratification in the way she flaunted this beauty. At fifty she still retains this tarnished image. She has not joined the jet-set or the blue-rinse brigade, she has little interest in motherhood, none whatsoever in grandmotherhood, though with her son just embarking on marriage that is probably the next thing with which she must come to terms. She is not a patron of the arts, still less a staunch supporter of her local church. And if she does good works it is more likely to be for animals than for the human race. Though she is shy of nude bathing now her figure is thicker set, she is not shy of her informal image. Let lesser women insist on flaunting their designer labels, even on the beach. Brigitte likes shorts, jeans, and the kiss of the sun. She lives from day to day, which is generally the approach of a much younger woman. She craves love, spontaneity and strong sensations. You can criticize it but, as the woman in the Colombe d'Or suspected, deep down, retaining the quality of your teens into middle age is not altogether to be despised. It is even a gift – a rare gift and a difficult one to share.

As I write this Brigitte Bardot, who was once mobbed by the housewives and pawed by the young men of France, is alone in her house on the Var coast. The treacherous sex-symbol has no current live-in lover. Her parents are dead, her sister lives in the North and for various reasons she has never really considered her son family. She has a posse of English setters, seven at the last count, of cats, rabbits, birds, flowers, and trees. She has the sound of the sea on her doorstep and of the Mistral in the reeds and the eucalyptus branches. She has her record player, her guitar, and her television set so she can watch *Dallas*, one of her favourite programmes. She has the townspeople. On the whole they are loyal to her, though she had a violent falling out with Mme Odette Giraud, the local florist, who took her to court last year for slander. 'Anybody who clubs her cat to death is a dirty bitch and a criminal!' Bardot shrieked in her shop, prompting Mme Giraud to demand £761 in damages in the local courthouse where, however, she lost the case and was ordered to pay costs. Bardot has a good acquaintance in the local police chief Georges Boeri and another in the local hairdresser, Gérard Montel, who sometimes house-sits one or other of her two local properties. She has sat for one local painter, Vincent Roux, and been idealized by a second, Andrew Quellier, as a sort of St Brigitte of Assisi. She is rather admired by local celebrities like Jeanne Moreau or the prize-winning novelist Françoise Parturier who know how difficult it is to grow old gracefully in the spotlight.

Since St-Tropez peaked in popularity as a holiday resort ten years ago because of her presence there, the local inhabitants are all interdependent with Brigitte, but none the less she is always the curiosity, the specimen wriggling under their microscope with whom they would not change places. 'She needs a strong man,' says Boeri. 'She doesn't trust people,' says Montel. 'She is very lonely,' says Roger Urbini who owns her favourite beach restaurant, L'Esquinade. 'Her problem is that all she wants to do is make love,' says Félix, one of her bridge set, who runs Tahiti beach. This is the stuff that myths are made of and once the myths have begun the truth is an irrelevant detail. Let's go back to the beginning and see how this sort of thing comes about.

Brigitte Bardot was born exactly fifty years ago around midday on 28 September 1934 in her mother's bed in Paris. Her parents' apartment on the fifth floor of the grey stone block at 35 avenue de la Bourdonnais was about 100 yards to the south-west of that other great symbol of modern France, the Eiffel Tower. It was not a grand or spacious home but it was fairly luxurious for a young married couple starting out in life. It stood appropriately enough in the road where Edmond Rostand died, creator of *Cyrano de Bergerac*, lovelorn serenader of the beautiful Roxanne; that is in the seventh *arrondissement* of Paris, near the river and Napoleon's tomb, a residential but central area with an energetic street life rather like South Kensington in London or the Upper East Side in New York. In the avenue de la Bourdonnais you had the feeling of being in the middle of things without being responsible for them. It was on the bus route leading from the embankment to the Invalides and opposite the apartment was a huge, noisy secondary school. When Brigitte was first wheeled out of the wrought-iron door in her baby carriage her eyes fell on the usual Parisian corner café, a small antique shop, and a beauty salon.

Inside the apartment oriental carpets covered the parquet floors and some of the furniture was reputedly genuine Louis Quinze. Perhaps these things were exaggerated. Louis Bardot and his wife,

Anne-Marie Mucel, both came from good backgrounds with a tradition of nice family life and a polite interest in the arts, but their position in society, whatever they might have wished, was strictly lower-upper middle class. The Bardots had a certain amount of money but they were careful with it. Anne-Marie, who was of Lorraine stock, studied dance in Milan as a girl but any thoughts of a career swiftly gave way before the prospect of marriage. She was groomed, beautiful, with fine noble features and dark blonde hair, a much more slender version of womanhood than her daughter would be. Louis Bardot was ostensibly the perfect match. He was not very romantic-looking, it is true, but bony and patrician like his wife (neither of them had any feature as vulgar as the Bardot Pekinese pout) and he had bad eyesight. But he also had a good future with the family chemical firm in northern Paris, which enhanced his appeal as a husband. He was sixteen years older than his wife – she was twenty-two when Brigitte was born, he was thirty-eight – and therefore well established in his business and in his personality. In his spare time he was something of a poet, which certainly helped to win over his artistic fiancée. He even won a prize for one of his volumes of poems at the French Academy. 'My mother used to say Papa went through life with a rose in his hand,' says Brigitte. 'It was a charming notion.'

It was by no means the whole truth. Louis Bardot was no fey dreamer. He could be pedantic, rigidly boring and quite obtuse when he wanted his own way. He thundered and raged until he got it and then felt ashamed of himself. The family found him alternately terrifying and ridiculously comic. When he relaxed at weekends in the country and entertained them with his impersonations of Charlie Chaplin he could be good fun, at other times he was overcome by a sense of dignity he felt appropriate to a *père de famille*.

The family over which he tried to preside included Anne-Marie's parents who were a very soothing influence. His mother-in-law, Jeanne Mucel, Brigitte's grandmother, was only nine years older than Louis with the same admirable aristocratic looks as her daughter. She proved the perfect go-between in stormy circumstances. She often turned a blind eye to Brigitte's faults. She adored her granddaughter and it was mutual. Her husband, Léon, who survived just long enough to see Brigitte's success on the screen, always said sagely that the cinema would not ruin

Brigitte unless the potential for ruin was already there.

The three generations were close in Brigitte's childhood. They all had nicknames for each other. Brigitte was Bricheton, further abbreviated as Bri-Bri. Her younger sister Marie-Jeanne has always been known as Mijanou. And, despite his blustering manners, everyone was fond of the head of the house, Louis Bardot, who did so much to shape Brigitte's future response to the men in her life. He was always called by his comic nickname of Pilou, French for flannelling. He responded by calling his wife Toty, which seems to be a corruption of aunty, never Anne-Marie unless he was cross with her. In many ways he brought to mind Charles Bovary, the pathetic but well-intentioned country doctor of Flaubert's famous novel, whose wife's rebellion against the life he offered her proved so tragic. *Madame Bovary* was written a century before, but if Anne-Marie Bardot had not known quite so well how to handle Louis he might have made her life a hell, just as Charles did Mme Bovary's. As it was he often did this to his daughter.

The world has come a long way since those pre-war days. You can see Bardot's blatant sexuality on the streets any day now, but when her parents were young you had to buy it in a brothel or in a work of art. Art was the word used by some for the Czech film *Ecstasy* which came out the year before Brigitte was born and in which Hedy Lamarr took off more clothes onscreen than Brigitte ever would in her heyday. That was not the sort of thing to which Louis liked to take Anne-Marie Mucel while they were courting. Where the women of his family were concerned he was quite strict and he became even stricter as the elderly father of two girls. Louis had been young during the roaring twenties but he hadn't really roared along with his contemporaries. Sexual licence just wasn't a universal prerogative in those days. It was limited to the rich and to the poor and Louis fitted into neither category.

The middle classes, of which the Bardots were staunch representatives, had nothing like the freedom which would come to everyone after the Second World War. Neither did they think they wanted it. In 1934 they were still ferocious guardians of the proprieties. They wanted to defend the fragile decencies which they had inherited along with the wealth of the industrial revolution and which in France had still not been eroded. It was possible to live very well in Paris when Brigitte was young. For American and British expatriates and tourists the country was a 'bargain-basement paradise', in the words of Paul Johnson in his history of modern France. For the French themselves life belonged more to the nineteenth century than the twentieth as we know it now. Even a moderately well-off family could afford staff. The Bardots had several.

In the French countryside, even close to Paris where her maternal grandparents had their home, nothing much had changed since the *early* nineteenth century and it was still un-changed at the height of the Bardot years, which meant that the moral revolution she endorsed seemed extra shocking. In country farms, in Brittany for instance, where it was fashionable for people like the Bardots to rent houses in the long summer holidays, families would live according to totally different time-tables to the towns – primeval timetables, though their clocks would be set to help them maintain the illusion of a civilized lifestyle. There were very few radios, no television, very little day-to-day contact with the printed media. The people were dominated by nature. There were still 3 million horses working on farms when Brigitte was at nursery school and the rustic life crept right up to the gates of the capital. On the city streets there were still nearly 1½ million horse-drawn carriages, as many as when her grandmother Jeanne was born. There was no cheap mass-production of cars and they were consequently only for the very rich. It was not at all a mechanized society so it is rather surprising to find the little Brigitte already recorded by a moving camera when she was at the crawling stage in 1935. Photography was Louis Bardot's hobby. Everyone with a little money to spare had the jack-in-the-box Kodak, but he had a cine camera.

You could find home movies in America at that time and they might be *de rigueur* among the families of Hollywood stars, but Paris was not Los Angeles and the Bardots were not the Fondas. In 1936 even a talented crystal-ball-gazer would have found it impossible to predict from the set of Brigitte's pout that the two families would end up practically related. In 1936 Henry Fonda's acting career had just started to be viable and his private life was about to follow a typical showbusiness pattern. When Jane and her brother Peter played with little Chris and Tom Mankiewicz, whose uncle wrote *Citizen Kane*, and with Brooke and Bill and Bridget Hayward, whose father Leland was the most successful Broadway impresario of his time, she was learning first hand that tragedy as well as success could be the outcome of artistic endeavour. The Mankiewiczs' mother hanged herself. Her mother, Frances Fonda, took an overdose. So did Margaret Sullavan, the Haywards' mother who had once also been married to Henry Fonda.

Little Brigitte by contrast had no inkling that these could be the wages of fame. This sort of behaviour simply did not go on in the liquid oxygen business in the French capital. The Bardots' life was routine. Louis plodded across town every day to an industrial estate in the northern Parisian suburb of Aubervilliers which lies on the road to Charles de Gaulle Airport just outside the porte de la Chapelle, where Joan of Arc prayed before she entered Paris, but there is nothing remotely uplifting about its squalid side streets and dreary thoroughfares. Today it is a North African ghetto full of sickly sweet pâtisserie shops and ethnic flea markets but Louis Bardot's daily round lacked any such colourful input. The rue de Pilier, where the name Bardot still stands on a plate on the door of an electricity sub-station, is an industrial wilderness. As M. Bardot returned home each night past the greasy workers' cafés and through the cheap red-light district in the rue St-Denis he must have been quite determined that his little daughter would have no need to investigate this particular part of the outside world. Though they had a good library at home the Bardots didn't encourage any sort of first-hand investigation; they were possessive parents who lived through Brigitte and liked her to stick close to the family hearth.

In the Bardot's sensible, middle-class circles a girl was groomed to be a comfort in her parents' old age, not to make her mark elsewhere. Louis and Anne-Marie would never naturally have expected a daughter of theirs to earn her own living and stand on her own two feet. Those Frenchwomen of Anne-Marie's generation who had made a name for themselves like Colette, Chanel, and Piaf, were all patronized initially by influential men. They were mistress-figures not respectable wives. Simone de Beauvoir, who would write about Bardot when they were both at the height of their powers, had found out that women could be philosophers if they had the grim application to persevere through the co-educational schools stimulated by a brilliant lover like Jean-Paul Sartre. Not many, however, chose the professional route. The French people were generally agreed that if they had invented civilization, culture and philosophy, these were pursuits to which the gifted amateur could make a stunning contribution within the

29

home. A nation of girls was educated not only to please men, a lesson which Brigitte learned in abundance, but to make life easier for them within a respectable domestic framework.

Apart from anything else most people were quite insulated from the experiences of others. The great age of all-pervading media babble had not yet begun. When Lindbergh landed on French soil in 1927 Louis Bardot and Anne-Marie pricked their ears up to American rhythms. In the early thirties they danced to tunes like Rodgers and Hart's 'Blue Moon' but they were much more familiar with French indigenous culture and events.

The Bardots kept themselves to themselves and they worried a lot about the state of the world into which they were bringing their family. There was a good deal of political unrest in France the year Brigitte was born with the government falling and people being shot in the streets. The Austrian Chancellor, Dollfuss, was murdered by the Nazis in 1934. Louis Bardot, who had been a teenager during the First World War, became distinctly apprehensive when Italy mobilized. Over the next five years he watched the *Wehrmacht* march into the Rhineland, invade Austria and make war an inevitability. The German presence never affected his business as an industrialist but it certainly affected the mood of the family, making it more conservative and fussy and determinedly French. The Bardots believed in the old order where everyone knew their place, and they were quite as class-conscious as the English are supposed to be. They even brought an English girl over the Channel to look after their new baby, which was a typical piece of Parisian snobbism at that time. The England she left that year was obsessed with a new symbolic European pastime – hiking. Complaints were rife about the naked opportunism of such bare knees and thighs and the mobility of hiking itself. Such opportunities would one day be personified by the little girl in the Paris crib. But in 1934 the expectations of M. and Mme Bardot for their first daughter were that she would marry the man of their choice and lead a reasonably leisurely life as mistress of a stylish household with domestic help. She would be mistress of another house in the country, where she would be packed off with the children for the three-month summer *congé*. The children would be a *devoir* rather than a delight. Their mother would rise late, be effortlessly well dressed and she would complain of a liverish headache every time her husband got her on the horizontal. If the Bardots were honest with themselves they would have to admit that she might have a few, very well-regulated affairs between the hours of five and seven in the afternoon. These would not make her happy but they would not make her all that sad either. She would be a respectable woman. Right from the start, however, Brigitte would show that she was not too keen on either respectability or rules.

2. Bewitching Scatterbrain

Anne-Marie and Louis Bardot had their very first conflict with the new arrival on the Friday she was born – she was a girl and not a boy. The new parents quickly picked themselves up after their initial disappointment and put the birth announcement in *Le Figaro*, the French establishment newspaper. Brigitte was to suspect that a certain apprehension lingered, which was to take the form of alternately cosseting and ignoring her.

She was a girl, which was crucial for the world, for if she had had an elder brother we would never have been troubled by BB, even if the exact combination of genes had met to produce her later. She would have had a totally different attitude to the opposite sex.

She was a girl. She weighed 7lb 6oz, an average child, if a little on the heavy side for the time and place. If she was blonde in her babyhood – several people who were not present unkindly maintain that she came into the world with three spiky black bristles on her bald head – it was not nature's plan that the blonde hair should last beyond puberty.

She was a girl and her mother rapidly had her future planned. Anne-Marie was exactly the sort of woman who can't wait to dress her daughter up, curl her hair and make sure, when the time comes, that she has the right nail polish to match her accessories and that all the boys respect her. This sort of woman is strong on image but not too good on reality. The new baby seemed like a fabulous little doll, a mistake made by most mothers. She was called Brigitte to comply nicely with the French ruling that the first names must be saints' names. Brigitte was also the name of a Celtic fire-goddess, a sort of premonition if you like, but not to Anne-Marie who had simply named her after her favourite inanimate object, a real doll she had lugged around during her own childhood.

The real-life doll was installed in a fantasy nursery. It was white silk and lace with Empire hangings and period furniture, a green chaise-longue, ormolu candelabra, carpeted with cream moquette and filled with stuffed animals. Baby Brigitte had a real cat called Crocus and a cage full of singing birds. She had the English nanny and a French governess. Scarcely five minutes' walk away was the huge open space of the Champs de Mars where the little girl could watch the boys playing boule on a Saturday afternoon and brush shoulders with pampered poodles.

When the family outgrew the avenue de la Bourdonnais they moved to a little square in the fifteenth *arrondissement*, the place Violet, a rather more robust area. Although it was a pretty, light, south-facing apartment, it did not suit the Bardots' aspirations. So they moved over the river to a nine-room flat in the rue de la Pompe at its intersection with the avenue Paul Doumer. Though rather a busy part of the sixteenth *arrondissement*, and still on a bus route, it was in principle a very good address. Bardot bought into the sixteenth *arrondissement* as soon as she earned her own money, though she could never live in the very best part of it until she married the millionaire Gunther Sachs.

The new apartment was very convenient for a young child. The Arc de Triomphe was within walking distance as was the Seine, where Brigitte and her nurse would watch the flat-laden barges pass from east to west on their way to the mouth of the river. On the cindertracks of the Bois de Boulogne, where the fashionable Parisians exercise their horses just as on Rotten Row or Central Park, they would watch the animals pass during the last years of peace. The children of the area learned to play with their hoops on the dirt pathways between the grass verges just as they had done for centuries. Even closer was the little green triangle of Les Jardins de Ranelagh, a pint-sized children's paradise where donkey carts line up on a Sunday to trundle the children of the *nouveau riche* round and round under the plane trees. In the summer they could watch the Punch and Judy show from a little green and white shack and buy ice-creams. Breakfast at eight, lunch at one, dinner at seven, so her childhood unrolled, the French middle classes like the middle classes all over the world taking their meals quite regularly whatever else might happen.

There was really no point in leaving the calm of Passy, as this part of Paris is called, especially during the war years when the occupying German forces would sing their national anthem every day just across the pont d'Iena, sending the same shiver up Parisian spines as the wailing sirens did in London. Brigitte was six by then, the age that compulsory education starts in France. But she was already a dancer and the rest of her education took second place to her mother's ambition for her to learn classical ballet. Though some of the best *lycées* in France, including Janson de Sailly, lay just around the corner, the competitive state system with its harsh academic discipline and ambitious pupils of both sexes was not for Brigitte. She went to a private school, Hattemer, an institution for well-bred young ladies, also within walking distance. The branch of Hattemer in the rue de la Faisanderie, which she attended until 1950 when she was sixteen, closed just ten years later, but the school lives on in the rue Spontini in the sixteenth, and in rue de Londres in the eighth *arrondissement*, where the present headmaster, M. Corbon, invited Brigitte to celebrate its hundredth birthday in 1984 just as she celebrated her fiftieth. The school expects great things from its pupils and can count among its old boys Jean-Paul Sartre and Giscard d'Estaing's sons. It did not, however, expect much from Brigitte. M. Corbon was a great friend of Pierre-Marie Quervelle, the man who taught her French and Latin which she gave up when she was fourteen. According to Quervelle, who died just recently, 'She was a terrible student, bottom of the class.' She had no aptitude for study at all. 'She won't go anywhere,' he said confidently. Her mind was elsewhere. By the time she was out of the primary classes she was virtually a stage child, going daily to her ballet school, once again within walking distance, to the rue Spontini.

It sounds delightful but she was not happy. She was bored. Real life seemed too remote in Passy and childhood not an apprenticeship but an unconscionable period of waiting. As soon as she was old enough to take stock she decided she was being ignored by her parents. 'I was always with a minder of some kind to take care of me. I saw my parents rarely, usually at railway stations.' Even in those pre-war days, when it was not as easy as it is now, the Bardots did move round relentlessly according to the timetable of their class. At weekends they went to the family chalet at Louveciennes near Versailles, which her grandmother had imported from Oslo at the time of the World Fair, the rustic life being the height of French bourgeois aspirations. It was and is a very safe area – 'sleeping policemen' in the streets prevent anything happening too fast. As a small child Brigitte loved the secure freedom and the benign climate of this part of the Yvelines, as the *département* is called, but in later years she considered it altogether too tame. Her grandparents' house was mere clapboard, the garden a suburban square, but on the other side of the street was a tiny château. What's more, up the road was the real thing, the magnificent palace of the Sun King, just the right distance for Sunday outings. The dramatic aqueduct, built in the seventeenth century to carry the water uphill for the King's fountains, passed right by the village. That, and the huge waterwheel which pumped the water out of the Seine, were much greater achievements for a child to admire. Versailles was just a healthy walk away through the outskirts of Louis XIV's hunting forests. His mistress's house, Maintenon, was a familiar name from the local street signs. Mary Queen of Scots had lived nearby as a girl before she married the French Dauphin. The area was full of royal history, and the royals, albeit dead ones in republican France, were the real heroes of a well-educated little girl of the time. Growing up in Louveciennes was a bit like living on the outskirts of Hampton Court and then discovering you were not, in fact, Anne Boleyn. Things were always happening just over the horizon in Brigitte's childhood.

In the summer the family usually went to Biarritz – not yet to the Côte d'Azur but to the bracing Atlantic coast to have the cobwebs swept away annually in the manner of all nice families. You can see families like the Bardots still, wrapped in their lambswool sweaters, sheltering behind sand-dunes from Brittany down to the Basque country with pink windburn on their faces and mud on their ankles.

In the winter the Bardots went to Meribel in the French Alps and, for all Brigitte's recollections to the contrary, she often went with them right into her teens. Still she felt resented rather than spoiled, held at arm's length in her nursery world. She remembers wanting to escape into a much more challenging world like Colette's adolescent heroine Minne, but she neither lived it nor put it on paper. When her nursemaid walked her in the Bois de Boulogne she seemed not to have noticed the twilight zone behind the trees where prostitutes still proposition passers-by. She didn't play truant or roam the streets like Sagan, who came from just as good a family, speculating on the destinies of people she saw sitting on park benches. She didn't long to go to the cinema like Jeanne Moreau, who was forbidden its wicked influence even though she grew up in a brothel in Montmartre which was the only place her hotelier father could get work during the war. Little Jeanne craned her neck to hear the soundtrack coming from the cinema next door and escaped from the poverty of her childhood by imagining what was on screen. Little Brigitte didn't really imagine anything much. She had no idea what might be outside the comfort of the Passy apartment and the sheltered life she led. She did not read much as a child despite the books in her father's study. That would be for later. When left to her own devices, which happened rarely, she was engulfed by a nameless fear. She remembers being all alone in the apartment at the age of eight and being so haunted by terror she vowed that when she grew up she would never spend any time on her own ever again. Terrified that she would incur someone's displeasure and be abandoned, most of the time she meekly did as she was told – until one day she rebelled. As a child Bardot never learned to protect herself from her mistakes because she rarely had the opportunity to compare her progress with that of her contemporaries.

'I didn't know a lot of children because my mother wanted me only to meet a certain kind of child – of a certain class and educated to a certain standard. I remember worrying a lot about that. I was shy and when these well-behaved children came round with their correct parents I was absolutely terrified. I was so terrified I used to get eczema.' Later she would get spots.

'In Paris, in that class, many parents were strict,' she recalls. 'But mine were stricter than most. They wanted me to become a very well-educated, cultured and I think, rather boring girl.' Despite all the fussing over appearances Brigitte was lonely. Her sibling, who arrived five years later, was too young to share and compare any of the stages of childhood with her. The sibling, moreover, was the wrong sex – another girl, a competitor not a friend. When the time came she didn't even go to the same school.

Brigitte also felt that Mijanou was unfairly singled out for special treatment as the younger child. One day when her parents were out and the maid was looking in the opposite direction Brigitte, who was seven at the time and playing cowboys and Indians with her two-year-old sister, pulled the tablecloth from under her mother's favourite Chinese vase which went crashing to the floor and shattered into pieces. The scene which followed is etched painfully in her memory. There was a terrible Gallic row followed by several cuffs around the ear. 'We children were then banished from the family circle. That is to say we were told to address our parents formally as *vous*, not *tu* from then on, because we weren't worthy to be their children. I was also given fifty whacks of the cane – I was often caned – naturally the baby got less.

'I took it very badly indeed. I couldn't get it out of my mind. I didn't feel I belonged there after that. It just wasn't my home any more. I vowed then and there that I would one day have a home of my own and no one would tell me what to do in it. Of course, I now have several. I have often thought that incident accounted a lot for my future lifestyle, wanting to be at home wherever I was, to have a choice of home but to be totally in control of my environment.'

Clearly Brigitte was neither as neglected nor ostracized as she felt and the proof of this is Louis Bardot's moving camera. Obsessed with both his hobby and his daughter, he delighted to take pictures of her at all stages of her development, beginning the day after she was born. Instead of the ubiquitous snap in the album of the naked baby on the piano there are thousands of moving frames of Brigitte, wriggling about naked on her baby blankets, playing with her bucket and spade wrapped up in a woolly cardigan on a draughty beach, posturing in granny sunglasses on a park bench and leaping all over the hollyhocks in her grand-mother's garden in Louveciennes. The results form a valuable collection which has stayed in the family ever since and helped to convince the adult Brigitte that her parents, to whom she became fondly reconciled before they died, were no more ignorant of her feelings than most middle-class parents and were perhaps a good deal more concerned than most with their offspring. We are all other people's fantasies and she apparently more than most. There she was, the doll-like Brigitte Bardot, her parents' property and a big fight ahead of her on behalf of all the comfortable children of comfortable people for the right to move further away from them than the complacency of the house next door.

Yet though she would change a lot of things in the future she would never change her name: Bébé she was right from the start. Actresses since then have in the naturalistic phase of the cinema made it up on to cinema marquees with improbable real names like Mary Steenburgen, but Brigitte was given the archetypal double initials, which usually emerge from studio conferences, as her very first identity. This was no accident. Despite a satisfactory marriage Anne-Marie Bardot was still smarting from the loss of her own artistic career. A pregnant woman, moreover, likes nothing better than to while away her months of waiting with her nose in women's magazines and entertainment sheets. The name which dominated magazines like *Ciné-Miroir* in 1934 was Simone Simon, an almost exact contemporary of Anne-Marie Bardot who became a huge French star that year. Michèle Morgan was coming up fast on the inside straight having changed her name from Simone Roussel. When it came to naming her daughter something rang a bell. Brigitte's alliterative initials were her first cue for fame, the first thing she had in common with Greta Garbo, who was every little French girl's fantasy the year Brigitte was born; with Charlie Chaplin who was her father's idol, with Marilyn Monroe who would be her own, with Danielle Darrieux to whom she would be compared, or Marcello Mastroianni and Claudia Cardinale who would be her co-stars. Cardinale acted in a film called *Les Pétroleuses* ('The Oil Girls') with BB in 1971, one of the last films in Bardot's screen career which was distributed in English-speaking countries as *The Legend of Frenchie King*. A blurring in the distinction between art and life – a common trait in a later generation which would be babysat by the media – was to be Brigitte's trademark and a liability perhaps later, for when she became vulnerable it was her very essence which would be threatened, not some fictional character. It all started in front of the amateur camera of her father.

This early brush with the moving camera gave Brigitte the habit of being the centre of attention, even more than most children. Brigitte as a baby was already a star. 'I never thought about the future,' she says. 'I still never think about the future.' If you believe there are no coincidences the future was obviously mapped out for her.

Bardot had lots of time to study what she looked like when the holiday pictures were shown at family gatherings and she has often said that what she saw did not make her all that happy. Though you can see the pout even then, the overall picture is a pretty average one. There are many prettier pre-pubescent children who never grow up to be half as attractive as Brigitte Bardot. She seems to have known this right from the start for when the annual school photograph was taken in *dixième* – the year she broke the Chinese vase – she longed to be the gamine child in the front row with straight hair and enough confidence to sit carelessly out of line. Brigitte had the archetypal plain look, the central parting and the frizzy hair scragged back with plain grips. She also had a ludicrous bow slapped on top by mother, the token 'If you are a girl you should wear curls and a bow', which was how things were done at the time.

Then there were the wire-rimmed spectacles. They were necessary because Brigitte even now is plainly astigmatic. Her right eye refuses to keep pace with the left. She still needs to wear glasses and naturally, like most women, she still prefers not to. Painters have described a squint or a wandering eye as one of the most attractive flaws a beautiful woman can have – and a flaw, for those teenage girls who like Brigitte longed for perfection, is always a perversely added attraction. But for the person who has it bad sight is never an asset and for a kid it is just a nuisance. To make matters worse for an embryo exhibitionist Bardot wasn't even the only one with the condition. Her best friend, Chantal, and her little sister, Mijanou, had wire-rimmed spectacles too. They were all also forced into identical white collars with identical button-through blouses and identical plaid skirts for another of the many photographers. In front of them is a line of identical bald-headed dolls with identical white bibs.

The world was amazingly static in those days. Countless families in five continents have snapshots in their albums of nice, well-brought-up little girls looking exactly the same as Brigitte Bardot. All their mothers put their hair in coiffes by day and rags by night and they all graduated from smocking and strap shoes into school uniform and stockings. Most of them felt old before they had even had their first kiss, weighted down by belts, braces, bodices, and bras. Standing before the mirror in the privacy of the bathroom they sometimes despaired that nature should be at such odds with convention. 'No wonder girls got the reputation of being dumb,' says a girlfriend of Brigitte's. 'You simply couldn't say a word at parties because you were concentrating all evening on your girdle.' And if all little girls throughout history have always yearned to be free rather than take on the shackles of the adult world, this was the generation which would achieve it for longer than most.

Brigitte's first taste of a sort of freedom was her ballet class. Whether or not it was a vehicle for her own frustrated ambition, one of Mme Bardot's first educational acts on behalf of her daughter was to summon the fashionable M. Recco from the chorus at the Opera, who moonlighted by instructing the daughters of wealthy middle-class families, to put her through her paces in the family drawing room. Later, when she was old enough to stand unaided, she was enrolled in ballet class.

There she discovered she was basically a physical animal. It was to be the making of her. Even now her figure and her features have coarsened she moves with enviable grace. She seemed liberated by the movements which strangled other children, for ballet was the universal first form of self-expression after finger-painting of the middle-class child. In studios and church halls all over Europe little girls learned to force their toes out and their bottoms in while their mothers ran up their tutus on hand machines for charity performances. Leslie Caron, born three years earlier than Brigitte into a similar family, had the same sort of upbringing. She remembers her childhood as a mixture of her own otherworldliness and of a terrifying responsibility as the harbinger of a couple's dreams, especially her mother's. Both children were enrolled in ballet school, a nice, acceptable artistic training for a girl from the Puritan stratum of society, which involved on the whole a good deal more genuine hard work than the theatre and not so much lying around in dressing rooms on casting couches. Girls like Leslie and Brigitte, who had an aptitude for these things, were never moved to tiny acts of rebellion like the rest of the population, like wearing navy-blue knickers under their tutus for their first stage appearance. Brigitte simply took off in the studio, her eyes fixed on some faraway dream. She became beautiful in the act of dancing and having tasted approval and indeed self-approval, she determined to have more of it.

Claude Bourgat, whose mother ran the ballet school in the rue Spontini, remembers that she was an exceptional little girl, enjoying at the time even the pain of performance. 'She was always smiling, she never showed the hard work that went into it and she had a very pretty body, which is something unusual for a child. She liked to be noticed and therefore people did notice her and especially her costumes.' Brigitte was a sprite even in her tartan Sunday frock, caught again by her father's camera in her grandmother's garden at Louveciennes, leaping around in the faster than real film saying 'Look at me, look at me', while other people did sensible things like weed the garden.

Like most children Bardot spent her childhood preoccupied with herself. She was not even particularly fond of animals in her early youth or sentimental about them. She preferred her stuffed ones. The momentous world events which scarred many of her compatriots made little difference to her lifestyle. The Second World War rolled right past her doorstep, yet to her it simply meant the departure from the nursery of her English nurse. Brigitte does, however, remember the war *being* her childhood in that way that gave a permanent, nameless fear to children of her generation which would come back to them again and again long after peace was declared. Brigitte felt fear while the war was on and can feel it still. 'Sometimes it comes back to me when I feel worried or in a bad mood. I remember the alerts in Paris, being awakened in the middle of the night and the basement where we had to go. I was afraid of dying there, I felt trapped and I am still terribly claustrophobic.' She was ten when it was over. The formative years had passed in a spirit of upheaval which would leave the adult with no comprehension of the value of routine in establishing a strong identity. She felt a little magic attached to the idea that she had survived. This was a story which would be repeated over and over again in small minds wherever Hitler was feared. It was to lead very convincingly to the possibility of establishing a revolutionary new identity and to the creation of the teenager in which Bardot played her part.

3. That Goddam' Girl

Bardot's first notable teenage act was a perfectly acceptable one –
but then it was only 1947 and the rebellious teenager had not yet
been patented. She was thirteen and she passed the exam for the
National Conservatory of Music and Dancing at her first effort.
At this point wild hopes were unleashed. 'No one expected to get
in first time,' she remembers. 'You might do it on your second
try.' A total of 150 children competed for eight places and even an
unenthusiastic maths student like Brigitte realized that this meant
about only one in twenty would be accepted. Bardot says she was
not the best dancer in the school but she was all the same pretty
good. With those first teenage stirrings of the possibility of an
identity away from the family she determined that she would
become the best at something, that she would be amusing or at
least interesting, 'otherwise you will be nothing.' She was still
obsessed with her dull looks, a subject she can be relied upon to
bring up even now. She hated imperfection – because it was not
interesting. 'I wanted the world to hear of Brigitte Bardot.
And they would have done, even if it was not in the way it turned
out.'

Many a teenage girl thinks this way. The new identity becomes
incredibly heady and the routine compromises embraced by most
of the adults around them quite incomprehensible. Everything at
the time is bursting, and rising in a frenzy of adrenalin and energy,
as if they are permanently in a state of first-night nerves, but they
know that if all goes to plan they will hear the roar of the crowd.
Lucky is the teenager who has an outlet for this confidence and
energy and Brigitte was one of the lucky ones. She had already
proved herself in a competitive world. She did not have the vague
dreams of unspecified fame which haunt today's young people,
created by the overwhelming power and hunger of the media.
Though, to the detriment of her soul and ours, she would become

the epitome of the media-created star, at the time she cherished a rather old-fashioned ambition – that of being a ballet dancer.

The man into whose guidance she delivered this ambition was a Russian exile living in Paris. He was fascinating to look at with hollow Slavic cheeks, pixie ears, solid thighs, and dark, romantic hair. He was also not very much older than she was. His name was Boris Kniazeff and he taught her dancing.

After her father with his camera, Kniazeff was the next Svengali in her life, and he gave her something quite as valuable as her familiarity with the camera lens. From a 'frozen, solemn kind of a child', (Brigitte's own recollection), the restrained girl with braces on her teeth learned to discard her clothes for a bodystocking and fishnet tights and revel in her own shape. The pictures of her from those days in legwarmers and leotards seem very modern now, in this age of compulsive exercise. Bardot was fit before any of us ever dreamed it could become fashionable. She suffered then for something that lay in the future. She will not, however, suffer today to attempt the impossible, the summoning up of a physical beauty that must always lie in the past. 'One thing is certain, I simply could not dance classical ballet today. There is no let-up for a serious dancer, there are no holidays.' She says this perhaps with a little sadness for the passing of time, but with no regret.

First she grew too big. She is 5ft 7in in her bare feet and barefoot is how she likes to be. Something else along the line deflected her from dancing though, which she began to realize was her mother's purpose for her, towards a destiny all of her own. The sceptical have called that something innate laziness. 'She thought the world owed her a vacation,' said one of the first producers who worked with her as a teenager. Whatever the temptations presented by the packaging of the young sex-symbol, he remained stoically unimpressed. There is about the full lips and now the fuller figure an air of such sensuality that it clashes with any concept of hard work. Her gift was at the very least one of timing. In a world which would shortly be given over to the masses her timely instincts were to hook as large a following as possible. Her bait was quite simple. As freedom for women progressed as an idea most girls would undergo the oddest of transitions. They felt insulted when their newly and willingly exposed bodies were praised by the opposite sex, insisting on a veil still but that it should be drawn over men's eyes rather than women's curves. Not Bardot. She had none of those phoney scruples that every showbusiness writer was to encounter with a yawn in the years ahead about wanting to be loved for her art rather than her body. In 1959, when her producer Raoul Levy squabbled with her over the future of her image, she simply broke with him. 'She has years of successes ahead of her as an actress not as a striptease artist. I know I am right,' he said – he it was who had produced her great scandalous success *And God Created Woman*. 'I should not drop those parts of my personality that the public love,' answered Mlle Bardot.

She had discovered something she could be proud of, something she owes to the training of that first Russian influence in her life. On the beach or in the garden you may see her now, walking just as she did for the camera, with the care of a cat, putting the front half of her foot down first as if to test the ground, pointing it slightly and resting the weight of her upper body as squarely on her hips as if she were about to perform an *entrechat*. In contrast to the timidity of most teenage stances, the one which she learned *chez* Kniazeff thrust the shoulders back and the budding breasts to the fore. It also arched the back in such a way that the eye of the onlooker easily strayed to the primary erogenous zone, the only one left to her as last in the line of cinematic sex-queens to make famous. Bardot was to shift the area of interest to where it mattered most.

In 1947 the crotch was probably rather more on Mme Bardot's mind than on her daughter's. It was the year of the New Look and Anne-Marie was looking round for a new look of her own. A mother does not give in easily at the sight of the first curves of her offspring. By 1948, when Brigitte was fourteen and Mijanou nine, Anne-Marie had the solution. She would go into the fashion business. With her team of seamstresses she adapted *haute couture* designs for those who weren't sure they could afford the real thing. It was also a way of trying to make peace with her daughter's new interest in her shape.

For Brigitte was pulling away from the nest. Her first real appearance in public was little more than a high-spirited dance round the camp fire to a country holiday audience. 'They paid for their tickets with chickens and eggs,' she remembers. It was in Fougères in Brittany, a country town surrounded by forest with a lot of holiday trade from the nearby Mont St-Michel. It was organized by Mme Bourgat whose dance college still puts on charity performances today so her pupils can dip their toes into the unsuspecting eddies of actual performance. On this occasion Mme

Bourgat had literally to push her star pupil into the spotlight. Waiting in the wings she was overcome with stage fright, the terrible *trac* as the French call it. She was white with fear, quite nauseous and suspected she had lost the use of her limbs so frantically she was trembling. It gave her no confidence whatsoever in her future as a dancer.

In years to come, when technicians were waiting and francs being lost, others would show less understanding about her hesitancy to perform, but on this occasion her teacher gave her exactly what was needed, a hefty shove from behind. Brigitte recovered her balance and instinct took over. The little girl who was so shy in herself discovered that she enjoyed the performance immensely.

That was why at fourteen she took her first job on the old cruise liner the *De Grasse*. She was one-third of an innocent cabaret, which also included a conjurer and the very handsome actress, Capucine, who was modelling cruise wear. Brigitte was doing what she did best at the time, dancing. Brigitte and Capucine shared a cabin. The cruise was not wildly appreciated as an idea at home but Brigitte seems to have prepared for it with more common sense than romanticism. She spent nights before the trip lying awake figuring out a way of remaining upright on the polished dance floor if the ship lurched from side to side. She stuck rubber soles on her ballet pumps. The sort of dances she prepared for the audience were lacking almost entirely in sex appeal. She faced front and smiled, and performed them with the innocent exuberance of the *midinette* or the cheerleader. More ingenuity, however, went into the costumes which she made herself, for her parents insisted that if she was going to fulfil this engagement she should bear the full brunt of the responsibility.

Thus, by the system of alternately playing out the rope and withholding it, has many a post-war, middle-class parent sought to bring a daughter, and no doubt a son, to heel. The world simply opened up before them, fraught with pitfalls as much as possibilities that had simply never occurred to them in their own youth. Bardot herself, naturally, saw no possible disadvantages to the cruise. She had a wonderful time and clearly looks back on it as a step in the right direction, which was towards a total severance of the umbilical cord endlessly being manipulated by Pilou and Toty. Capucine and she spent most of their time giggling, which is what healthy young teenagers enjoy doing more than most other things despite their parents' darkest fears. The main source of mirth was the fact that their cabin was very small and between Capucine's costumes and Brigitte's there was not much room for their owners. 'It was like a Marx Brothers film,' says Brigitte, who knew about such things from Pilou. The cruise earned Brigitte 40,000 old francs. She was a professional entertainer.

Back in the rue de la Pompe Mme Bardot tried to amalgamate the careers of mother and daughter. She gave up asking Brigitte to pay more attention to her Latin verbs and set about dressing her in the fashions she imitated. Young fashions were innocent and fun. They had high necks, full skirts, and indeed the element of fashion, or at least high fashion, was at a minimum just after the war. The step that Madame took, which was going to make all the difference to her daughter's future, was not to allow her to wear fashionable clothes but to allow her to model them. She it was who directed Brigitte's steps towards the catwalk. In doing this Mme Bardot actually pre-dated two current fashions by forty years.

For the models of the forties and fifties were not fourteen years old as they are quite likely to be today. In the 1940s children were wholesome by contrast, at least as far as their public image was concerned. They were goody-goodies, even those few who were ambitious enough, or whose mothers were, for them to get on-screen. Little Shirley Temple, just five years older than Brigitte, had got the Americans through the Depression and their war effort by creating an innocent vision of hearth and home and the brave young and cute future generation clustered around it. In 1947, the year Brigitte got into ballet school, Shirley was nineteen and making *The Bachelor and the Bobbysoxer*, which tells you where American girls were at. Shirley was cast as an impressionable young girl with a crush on Cary Grant, whose salvation is engineered by her elders and betters. In those days, there was no doubt about it, elders knew better. In 1949 she would enact almost exactly the same story playing opposite David Niven. There at twenty-one she is still portrayed as an innocent, even in America which was about to give the world kissing and petting in the backseat.

Today French magazines aimed at girls barely in their teens offer advice equally on clothes and contraception to make the Anglo-Saxon mother blanch. Such things were completely un-thinkable when the century was in its middle years. At fourteen in

England any good middle-class girl was streaking her way up the left wing with a hockey stick and being groomed for the school leaving exam, not the coming-out dance. France was much the same. A girl did not put on her first long dress until her late teens. It was strapless, white, the colour of the virgin, and moved quite independently from the body it encased. The rituals were well defined. The fashionable girl carried a clutch bag so her hands could never stray, she had sloping elegant shoulders and a long neck and she had to stand up straight to keep her hair tidy on top of her head, which gave her the profile of an alarmed goose. It also made her look a good deal older than the oldest teenager. She looked so proper she was almost regal. Models married barons and earls. There was nothing new in having ambitions for your beautiful daughter but it was new to bring her out before the age of consent.

This is effectively what Anne-Marie Bardot did. She also did it to music. Brigitte *danced* down the catwalk in anticipation of the fashion shows of the liberated sixties. On her head was the millinery of Jean Barthet.

It will certainly amuse students of the cinema that both Brigitte Bardot and Greta Garbo – Greta Gustavson as she was at the time – were propelled towards their cinema careers by modelling, of all things, hats. Brigitte, for one, has hardly ever worn one since, even in the high sun. But she has always liked to think that she has conducted her career, including her retirement from the cinema, as gracefully as Garbo appears to have conducted hers. It appeals to her that Garbo has been able to amass a great deal of money, a great deal of fame and yet remain elusive. Moreover, that above all she has eluded the cinema, which is so compulsively dangerous to those who allow it to be. Bardot may succeed in imitating her in retirement but that and hats is just about where the comparison between them must end. Garbo was photographed wearing several models in a Stockholm store catalogue where she was working as an assistant at the time. Bardot pirouetted down the catwalk to the tune of *Swan Lake*. It was very much Mme Bardot who engineered the event; Barthet himself failed to see the advantages.

Over and over again the story of these first few years is that men, as opposed to women, felt remarkably few vibrations from the gamine. They were not yet susceptible to the tomboy type which Bardot, the elder daughter, represented, vessel of all her

47

parents' hopes for the son they never had. Men were the seducers of the era not women, who were either remote cabaret stars or homemakers. The innocence of the young was not yet in season. In the very near future the Lolita syndrome would be discussed at length in the most academic terms. In fact it became more acceptable if you did discuss it in academic terms and cast an actress like Carroll Baker, who was known to be more intelligent than most, in the role of the seamy sex-kitten Baby Doll. That was in 1956 by which time the American cinema had been affected by Brigitte Bardot. *Lolita* itself, written by prize-winning novelist Vladimir Nabokov, was not filmed until 1962. It would be permissible again – for the first time since the days of Alice – to fancy the young, as long as you had a good story to back it up. The new story (it would be rewritten again as real life paedophilia raised its head) was that the brazen, knowing sexuality of the pubescent child, masquerading treacherously as innocence, could enslave adult hearts and minds without any terminal guilt attaching to the latter. Not knowing that he could have become a trendsetter, Jean Barthet was very slow to catch on to this aspect of Brigitte. He thought her gawky and ill-at-ease with herself, though he relented a little when he saw her dance. He was still in the grip of the fashion at the time, which thought you actually had to do something to earn a living. He didn't know you could just be, and more than that, that you could just be young.

Roger Vadim in his book *Memoirs of the Devil* describes very well the excitement of anticipation among the young people of Paris at the time. Though he had not yet met Brigitte there was no doubt that a lot of people were getting ready for the experience. Young people had had enough of watching the older generation making a mess of things all over the world and those in Occupied Paris had good reason to feel particularly vulnerable. All over Europe students left the universities because they felt old before their time; they wanted to get on with real, not theoretical life. They had seen the fighting and now they wanted to experience something good before it was too late. They started to claim their rights as well as pay their dues.

Popular culture was their battlefront. Vadim, older than Brigitte and with a family who had always let him out on a long string, lived a life of jazz cellars, cafés *klatsches*, midnight raps and sophisticated sex. The young in France were financially resourceful, they knew how to manipulate the liberating armies and they turned their faces to the New World because of them. Just as the New World turned its face to the Old which it had saved. Sinatra, the first international mass youth idol of all time, was more popular in those days in France than in England. In 1949, 800 girls barely older than the fifteen-year-old Brigitte were members of his Marseilles fan club together with 300 young boys.

Girls of all nationalities behaved very badly around Sinatra in a way Al Jolson had never inspired or even Maurice Chevalier. With Tino Rossi they worshipfully threw their coats down on the ground for him to walk on, but with Sinatra they became rapacious. They begged for locks of his hair and sent letters imploring marriage, believing him miserable in his existing marriage. In 1943 he was getting 3,000 fan letters a week. In 1946, when he was voted the most exciting man in the world after President Eisenhower, he sent out 3 million pictures of himself to those same fans. He was earning £250,000 a year and though he was twenty-seven, with his frail frame – rejected 4F for military service because of a perforated ear-drum, an ironic thing in a pop-singer – he looked years younger. In 1947, the year Brigitte got into the Conservatory, his fan clubs among young people around the world totalled 2 million. Meanwhile the older generation were labelling him a Communist. It was difficult to ignore the message that young people were closing ranks in a mass movement which the older generation feared threatened society.

When we, the great audience generation, later suspected there was more to life than a predictable marriage followed by responsible parenthood, when we knew that our younger generation would sap our strength and will just as we had done to our own parents, when we were reluctant consequently to adopt the roles of parenthood, when we rejected the act of growing up and, Peter Pan to a man and woman, were still rejecting it in middle age and aping the fashions of youth, we had role models. We had Elvis Presley and Natalie Wood, who engineered their disappearance from the planet before their appealing acts had to be totally rewritten with the responsibility of experience, and others who had not even wanted to survive the first flush of youth to be tamed by any subsequent reflections: we had James Dean, Françoise Hardy, and Eddie Cochran. We had the near death of Françoise Sagan.

Brigitte, when she was young, had no such role models. There were trends which could be absorbed by the astute child but no starry-eyed or wild representative of youth had explored all the pitfalls of the path, stumbled, fallen, picked himself up again, shown that you could survive, though you might choose not to, and that the rough exchange for your own brief life could be a sort of immortality. Her development from the grey, dormant chrysalis of the chastened post-war scene into the brazen butterfly who was BB, the outrageously beautiful baby, and who wanted always to be BB beyond compromise, who even now says she will always be BB over and above Brigitte Bardot, was a pioneering act.

4. The Bear and the Doll

It has always seemed incredible to me that Roger Vadim, a man who even at the age of twenty-two had a good deal of worldly experience written across his face, could say the following to Mme Bardot and get away with it. 'Madame,' he said one day not long after they had met, 'wouldn't it be fun to take your daughter and make it seem as if she had gone off the rails.' He has been quoted as saying it and she has been quoted as quoting him saying it; it has become part of the history of the downfall of the till-then virgin Brigitte. 'My daughter with her typical religious and bourgeois upbringing excited Vadim,' Anne-Marie is said to have said, just like that as if the rest was inevitable. Mme Bardot is now laid to rest and Vadim is not contradicting such a good quote from his youth.

Surprisingly Mme Bardot did not show Roger Vadim the door. She heard him out and in effect she connived. 'As an Aquarian she must have had a liking for the unexpected,' her future son-in-law said later, though nothing as respectable as marriage had been proposed at the time. The cast list thus suggested consists of an exceptionally charming Vadim, an exceptionally strong-willed Brigitte, and an exceptionally ambitious and frustrated mother. Louis Bardot by all accounts had a much more suspicious nature where this rival for his elder daughter's affections was concerned. He took Vadim to his desk, unlocked the drawer and showed him a pistol. 'If you lay a finger on my daughter I shall not hesitate to use this on you,' he said. Mijanou the younger daughter remembers this with something a little like envy now. 'Everyone always did adore Brigitte.'

For all these extreme reactions Vadim had no particular designs on Brigitte when they first met. He had been shown a picture in a magazine and had written to the girl at 1 rue de la Pompe on behalf of Marc Allegret, the director who wanted to make a film about the young, post-war generation. The letter was as hackneyed as it could be: 'Would you like to go into films?' it asked. 'If you would and it would interest you to make a test, telephone me. My name is Marc Allegret.' It was sent express. To a little French girl – and her mother no less – it was the equivalent of a summons from Louis B. Mayer. Anne-Marie later said: 'I decided to play the heavy mother because I didn't really want her to go into films at all. I wanted her to keep on dancing.' All the same she ignored her husband's advice and telephoned Allegret.

Allegret had been shown Brigitte's picture on the cover of the fashion magazine *Elle*, an assignment that had resulted from her modelling. He was not the sort of man a *bonne bourgeoise* would get to meet in a lifetime of family dinners. He was a legend in the French cinema for his knack of directing artistic films which made money. He it was who had made a sex-symbol out of Simone Simon in the year Brigitte was born with the film *Le Lac aux Dames* with a screenplay by Colette. An educated man, son of a pastor, he came from a big, close-knit, and influential family who were genuinely interested in the arts. He had always kept his eye open for new stars. His formula was to team a beautiful young thing with some old and tried talent. He gave Michèle Morgan her first break in *Gribouille* with Raimu, the great French music-hall character actor. He discovered Jean-Pierre Aumont, the brilliant leading man of *Hôtel du Nord*. He surrounded himself with young assistants with equally keen eyes. Allegret was then in his late forties and Vadim was his link with the younger world. He was fascinated by the rootless young people who gathered on the Left Bank in the first days of peace, bumming successfully off café owners and well-heeled customers. It was a brilliantly mixed society, which included the more unusual, older generation who had always felt at home in the university area of Paris. Vadim knew Colette herself, whom he used to visit in the gardens of the Palais Royal where she spent her last years; he knew Cocteau and Gide, who he says compared him to his brilliantly unprincipled character, Lafcadio in *The Vatican Cellars*, the man who could get away with any crime. Gide was the in-name to drop at the time, before he was dropped in favour of Sartre, and Vadim was determined to be in.

In London, which has always been both more compartmentalized and diffuse as a society, it is difficult to imagine the optimism with which people like Vadim fashioned their future out of chance meetings in the depressed days just after the war. Paris was a small society then as now and you could literally meet anyone over a drink which, with no licensing hours, could be made to last the whole day, if you chose. Politics, philosophy, and the arts were all a part of their conversation and the great prize for the quasi-penniless young people who shared their food ration tickets and tried to scrounge a few francs with their guitar-playing, was a couple of days' work at the film studio in a crowd scene or, better still, as a *silhouette*, a minor speaking role. The least you stood to make out of it was 120 francs a day – you could also dream of being spotted and becoming a star.

The watchword was liberty and no doubt the war had something to do with that. Roger Vadim Plemiannikov was truly an urchin of the hostilities. The records say he was born in 1927, sometimes his birth has been put at 1928, and Vadim has claimed he was seven in 1937, making him a creation of the disturbed thirties. His father, Igor Plemiannikov, was a white Russian officer, a talented pianist who fled to Paris after the revolution. There he made an unimpressive living in the *boîtes* and bordellos of St-Germain des Près. He finally married a French girl who seems to have had both beauty and initiative, which was just as well for Igor's was to be a brief and unfulfilled life which left his son with little more than some fascinating background material. Igor had studied at the Warsaw Conservatory and Vadim's paternal grandparents still lived in Warsaw when the boy was born. Vadim claims to remember taking his first steps in a snow-covered garden in the Polish capital at the age of ten months. Precocity has always been much-prized by Vadim and he encouraged it in Bardot when they met.

At fourteen months Vadim recalls some early practice in bargaining, over a sweet. His father insisted that he ask for it in Russian. Vadim's career at this time was already taking on international proportions. Igor had become a naturalized French citizen before his son was born and a minor French diplomat. The early thirties, when Vadim was either five, four, or two, depending on whom you believe, found the family living in the consulate in Alexandria. It was here that Vadim made a significant discovery which, pooled with Bardot's sexuality, would ignite the Western world. A Muslim maid, surprised by Igor Plemiannikov without her veil, picked up her skirts to cover her face in the presence of the two French males, thus revealing most of her private parts.

Igor laughed. Vadim says: 'I had just discovered that the rules of decency as applied to the feminine body were rather variable – they seemed to depend on geographical location and religion.'

He also discovered a taste for living dangerously. He remembers vividly that Europeans were being crucified in the Egyptian streets in the early thirties during a spate of nationalist fervour, that one of the tradesmen who came to the house caught the plague and one of his young contemporaries died of cerebro-spinal meningitis in the family drawing room. Such things would have been unthinkable in the sixteenth *arrondissement* where Brigitte was simultaneously taking her first steps in the world. For a brief period Mme Plemiannikov sought sanctuary in France with Vadim and his older sister Hélène but she was soon back with her husband abroad, this time in Mersin in Turkey near the Syrian border. There life went on as usual with a public hanging every three weeks which delighted the young boy. He also enjoyed the time he was kidnapped for political reasons – typically he fell on his feet and was given the best bedroom in a poor Turkish house – and becoming intimately acquainted with the remains of several thousand French soldiers buried in a mass grave. Back in France his father dropped dead in front of him of a heart attack. His life insurance had just expired. Vadim was seven, nine or ten, a hungry angel.

Vadim relates these stories with relish but it would be wrong to conclude that he was totally insensitive. He seems to have loved his immediate family, including a stepfather not much older than himself and to have sought in vain all his life to re-create a similarly close-knit group of bohemian spirits. He was never ghoulish, rather condemned to be full of the detached curiosity which has always prompted him to be a writer. His first character as an adolescent and indeed his last as a grown man in his recent novel *The Hungry Angel* was the wise Sophie, a name which Bardot would take for herself as soon as they became close friends. 'Poor Sophie is suffering too much,' she would cry in the third person like a child when her parents prevented them from being together. (The use of the third person by an adult is always an attempt to play at make-believe and avoid direct confrontation.) 'Please do something, she can't go on living like this,' she would urge. When she wrote him love letters she signed them Sophie. Macabrely the original Sophie, the twelve-year-old girl who had inspired the name, was dead. Vadim, not much older than her at the time, had seen her lying across the rear wheel of a tram, naked from the waist down, crushed by a German explosion in Toulon, such a perversely erotic image that it is worth noting that Sophie is the name of one of the heroines of the Marquis de Sade. It is also the name of the original naughty little girl in the famous French children's story by the Russian-born Comtesse de Ségur. Vadim brought to his relationship with Bardot a lot of numbing, first-hand experiences from which Brigitte had been insulated. He had salvaged from the war an unusual imagination and a low boredom threshold.

While Marc Allegret studied the fourteen-year-old Brigitte in his usual impassive way in his living room off the Champs-Élysées, she studied Vadim. 'Well, he was entirely different from anything I had ever seen before,' she says now. 'We were simply not used to anything so romantic and good-looking. All the boys I knew had spots and glasses. They were all going to be medical students or engineers – what we call the Thomas Diaphorus type. I said to my mother afterwards, "Did you notice that queer-looking man? He's got a very odd face, don't you think?" ' Mother agreed. All the same Vadim looked fairly clean cut compared to what parents would be asked to condone in the name of creativity in the near future. His hair was relatively short and well-kept. They thought it too long, of course, they could see he had not been overfed and they also took a dislike to his open sandals. His long, thin face gave him an intense, lugubrious look fashionable for the time, which its owner liked to compare to a character out of Dostoevsky. Despite his itinerant childhood Vadim was much better read than Brigitte and was always modelling his life on literature. He certainly never lacked self-confidence and was determined to succeed. Like most people who come within a ghost of such ambition in the film business he liked playing for high stakes and he could charm the birds off the trees. Brigitte too, it turned out, liked playing for high stakes, though till they met she hadn't determined what they might be. 'I couldn't take my eyes off him,' she says, 'he seemed so strange. He talked as if the world were his, and everything he said was fascinating.' She threw down the glove almost immediately. 'We flirted. It wasn't the first time I had flirted, even though I was only fourteen, but up to that time my flirtations had not been serious.' She left the older people talking and drew his attention to her by wandering out on to the balcony in the summer sun. He followed her. 'I love balconies,' she said. 'Why?' asked Vadim. 'Do you have to have a reason for loving?' she asked. When girls make an excuse to use the word love, the feeling which inspires them is never theoretical.

Vadim had been there before. He had lost his virginity at sixteen with a student actress in a Normandy hayloft on D-Day, when according to him the barrage made the walls and ceiling, if not the earth, move. He had also fallen in love in the best way, which is at first sight, with a sixteen-year-old girl called Nicole. Vadim saw her as 'the incarnation of sexuality'. She moved in with him briefly in his mother's flat, left him and was never heard of again.

By comparison his first impressions of Brigitte were coolly analytical. In his autobiography *Memoirs of the Devil* he describes the girl who was the daughter of a liquid oxygen manufacturer as if she had royal blood. Her dancer's training made her hold her head up proudly at all times, and the alert eyes which followed his every movement seemed feline to Vadim. All this was in complete contrast to a mischievous sense of humour. She could be direct without being aggressive and make fun of her mother's pretensions without showing disrespect. As to her looks, she was just a girl whose hair was on the dark side, who wore no make-up and very simple clothes.

Those straightforward observations mark the first recorded description of the girl who would drag the reputation of all women from the pedestal to which they had previously aspired, who would do it willingly with no economic pressures upon her, who would pounce without a frisson of regret on that page in history which was just about to be turned by someone, anyone, and would claim it for herself. In liberating women she would undermine the mysterious power they had to retreat into the sanctuary of their bodies, which rare sanctuary only they could grant, and she would destroy the Judeo–Christian myth of womanhood only to expose a dangerous truth, buried purposely in the realms of antiquity by the guardians of society, which is that women, driven by their powerful sexuality, can be fickle, selfish, and shortsighted while the bloom is on their skin and set themselves up to be their own worst enemies when it is not. Shrewish, illogical, imperfect, they hold men while they can in a tyrant's vice of perfectionist expectations. Brigitte, once aroused, was determined to get her man. Vadim saw her only as a means of pleasing Allegret, who had commissioned a film script from him.

He agreed to coach her for a screen test. 'Rather dark, no make-up, simply dressed,' if you remember – certainly not blonde. Basic *Pygmalion* material.

All that happened in July 1949, according to Mme Bardot, who seems to have left the meeting with the distinct impression that she had got her own way. Brigitte had had her little brush with the cinema, her ego tickled by the meeting with one of France's cult directors. Now nothing more would be said about a film career. Vadim remembers things differently. Allegret normally plucked his girls from drama school but Brigitte had no dramatic training. Vadim made arrangements to rehearse the girl once a week on Wednesdays after dancing class till she was ready for her screen test. He persuaded himself that the mother would go along with this so that Brigitte could enjoy the illusion of independence before settling down with a nice diplomat, or, prize of the sixteenth *arrondissement*, an engineer. Well, Vadim had toyed with the idea of becoming a diplomat like his father. He had been to the School of Oriental Languages and was about to take an entrance exam to the Foreign Service when he got sidetracked by the idea of drama school. Auditioning with the part of the madman in Courteline's *Le Commissaire est Bon Enfant* he was accepted along with the mime Marcel Marceau straight into the senior class of the Charles Dullin school, one of several Paris stage schools owned by private actors who were steeped in the declamatory tradition of old-fashioned French theatre rather than cinema. Acceptance to the Dullin school meant that they could get practical experience as extras on stage at the Sarah Bernhardt theatre.

Extra, however, has never been a word in Vadim's vocabulary. Twice he failed to turn up when so cast, once by Dullin on-stage in *King Lear* and once by Allegret in a film. Both were sacking offences but on each occasion Vadim seems only to have singled himself out for favourable attention. Allegret indeed commissioned the footloose youth – he was nineteen, twenty-one, or twenty-two at the time, 'the youngest screenplay writer in France . . . perhaps in the world' – to write the script about other footloose youths in which he planned to star the baby Bardot.

Rehearsals for her screen test took place at the flat of the dark and handsome actor Daniel Gélin in the avenue Wagram, where Vadim, who always hops from friend to friend, was living temporarily. Brigitte was keen and innocent enough to arrive on time, which would not always be her habit in the future. After some coaching, however, Vadim was still not convinced she was promising material, though his impressions were prophetic. She was too independent and impatient to bother learning any of Charles Dullin's acting techniques. 'She could imagine a character in any situation as long as that character was herself.' This would be very important to her career, for the world which had been straining towards the cult of the individual, towards naturalism and away from the grand conventions of the nineteenth century, would make this jump with the new generation. Being herself Bardot would later enjoy her greatest success, though Vadim had yet to come to this conclusion. Was it the cynical pursuit of his own career that led him to spend a lot of time in this apparently unpromising young girl's company? In his novel *The Hungry Angel*, which appears to be almost wholly autobiographical, the Marc Allegret character is obsessed with the Bardot figure, and the angel, a devil in disguise, enjoys no little satisfaction in seducing her away from the older man who gives the young couple his blessing in order to keep access open to the girl. Vadim studied Bardot in her dancing class where he would meet her after school. In front of the mirror she was magnificently free.

In front of the camera she was leaden. Also, like most teenagers of the time, she was prematurely middle aged. 'She spoke as if she was wearing her mother's denture,' said Allegret cruelly. Pierre Braunberger, the money man, if not Allegret the would-be director who had seen talent blossom under his tutelage, dropped the idea of casting her and Vadim's film *Les Lauriers sont Coupés* was postponed indefinitely. Vadim, though ever charming when he recalls those days now, must have been more than irritated at the time. It was not the first time a girl had tested for the film he wanted so much and failed. Even before he met Brigitte he had run across Leslie Caron on the cross-Channel ferry. Thinking her very distinctive, he had persuaded Allegret to go and see her on stage in Paris in Roland Petit's ballet *La Rencontre*. Then too it had been the producer, Braunberger, who gave her the thumbs down. He was wrong about Caron, who was spotted just about that time by Gene Kelly and whisked to the United States following *An American in Paris*. Braunberger was not convinced that it was enough for these girls just to be young. Vadim came to the conclusion he was on the wrong track and put the fourteen-year-old Bardot very much on the back burner.

Until one day he was bored. It was early autumn and he was

alone in the Gélin flat where the telephone had been cut off as he recalls it. Down in the café he ran through his address book and his small change. With his last twenty-franc piece he called Brigitte. Though all of Paris was willing to abandon him that day, he was touched that she was not.

According to Mme Bardot the screen test did not take place until after that fateful telephone call. Perhaps she was protecting her maternal reputation, perhaps not. Brigitte was strong-willed and might not have jumped at the opportunity of seeing the young man having once failed him. Either way it is agreed that Anne-Marie and her husband Louis were not in Paris when the two young people renewed their acquaintance. They were either in Biarritz or in Bougival, the suburb where the grandmother had her chalet. The grandmother meanwhile was looking after Brigitte and Mijanou in the rue de la Pompe. Vadim remembers there was a fourth person in the flat that day, a rather feeble contemporary of Brigitte's, an admirer although she was only fourteen. But nothing serious had passed between them and he became immediately resigned to losing his paramour, leaving the field open to Vadim who seemed a grown man to the girls. All parties concerned including Vadim were entirely satisfied with the first impression he created on the materialistic middle-class home, which was that there was some danger to the family silver. Their thoughts then turned to the daughters. After Vadim had reappeared several times in the space of a week Mme Mucel thought it worthwhile to alert Brigitte's mother, who immediately took a train and returned from holiday. She found her daughter forever altered. Brigitte had kissed Vadim.

Is a kiss enough to change a life? In those days, when mothers prized virginity on marriage, it was indeed. Coupling was not a subject of discussion, yet on every level it would have been an interesting one. Middle-class French mothers were still telling their daughters that little boys were found in cabbage patches and little girls in rosebeds. But it was not only a question of an anatomy lesson. The strength Brigitte had begun to feel in her dance classes seemed to belong uniquely to her. There are no influences on the adolescent girl comparable to the power she begins to feel in herself. It comes about all of a sudden when the body has matured though the mind will be a lifetime in the making. Many people have written of the diffidence of adolescence but they are wrong to forget its other identity as a moment of release. The child woman has a brief, wonderful glimpse of immortality. She is on the edge of a great adventure where she is chief protagonist and author of the script. There are no bargains and no co-stars. There is only the most compelling freedom. Yet the direction in which this freedom compels her is towards the imprisonment of the first kiss.

Why imprisonment? You need two to do it, that's why. In the future Bardot would be overwhelmed by this need to ensure a willing supply of fresh young flesh to succour her own. For even as the young man prepared to leave, the question loomed, when would he return? You may kiss the mirror or a photograph, and Brigitte did, you may embrace a memory and like Brigitte you may languish and pine. But you will not summon up the same adrenalin on which you are now hooked, only a void of with-drawal symptoms and in the pain of these the high-flying freedom of the single-minded is forgotten. Once you are coupled it is a long time before you will ever be single again.

Bardot, of course, like everyone else, saw only a more intox-icating freedom at the time. Where she had been struggling to define her new freedom in relationship to past dependencies – on Anne-Marie and Louis, on her nice school Hattemer, and the familiar suburb Bougival – her freedom all of a sudden had a focus and a name, a foreign name. Roger Vladimir Plemiannikov. She would call him Vadim. She immediately transferred to her new idol all the romantic attachment which had lain latent since the powerful child had come to realize the older world had feet of clay.

It all happened in the space of a kiss in the hall. Grandmama, whom she loved as she would later love a lot of older people, left the young couple alone in that spirit of envy, excitement and *laissez-faire* the old have when they know nothing in the world matters that much. To Brigitte the kiss was the most hopeful and the most exciting thing that had ever happened to her, it was also the most dangerous and most sorrowful, arousing the sense of fear always attendant on a need. Could a kiss mean all this so that the nights could never again be used for sleep? And what lay beyond? Anne-Marie and Louis, like most middle-class parents, had not found a way of alerting their daughter to this mystery. She came to the involuntary conclusion that they had betrayed her, that she was a changeling child able only to share her guilty secret with the man who had revealed it to her. When Anne-Marie came back from holiday she had not yet gained a son but she knew she had to court Vadim, despite his potential to corrupt, for she had already lost a daughter.

On her fifteenth birthday, on 28 September 1949, Brigitte, who had already been kissed, stood in front of the full-length mirror in her parents' flat and took stock of herself. She saw a tiny waist: 'Yes, that will be all right.' The legs passed inspection as well. 'But my bosom! I had twice too much. And with my nineteen-inch waist it looked ridiculous.' Unlike many teenage girls who feel helplessly threatened by their new shape, Bardot was proud rather than ashamed of it. If she needed any excuse to replace Mme Bardot's ambitions for her with her own she had now found it. Neither a ballet dancer nor a model would be much served by her over-large superstructure. The same feature, however, was no disadvantage to a lover. It was quite clear to her at this moment in which direction her future approbation lay.

If she had not turned Vadim's head already, he certainly began to take a more sensual view of her now. 'She had a way of being very free with her body. And her mind. When I say free with her body I am talking about the way she would walk, move, look at people, sit. She was also for a little *bourgeoise* in a certain way very revolutionary. She approached life, any kind of problem, with a really free mind.'

Her main attraction was that she was very different from all the other girls he knew, fringe members of society who gave themselves up freely to bohemian experiences. One moment he felt like corrupting her as he had explained to her mother, the next he felt warily protective. Brigitte, who had always felt protected, rather favoured corruption. Her main problem during her sixteenth year was how to belong totally to Vadim. She wanted to understand fully all the mysteries of her sex and she could not rest until she had done so. Even thirty years ago a girl might well have felt like this but most, even before the great event, could also understand that this new knowledge might entail an onerous responsibility. Thus they were nearly always able to find an excuse for postponing it, to linger in their girlhood until the time was absolutely right. They were not thinking of the children they might have as a result and the consequent need to marry. Even in the days of imperfect contraception a young girl never imagined she would fall prey to such practicalities. She is a free spirit remember, on whom the discovery of the body is forced by her arch enemy, time. If nature postpones the discovery she is lucky, for she has time to hone the sense of her own identity – which will be the only thing that remains with her till the end. Bardot was robbed of this time, not because she was bound to grow up quicker than anyone else but because she came into contact with a man who made her feel like a woman and who, for a while at least, seemed the substance of her wildest dreams.

In these days of mixed schooling and stereo sex education it is difficult to imagine the tricks played by girls' minds when these sorts of experiences came together. Bardot was a girl from a family of girls. She knew nothing at all about boys. The decent, mythical end of love between the sexes was the plighting of eternal troth. But she was not even of the age of consent. Vadim was allowed to pick Brigitte up from her parents' flat and take her to the cinema as long as they were accompanied. The role of duenna often fell to Mijanou, just ten years old and already fed up with playing second fiddle. That, alas, was the part the Great Composer had written for her. Scholastically bright - she left her *lycée* with good qualifications - she was a pleasant-looking child who would grow up into an equally pleasant-looking adult. Her hair was always a little redder than Brigitte's, her skin paler and on the freckled side. She inherited the patrician features of her mother and father, as a grown-up she was to be slightly smaller than her sister and lighter in build, but the real difference between her and Brigitte has always lain around the mouth. Mijanou's was tight and slightly pursed whereas Brigitte's retroussé upper lip, apparently permanently proffered to the world in a suggestive gesture, would give rise to the story that she, amongst all actresses who are traditionally careless with their favours, would invent the theatrical custom of the ubiquitous kiss. Mijanou had to determine what to do about such an unfair distribution of charms at an early age. If her sister kissed her boyfriend even in the safety of a public place, such as the Métro, she told her parents and there was trouble.

The stage was set for a pitched battle with the family and by the time it was over many many years later it would have proved itself a pyrrhic one. They didn't send her away to take her Bac, which she never completed - perhaps they felt they could not. Headstrong young girls are very tiring to the middle-aged. They didn't even insist she stayed on to take her Bac in Paris. Her mind was obviously elsewhere. But they did insist on managing the love-affair. They were giving with one hand and taking away with the other, a favourite trick of the fainthearted and pity them you might, but the seeds of discontent were sowed in Bardot for years to come.

Between her last lesson in school and her dancing class she arranged to meet Vadim for secret trysts. He has written about the physical things that lovers do together to pleasure each other without the commitment of an ultimate act. This might have been enough for him, a bystander with a bohemian life elsewhere, especially as he had taken to heart her father's objection to their relationship. Often, after their meetings, he would not even accompany her home, particularly if they were later than they should be, for fear that Pilou would be standing on the seventh-floor balcony armed with some missile which he had every intention of throwing. No wonder Brigitte felt obliged to provoke Vadim to declare his responsibility for her. Little by little she ensnared him with the passionate will to be loved which would become legendary in later life. Another girl, more shrewd or less passionate, might have shrugged her shoulders and gone back to her ballet classes but Brigitte, having spotted an object of her very own desire, was determined to have her way. Women's desire to seduce is at least as strong as that of the opposite sex. They will promise their man eternal devotion in return for his sponsorship in the world and when this brilliant vision is not fulfilled they will rail not against the practicalities that come between them but against the man himself for personally engineering their disillusion. Thus many a man who has never been a lover of the great Bardot has seen the woman in his life as the Devil's work, has spotted that his own Faustian contract was an eternity of sadness for a brief moment of triumph.

'Am I a woman now? Is that it?' Bardot asked Vadim one day after they had stolen some time together.

He laughed because he was still deliciously in control. 'Only twenty per cent,' he said. She asked him again and again each time they met. One evening he said 100 per cent. 'She began to laugh and clap,' Vadim remembers. 'She opened a window and shouted to the street, "That's it. I am a woman."'

By the time Bardot was sixteen she was still a brunette but she was almost certainly Vadim's mistress. The exact date of the act is veiled by both protagonists in the decency of the past, but her sea-change had happened in the most tentative circumstances and from time to time she was overcome with unstable melancholy. 'What does it mean being a woman?' she would ask. One thing it meant to a *petite bougeoise* was the right to be with her lover in security all the time and she set about doing everything she could to force this next issue, bearing dramatic tales of her parents' threats back to a rather squalid little love-nest under the eaves at 16 quai d'Orléans, where Vadim had finally set up a home of his own with a Chinese cook and the actor Christian Marquand.

Looking back now it is easy to see that she was disappointed. Women have lost their virginity in worse circumstances and with worse consequences but even those might seem more acceptable to a romantic sixteen-year-old than the hypocrisy of a non-event. Middle-class parents reining in their daughters with a last jerk against the tide of changing moral fashion made a nonsense of their reasons for making virginity such a great prize. They invoked the wrath of God and the icon of purity when plainly the great post-war pursuit was blatant materialism. This did not go unnoticed by the ungrateful generation on whom they lavished it. The expanding bourgeoisie was a curious half-caste, created everywhere by superior universal education, the knowledge education imparts was still regarded with the utmost suspicion. The Bardots, pillars of society, were basically ignorant, like millions of other similar families all over the world. To break down the barriers of the comfortable fiction within which they lived seemed to them like an incitement to hedonism. They told their children nothing and were surprised when they found out. They lacked the basic psychology to alert them to the fact that their daughters were bound to pick forbidden fruit. Vadim's family, hit by some of the obvious tragedies of life, was bold and pragmatic, not so Bardot's, full of received truths which were just about to be re-examined.

From its beginnings the bourgeoisie was proud of its image of stultifying self-righteousness and devoted to the outrageous hypocrisy necessary to uphold it. The sixties and seventies would expose this hypocrisy in a mass movement which was a mixture of idealism, sentiment, and naïvety. Bardot smelled this change more than a decade before it happened. If society was in an inflammable state, Brigitte was like a firelighter. She had a head start because by an accident of combined fates she had found out these inconsistencies while she was still young enough to care passionately about reconciling them. She had always been the centre of attention. Yet her greatest discovery, the pleasure she had invented herself with her lover, the joy her parents had never revealed to her because they knew they would lose her that way, had to remain a secret. Her vengeance against all those people who had disillusioned her with their miserable furtive approach to her finest hour would be henceforth to bring the most intimate details of her private life right out into the open for even strangers to see. She didn't know these things yet of course, but by the time she had won her parents' permission to become a respectable bride, the switch had been thrown which would expose her instead as a goddess of naked lust.

5. The Novices

If in retrospect Bardot's childhood was a sort of bondage, it was nothing to the slavery she was now embarked upon. There are many clues to her future instability in the unsatisfactory relationship between her and Vadim before they were married. Yet at the time it appeared to her the most satisfactory thing in a life which was one of accumulated frustrations. She had no qualifications other than her appeal to Vadim and declined to pursue any. She had no confidant other than him. Her sister was too young, her parents were her enemy. She neglected her schoolwork and gave no thought to a career. Her height and her figure had snatched away any chance of being a classical dancer. She had failed her screen test and even if she had passed it she was convinced her parents would not have allowed her to stray far enough away from them to make a film.

Looking back on the choices she had as a young girl, she has said many times that she should have married an ordinary man and lived the family life of her parents. 'I feel that I have missed out on life,' she said rather prematurely at the age of twenty-four, 'I should never have made movies but now I am in the rat-race. At eighteen I should have married someone stable, a real companion. We should have had children, a villa at Arcachon [between Biarritz and Bordeaux, the archetypal spa of the Atlantic Coast], and a lot of togetherness without dramatics. That would have been marvellous. But in love I have never counted . . . ' Had she set her heart on someone with the same marginal experience of life as she had, he might have introduced her gradually to her womanhood and it would have been a different story. A more delicate, older man might have made her happy had he crossed her path. But no one appeared in her life at that time who could persuade her of the gentle virtues of her background. The plain fact was, she was not in love with a man who could live her parents' life.

Vadim did not want anything so predictable. He couldn't really put his finger on what it was he did want except personal success. Though romantic in his imagination, his appearance and his connections, he was like most men who aim to succeed, completely practical. This in the end would start to prey on Bardot's sense of self-worth. The priority in his mind was not a wife he could not afford. In this he was an ally, if an unwitting one, of the senior Bardots. 'You must understand,' he wrote in the letters they exchanged at the time, 'that your parents really do love you but they are scared I am not going to make you happy because I have no situation and no money. Don't be afraid. It will be all right. I promise you. Vadim.' The tears fell on those words and on the answers which Brigitte wrote, so genuinely laden with emotion that she seemed to have an impressive writing talent. Years later Gunther Sachs noticed the same talent and treasured her letters long after he had parted company with the writer. As for Vadim, he has kept their correspondence to this day for, having read them and wept over them, Brigitte returned his letters to her lover for safe-keeping because she was so afraid of her father. Everybody seemed to know where they were going except Brigitte, whose future was not in her own hands. No wonder time hung so heavily. She was not even allowed to partake to the full of her lover's social life because of her father's midnight curfew. She snatched her love life in Vadim's garret and when he went on to the jazz cellars of post-war Paris she returned home half across the town to her lonely bed. While she loved company and was denied it, he had access to the sort of people who could not but arouse her suspicions if not her jealousy.

Vadim was enthralled by everything in those days. Everyone he met seemed to have an exciting future or an exciting past. His natural habitat was far removed from respectable Passy. His tiny little flat under the eaves where he had made her into a woman, though unimpressive on the inside maybe, looked right out over the Seine on to the rear elevation of Notre Dame in the oldest part of Paris. Steeped in the cinema as he was, he could practically imagine himself looking into the eyes of Charles Laughton as the hunchback bellringer up in the cathedral tower. A short walk over the river the entire street theatre of St-Germain beckoned him. Dissidents, fire-eaters, foreigners, outsiders of all kinds have gathered there over the centuries. The Left Bank, left-wing scene had hardly abated throughout the Occupation, indeed in some ways it had been stimulated by the Nazi presence in the capital. In the Café Flore on the boulevard St-Germain resistance was a way of life – against anything solid, predictable, bourgeois – in short the entire atmosphere of the Bardot home. Many of the young people who gathered there religiously every day around noon had no choice in the matter. They were ostracized from their own societies by some accident of birth or politics. They were international: Italian anti-Fascists, Spanish Republicans, Communists, Trotskyites, and many of them of course were Jews. Though they came from such different backgrounds they were passionately loyal to the idea which had brought them all together, often calling each other by the intimate *tu* at first sight in a way that the coldly correct Bardot family, who had told their daughters to say *vous* on account of a broken vase, could never imagine. They may have been poor but they prided themselves on their vitality and resourcefulness. If they had to eke out one lemonade till dinner time there was no shame in that. Picasso might come in in the meantime and buy them dinner because he felt in need of the attentions of a young courtier that night, or the sculptor Giacometti, who could put a meal on a patron's account. They lived from hand to mouth off the unexpected. There were no orthodox fashion plates among them like the teenage Brigitte dolled up in gloves and Eton collars from her mother's collection. They wore dirty polo-neck sweaters, old corduroy jackets and they could not afford to send their trenchcoats to the cleaner's. The women wore no make-up and if there were in fact very few women among them that was no comfort to Brigitte, for those that did gather there obeyed a quite unconventional morality.

Sexually and in other ways you could not predict their behaviour by the standards of Passy. Some of them hardly worked at all, they even turned down work if it didn't suit them. They discussed the theatre and the cinema at length but from an intellectual point of view which simply was not Brigitte's. They idolized Jean-Louis Barrault, who was putting on his own productions in attics if need be, and Jacques Prévert the screenwriter who helped him find his touching brilliance in *Les Enfants du Paradis*. This was serious competition for a girl who refused to pass any exams and who knew only that she enjoyed being looked at. There is a sense in which theatre people love the life of the troupe as much as they love the limelight. Even as a teenager Brigitte had not been that sort of a person. She had been the star in her father's life, now at last she was the star in Vadim's and that was how she wanted to keep it. The trouble was Vadim knew so many stars. He hung round all the places where such people went and encountered, if only briefly, both those who were established and those in embryo: Ernest Hemingway, Prince Aly Khan, the future President Kennedy, Marlon Brando. He knew equally well Jean Genet, the Rothschilds and Hélène Lazareff who created *Elle* – and Bardot too for that matter, by first using her on the cover of her magazine. The one that had prompted his letter to Allegret.

The day that happened everything seemed set for success, in the fatalistic way of which Bardot, as an involuntary member of the self-effacing middle class, best approves. One day, just after she had climbed down from an enthusiastic reception on M. Barthet's catwalk in the Galerie David Drouand, the telephone had rung at home for Mme Bardot. It was the editor of the 'Junior Miss' section of *Jardin des Modes*, Mme de la Villuchet, who as it happens was Mme Bardot's cousin by marriage. She asked to borrow the fourteen-year-old Brigitte to stand in for a model who had gone down with measles. The next thing that happened was that *Elle* itself phoned. They wanted to use her on their cover. The request occasioned much soul-searching within the Bardot family. Brigitte was still a schoolgirl and it did not fit in at all with Pilou's theory of life for his daughter's face to smile out at the whole of France from the bookstands. His wife, like most women, was a natural stage mother. Her main problem was not reconciling herself to the idea of Brigitte as a cover-girl but reconciling her husband. She decided to say nothing and let events speak for themselves. Meanwhile her bourgeois modesty was satisfied (her French thriftiness can't have been) by *Elle*'s offer of a small fee – accounts vary from nothing at all to 5,000 old francs which Brigitte judiciously spent on a book for her father and pigeons for herself. Mme Bardot could comfort herself that her daughter was not a fully-fledged professional cover-girl. There was also an agreement that only the initials of the child, not her full identity, be disclosed. BB was born.

In the event it was not a very daring photograph. Brigitte, in a plaid dress and pony-tail, was the demure daughter-figure in a mother and daughter shot, which if anything calls to mind the sort of photograph used to promote a post-war knitting pattern. What *Elle* had anticipated was not a new form of beauty to rival the current heroines of the international cinema – Rita Hayworth, Jane

Wyman, Ava Gardner, Jean Simmons, Maria Schell, and Sophia Loren – but the youth cult. Vadim, forced to become the man in the family at the age of eight, was a founder member of that.

Elle's legendary success on three continents over the next twenty years was as the definitive, stylish young people's magazine. Well-bred daughters of affluent fathers pored over its fashions over tea at boarding school and those who had enough influence with Papa brought the right clothes back from trips to Paris. They wore them in the underpaid prestige jobs favoured by the middle classes for their daughters in those post-war days when young ladies did not necessarily expect to go out to work. That they had access to *Elle* at all was rooted in the fashion for finishing a girl on the Continent, where she would learn at least how to order dinner in the best restaurant in three languages and try on an outfit in a boutique. The need to earn money may have been entirely vulgar but it was agreed that a girl needed something to occupy her before marriage to keep her out of trouble. You couldn't keep her corseted indoors any more sewing samplers or fire·screens, but in her Chanel suit, her sling-back, two-tone shoes, her gilt chains, and her pearl ropes she could grace a 'nice' office as a general factotum or receptionist.

Before Biba, before Mary Quant, before the apotheosis of Levi-Strauss there was only Chanel to symbolize the freedom of attire needed by the young working woman and *Elle* was the Bible that glorified her. Mothers saw only the well-groomed aspect of her fashions and turned a blind eye to the fact that their designer was the darling mistress of more than one upper-class bounder and that her nickname Coco derived from her passion for cocaine highs. Those who could not afford real Chanel, or even a pale shop-bought imitation, sat for hours at their mother's sewing machines to reproduce one. Women were all waiting for a new image which would flatter the young and be affordable. The funny thing was that when the image became affordable, so would the women. They would become cheap in the old-fashioned sense of available, though of course in the new egalitarian world this became a virtue. Availability was deep inside respectable young women at the time, just put there by the force of history. And availability in young women was naturally what interested Vadim, who was able to argue the virtue of it by defining the timely yearning women had to take the centre stage and by appearing sympathetic to it.

70

What was about to happen to women would not be easy for every man to understand. There were those who would resent the competition in the workplace and those who would feel the future of society adversely prejudiced by women's absence from the home. There were those who, try as they might with their minds, just could not respond with their bodies to a more militant fairer sex. They became impotent and confused. There were those men who became sexless before the new woman and those who decidedly preferred their own kind. But Vadim had no fear of women and no fear of strength in them. He had grown up with a mother and sister who had always had an enterprising response to life for as long as he could remember. If the majority of women could be persuaded to take responsibility for themselves, more-over, he realized that for men of his sort of lusty character the way would be free for more adventures and less guilt.

In mulling over all this he conceived a heroine of the times.

I had an idea of the type of woman I was looking for. I wanted to express a certain type of femininity which I thought was new. Women have always been conditioned to a form of slavery towards men. Ultimately the man may become the slave, but it doesn't begin that way. In the past women have achieved their power over men in a variety of purely feminine ways – using charm, coquetry, trickery if you like. But I feel that the young girl of today – the sixteen- and seventeen-year-old – has a masculine mind. She wants to be free to love as a man does. I am not speaking of the career woman, the intelligent woman or the blue-stocking. I am interested in the girl who is not very brilliant, who takes her freedom with both hands and expresses it in the way that comes most naturally to her – particularly in her relations with men.

But could things really change between the sexes? Thirty years after Vadim's definition of the new, masculine woman some people are just beginning to suspect that most women, as well as the men in their lives, must pay a price for their attempts at playing superwoman. 'Sometimes, because a girl is not very intelligent, things get out of hand and she finds that she can't always control the situation she has got herself into, or her emotions,' he said prophetically, 'As her approach is more direct and masculine, her power over the man is necessarily diminished.'

It seemed inconceivable at the time that this would happen to Bardot, but we shall see that it did. In the meantime the nature of young women was what interested Allegret and it was the *Elle* cover, pointed out to him by Pierre Braunberger, which led to the meeting between Brigitte and Vadim.

After this rapid and encouraging start, however, nothing had happened. With childish delight Brigitte organized a crocodile of schoolfriends to take a circuitous road home from Hattemer past all the bookstands in the sixteenth *arrondissement*. Bardot says she saw the writing on the wall, the inherent weakness of a dependency on showbusiness, that very day. She was a star among the girls in her class but even so the people in the bus queue failed to recognize her as the very same cover-girl who was on their magazines. Comfortable child that she was from a sheltered home, she simply did not know how obtuse the world could be. She didn't even know that it is a point of pride among such people as M. and Mme Bardot not to seek distinction but to have it thrust upon them. She did not know that hard work was not a subject of shame. No one therefore did anything and an opportunity was lost.

Had Brigitte been allowed out into the world perhaps she would have discovered her identity for herself much sooner, to shed real tears of hurt and happiness rather than the corroding tears of frustration. Temper tears, the device of childhood, seemed to be her only weapon, but then Pilou and Toty had never schooled her to plan rationally how to get the things she wanted because she had always had them. It had been their pleasure and their pride to give them to her. Now she wanted her freedom from this arrangement the tears couldn't be allowed to work and her mood became more and more dramatic. She was leading a tortuous double life with no let-up in sight and there is nothing the average teenager likes less than playing a waiting game. In later life she would punish the whole world for how it treated her in the transition period in which they were both caught while the power was being transferred to a younger generation. For the time being she was simply trapped. It is in the appalling, dulling frustration of the teenage years, which she shared with so many middle-class children at this point in history, that the secret is to be found of the future explosion of their apparently wild, lawless, immoral notions. The rebellion surely didn't take the adult generation by surprise, since their fear spawned it, but they bitterly resented it for having lost out on it themselves and created the biggest generation gap in history. They had lost out all along the line. Victims of two wars, they had to persuade themselves they had been martyrs for a decent cause, the perfect future of their young. The breaking-point came when their young didn't want their vision of perfection.

The stress in Brigitte's case was both mental and physical. Every time she suffered an attack of hopelessness or frustration she came out in spots, which further undermined her endeavours. It was not an easy period for anyone to the point that even Vadim, who arguably had the best of both worlds, felt the need to escape for a while. Each time the couple were parted by his career Brigitte's passions and tantrums increased. She, who had always lived that way, seemed to think they could live on love alone. He knew otherwise and wore himself out juggling their two interests. Marc Allegret, who had taken him to London with him once to work on the film *Blanche Fury*, asked him to go again. Useless though he knew it would be, Vadim went through the motions of asking the Bardots to let Brigitte accompany him. They refused. The confrontations became worse. Finally an exhausted Vadim announced his intention of going to the South of France alone to complete a screenplay. It was there that his mother had taken the family after his father had died and though they had lived from hand to mouth Vadim had happy memories. Perhaps his intention was even to rupture the frustrating arrangement by which he, who had struggled for a living since he was a boy, was strapped to a histrionic schoolgirl. Vadim has never confessed to this, only hinted that it was Brigitte's idea to get married and that the idea did not entirely appeal to him. Brigitte seems to have sensed something terminal in his departure. It is very much a part of the Bardot myth that as he was steaming towards Nice, resisting any fleeting temptation to retrace his tracks, his young mistress was lying on the kitchen floor with the gas oven turned on in the midst of the first of several suicide attempts.

The attempt in someone so young was taken as genuine but there was a sense in which it did not unnerve the older generation nearly enough. Bardot *mère et père* and little Mijanou had gone out to see the new illuminations of the Paris monuments, all the rage after the dull nights of war. Pilou, as was his nature, planned the outing to these familiar landmarks as if it was an assault on the Khyber Pass, robbing it totally of the spontaneity which was his daughter's watchword. They would take the family car and drive past the Arc de Triomphe, down the Champs-Élysées, round the Palais Royal to Notre Dame and the Opera House, they would eat in a mid-town restaurant he had in mind and would be back home in just under four hours well before midnight. Brigitte declined. She loathed such assiduously planned family outings and had something much less bourgeois on her mind. To get her own way she feigned a headache.

It is not a great distance from the rue de la Pompe to the Trocadero but by the time the family arrived there they felt the pull of home, or perhaps the pull of Brigitte, for she has always exploited her ability to focus other people's attentions on herself. It was a colder evening than they had expected. Mijanou wanted a coat to wear. Anne-Marie, moreover, guessed something was wrong, or so she said in retrospect, though she usually declined to discuss what happened. It must indeed have been horrific. When they arrived at the flat they discovered their elder daughter unconscious with scarcely fifteen minutes to live.

Such an event obviously begged a radical rethink within the family, although they seem to have done less thinking than Brigitte, who had exhausted herself in the process. In a sense the near-suicide was the last really spontaneous act of her life. Spontaneity, when regained, would become an act. 'Something in Brigitte broke and she has never been the same since,' Vadim has said, looking back on that period. She became a sullen automaton in the face of everyone's reiterated plan for her future, which was no plan except waiting. Meanwhile her parents prayed for a suitable banker to turn up who could show this troublesome Russian the door and whisk their beautiful daughter off her feet. Though rescued from the brink by the family doctor, who arrived to administer oxygen, she lost both her will to live and her *joie de vivre*. She went through all the motions like a walking ghost and it didn't seem to matter who issued the commands. It might be her father, it might be Vadim, whom she summoned by letter from the South of France and who returned to find himself engaged to be married, but not until Brigitte was eighteen, of course.

Far from being horrified by such female blackmail, Vadim was fascinated by all the details of Brigitte's flirtation with death. He pondered over every last bit of her account of the event, over every minute introspection as unconsciousness had closed over his teenage mistress, indeed his insatiable interest encouraged her introspection. There was to be no covering up of the experience. It became the most important thing that had ever happened to the two of them. What might have been a mere teenage love-affair quickly forgotten in the aftermath of active life had Pilou really made good his threats and sent his daughter off to an English boarding school, was transformed into history because of the bizarre interaction of all the personalities concerned. Pilou could not bear to part with her even for her own sake. For Vadim, here in this near-death was the real stuff of the universe, the raw material that had got his imagination working ever since he had seen the mangled original Sophie near the tracks in Toulon – the death that was the proper end of desire, as described by de Sade and a host of Romantic poets. If she had not been so before, Brigitte was rapidly becoming an interesting vehicle for his ambitions. His dramatist's ego was not only immensely flattered that he could provoke anyone to a terminal act, he also studied its implications like a scientist with a beetle under a microscope, like a novelist, a journalist. For a journalist is what Vadim was about to become.

In none of the biographies that were written about Brigitte Bardot in her heyday did anyone bother to note the role of one particular magazine in her ascent towards immortality. It is hardly a cynical revelation, considering the intense interrelation between the people who write contemporary history and the public who create it and react to it in these days of media saturation. In the nature of this media bridge between the star and her public lie many of the explanations for Brigitte's future elusiveness and instability. The magazine with which Vadim became associated the day Pilou and Toty agreed to his betrothal to their daughter was *Paris-Match*. In France it was no disgrace to be an ally of the magazine which would even introduce Grace Kelly to Prince Rainier at a private audience during the Cannes Film Festival. Pushy, splashy, to this day an icon of photo-journalism, in the fifties it offered a prototype vision of the world as seen through the lens of a new kind of photographer, the omnipresent *paparazzi*. Its inside information came from all kinds of people who were not actually journalists themselves. They were gamblers, gossipers, gigolos and they had access to all kinds of information from hanging round the high-rollers which, put together, made a reasonably accurate photo-fit picture of society for *Match*. Being round the magazine's offices on the Champs-Élysées with a tale of what happened last night was one way of picking up some extra income for fringe members of fringe professions. If you were good at it you might be put on the payroll. For Vadim, who was struggling along barely well enough for a bachelor in the world of the self-employed, it was the nearest he could get to a steady job. A steady job was what he needed right now because Pilou had decided that he could only marry his daughter when she was eighteen on two conditions. The first was that he become a member of the Roman Catholic Church (he was Russian Ortho-dox), the second was proof of a regular pay cheque.

In *Bardot, an Intimate Biography* the late Willi Frischauer wrote:

> The first time I heard of Vadim was in the autumn of 1952 when his name cropped up in a small Paris bistro where I spent some evenings with Jean Roy and David Seymour, both established photographers closely associated with *Paris-Match*. Among the young writers on the magazine, with whom Jean and David had dealings and drinks, was Roger Vadim. He might not have attracted so much attention among his eminent colleagues on the magazine had he not been talking so persistently and per-suasively about Brigitte Bardot, his protégée – fiancée was not a word to bandy about in such company – whom he described as a phenomenally handsome, exquisitely talented young dancer and actress.

Vadim, it seems, lost no time in flashing snapshots of the girl to everyone who would look at them. Actually Frischauer caught up with this fact rather late in the day. As early as 31 May 1952, *Paris-Match* had as its cover a picture of the Bardot girl.

Again it is a sweet picture. Bardot looks more like Heidi than Harlow. She has a little plait, a blue scarf round her throat and a high-necked red blouse. She is sitting in a meadow full of kingcups, clutching a sheaf of them in her arms like a doll. There is a look in her eyes which is not that of a virgin, but only a soothsayer could have predicted what such a child would become. The copywriter certainly had no idea, for the cover line reads 'Brigitte Bardot, the new Leslie Caron'. Even though she had gone to America, the delicate, demure Leslie Caron would always be an anachronism in popular entertainment in a way that Bardot would never be.

Almost exactly a year later *Match* had her on the cover again, this time looking much more knowing. She had been married to Vadim for six months and there was now no shame in her legalized sensuality. His promotion of her was not the action of a modest or jealous lover who could not believe his luck. As soon as he accepted that they were going to be married, he started to put a formidable plan into action, to which Brigitte, in her sleepwalking state at the time, and used to doing as she was told by the people she loved, agreed. By now she seems to have known herself well enough to realize that acting was not going to be easy for her, but not well enough to do anything about it. Nothing would be as easy for her ever again as it had been when she was a child, idolized despite her gauche looks. Nothing would be as easy for any middle-class child and how they resented this turning to sex and drugs as a substitute for the easy childhood gratification to which they were accustomed.

Like most of her spoiled generation Bardot hated difficulties and disappointments. She encountered them immediately in the professional world. Her nerves were bad, her skin erupted and she forgot her lines. In her first and last stage play a year after her marriage she says she forgot a whole act of Jean Anouilh's *Ring Round the Moon* at one performance. She was playing a major part, Isabel. 'The actor stood in front of me open-mouthed because he had no idea what I was saying. He wasn't even on in the last act and I had suddenly launched into it in the middle of the second. After a while the actor who actually was in the third act got the message and came on stage and we simply carried on from there. We even skipped the interval. The audience went home an hour early. They hadn't the faintest idea what was happening.'

Now she can laugh at the things that happened to her but at the time she went through them as if in a bewildered dream. If this was the price of freedom then she would pay it now, but she would store up the revenge of contempt for all those who were thwarting her. If she had made a shortlist at the time it would have included Mama and Papa and all those producers and directors who failed to be seduced by her personality. It might have included the public at large, certainly the entire *bonne bourgeoisie*, but not even she would have guessed quite yet that it would also include her saviour Vadim, the man who in her own words 'liberated' her from her 'bourgeois prison'.

To do so he first took Brigitte out of dancing class and enrolled her in drama school *chez* René Simon, which was like taking advertising space in *Variety*. French film people automatically turned to Simon when they had a part to cast. Every starstruck little girl wanted to be accepted by him. The trains coming into Paris were full of teenagers, their heads full of fan-magazine gossip, determined to head straight for his school and dazzle him with their personalities. Pupils remember him as a small, brown-haired man with an intense, nervous manner who did not waste words, but who, when something thrilled him, could be eccentrically noisy. He was given to setting potential pupils pieces from the classics for their auditions, but no one had any idea what he was really looking for. He just knew it when he saw it and part of it was no doubt a willingness to learn. He worked his students hard and demanded total dedication to the illusion of theatre, which they achieved by working without sets. Simon was both critical and practical and his methods often startled his pupils. He was quite as likely to set a difficult schoolchild's tongue-twister for homework as a high-flown, romantic speech. He knew the acting business from top to bottom and all the traps of the theatre and was always warning his pupils of the danger of the kind of fame which comes too soon. It can stop you really working at your talent, he would say and he would quote examples of people who had fallen in this way by the wayside. His catchphrase was 'respect for yourself and for others'. Only when that respect was gained did he think the spark could travel between the actor and his audience.

Brigitte did not stick around long enough to learn these lessons, which might have stood her in brilliant stead added to the spontaneous talent that she showed as a beginner. To this day she has no time for René Simon. As far as she was concerned he had nothing to teach her, even at the age of eighteen. Other pupils agree that he was vulgar, it was a way of attracting their attention and getting things into perspective. Brigitte, who can swear like a trooper these days and, according to Vadim, could even as a fourteen-year-old girl, says she loathed his vulgarity. Though his lectures would go on for a couple of hours with other teenagers hanging on his every word, she simply remembers the high-point of his lecture to her being the words, 'As long as a man can still watch himself piss he is still young.' He paused to let that take effect and Brigitte walked out. 'I didn't see the point of listening to that sort of thing,' she says, 'I wasn't used to language like that. As far as I was concerned I might as well stay at home.' Another broadside had been launched against the icons of her future profession.

Having failed with Simon, it is said, though not by Vadim, that he touted the film test done for Allegret around Paris, showing it to anyone who could possibly be interested. Vadim, gallantly, if you like, or in the interests of the product from which he benefited, has never laboured the connection between what was on screen and what was behind it. But one thing is certain, when he needed publicity for any venture he never forgot his *Paris-Match* connections, though he may have worked for them officially for only as long as he had to to comply with M. Bardot's image of a suitable profession for a son-in-law. He wrote in his memoirs that he had wonderful memories of those official three months in journalism, exaggerating on the face of it what was a very routine job at twenty pounds a week, first as a rewriter for which his editor Hervé Mille spotted he was very well equipped, and then as a reporter.

Those who love the stain of printers' ink, the heartbeat of the presses, the classlessness, the instantaneous demands and the daily unpredictability of journalism will recognize what it held for a man who didn't like his life to go by without feeling every second of it. His days at *Match*, before deadlines were eroded by union requirements, personalities undermined by chequebook journalism, and scoops consigned to history by militant public relations officers, were characterized even in his sophisticated circles by a total absence of cynicism. He had unexpectedly stumbled on an adventure. Vadim's gang, his musketeers, trooped like all young recruits at historical events and boring rituals alike. They got the world down on paper, but they were madcaps and many paid the ultimate price of too much hard living. Jean Roy died at the wheel of his jeep on the Suez Canal, the handsome Jean-Pierre Pedrazzini was mortally wounded in Budapest, the witty Eric Bromberger was killed when he fell down the stairs at the magazine's offices in the early morning. The list seems endless and heartbreaking: one was killed on the road, another in an aircrash, another was blown up by a landmine in Indochina; the poet André Frédérique committed suicide.

Sentimental Vadim, drawn to death, the ultimate drama, neglects to say that a lot of his contacts survived and were to be useful to him for some time to come. *Paris-Match*, which supported her as a young bride, was to dog Brigitte's footsteps in future years wherever she went. When I first met her in Paris it was *Paris-Match* which was responsible for the meeting. When I met her again in Hollywood, *Paris-Match* was there. *Paris-Match* was everywhere in those days. Brigitte liked the fact that its representatives were young, handsome men who sat at her feet and hung on her every word, even if they did intend to reproduce them the next day. But she could never entirely relax, not knowing quite what stunt they would pull next. Vadim never grew too grand for journalism, to despise it or to fear it – as others do if they can't manipulate it – as contrary to the imperious interests of showbusiness. Vadim thought he could manipulate the Press and the evidence was in his favour. He never felt the need to protect his private life from it. He had no private life that was not public and he believed there was no such thing as bad publicity. That was to become a big difference between himself and Brigitte. As late as 1983, when it was rumoured that Bardot had made a birthday attempt on her life, he still found no difficulty in bringing himself to write a piece for *Match* again, reprinted in England in the *Daily Mail*, explaining to those readers who like their journalism totally predictable why his former wife would never be happy.

In 1952, however, he struck a more original note and it was this to which people responded. Bardot was finally hired by the producer, Jean Boyer, to play in her first film, the story of intrigue in a village inn in Normandy called *Le Trou Normand*. Though Brigitte herself has never said she was satisfied with the results, her performance was certainly not all bad. She was fresh, cheeky, and funny, and the critics and the public saw this immediately. She was also, as she would be throughout her career, more or less playing herself. Well, she had rejected any idea of drama lessons, the *sine qua non* for a star rather than an actress. The young girl, whose ripening physical attractions play a part in the intrigue surrounding the ownership of the inn, leaves the village at the end of the film to become an actress. In naïveté, in experience of life little Brigitte was still a village girl with ambitions merely to be noticed.

The film, in which all the characters appear to Anglo-Saxon audiences to have straw in their hair, has never been shown in Britain and only made it to the United States (retitled *Crazy for Love*) at the height of Bardot's fame when film-goers found the absurd plot no hindrance whatsoever to an appreciation of the lady's figure. In France the film is part of a long-standing naïve comedy tradition which crops up perennially even today and is always bankable for a local market, just as the Ealing Comedies could be revived in England. In some ways it is no disadvantage to a country's film industry to have an unsophisticated, insular audience perpetuated by indigenous-language films in which young talent can get a grounding. Brigitte, in her first film, did not feel insulted to earn about £220 for a good deal of screen time and fourteen days' work. She was, however, horrified to learn that filming was not so very different from the rest of her life at that period, consisting mostly of the one thing she was not good at – waiting around. She waited for the lighting cameraman, for the director, for other actors, for her particular scenes and when it came to them she was chopped off in mid-performance because of something apparently quite trifling such as continuity or a hair in the gate.

Moreover, though it may be easy for many people to make a quick first hit in their profession, as time goes on they become weighed down by the implications of their knowledge. So it was with Brigitte. 'Everyone was kind enough to me, helping me over many difficulties and making what I did not like more agreeable. But as time went on I felt I was acting more and more badly – fantastically badly. I thought a film was made from the beginning to the end and not in disconnected little bits. I had thought that on the set I would be able to forget myself and my surroundings and give of my best. But it was nothing like that at all. I didn't like my part from the start – a little witch of a girl, somewhat vulgar, a little boorish, and very sensual – but that it seemed was the star role of the picture and I was told by everybody that this was a big break. So you see, film-making was not at all what I had expected. I felt let down. Was it always to be like this? I wondered. I had my dream shattered. And the film was terrible.'

Brigitte never forgave anyone for shattering a dream and she prepared her revenge. Many actors have described the feeling of performing to camera as though they were making love to it, the activity which Brigitte was soon to define as the one she liked best in the whole world. But this constant coitus interruptus of professional film-making was frustrating in the extreme, not at all what she had been given to expect when Papa Bardot had trained his amateur camera on her every natural movement or when Vadim her lover suggested that with his grooming she could be the constant focus of everyone's attention. If she was good enough for them, whom she loved, why not for everyone else for whom she had no regard at all? Though people found her diffident and difficult, she was motivated by perfectionism. No doubt the middle-class lesson had been learned that if a job is worth doing it is worth doing well. She wanted to be perfect for Pilou, for Vadim, or herself, as if she would simply cease to exist if she could not convince them how good she was.

Still, just as she was terrified about her first dance performance and had grown to like it, there was something she liked about filming. She liked being the subject of attention. Bardot began to suspect from her very first essay in acting that film-making as an activity ceases to exist without a subject to focus upon, that she was a plausible subject and could therefore call the shots. It was this self-confidence that shone through her performance and enabled her almost immediately to get another part, the leading role in *Manina, La Fille Sans Voile*.

Bardot was still living under her father's roof when *Manina* was being made and Pilou was furious. The film was not shown in England until seven years later in a shortened version with the appropriately bawdy title of *The Lighthouse Keeper's Daughter*. In America it was called *The Girl in the Bikini*. Papa Bardot seems to have suffered like most other people of the time from the illusion that he was seeing his daughter in the nude on film. In fact for the most part she was covered, if only by a skimpy bikini. Nonetheless this infuriated Louis Bardot, who could see what was coming and felt strongly enough to take the matter to court and win the right as guardian of a minor to see the film and suggest appropriate cuts. For Bardot it was her very first initiation into the role of the law and the lesson would not be forgotten. For Pilou it was the culmination of all their falling out. Brigitte didn't seem to care and the difference was that she no longer had to. She was about to be married. Pilou could demand final editing rights in the interests of the family image, he could thunder all he wanted, in fact, but he discovered that no one paid him much attention in the end. His daughter appeared to shed her previous loyalties as easily as she had shed her veil, and more, in *Manina* which was filmed on the beach in Tangier.

Of course her apparent insouciance was not real. Her family connections have lingered throughout her life, torturing her at times and providing her only real solace at others. They have been so powerful that they have prevented her from creating a real family of her own. Brigitte has always wanted to be someone's little girl, not someone else's mother or wife. In that too she anticipated the feelings of a generation who would not go to the altar willingly and would discharge parenthood as if it were sisterhood. An impossible little girl perhaps, headstrong, petulant, selfish and sometimes far from rationally lovable, just to prove that she was completely irresistible. In this she has been aided by the whole climate of the times, the climate she and Vadim helped to create.

One person did pay Louis Bardot some attention, though not the sort he might have wished – his future son-in-law. Vadim told his friends at *Paris-Match*, who no doubt told their friends in the rest of the Press, the story of the irate father and the bikini-clad beauty and, not unnaturally, they wrote about it. They were not *entirely* flattering. Raymond Cartier in *Match* itself said her acting was bad, as were her roles, that no one could understand a word she said and that she was no classical beauty. The critic Paul Reboux was even more scathing. 'She is not pretty. Her lower lip is too thick. She has enormous eyes and the face of a skivvy.' Enormous orbs of the Tretchikoff variety, suggesting vulnerability and greed, were not as prized as clever almond eyes at the time.

It was what Brigitte had always feared since she first looked into the mirror as a child. She hated criticism and she began, not for the last time, to look round for people to blame. She blamed the entire acting profession. She said she loathed the acting experience, or at least what had been expected of her in *Manina*, which was a sort of feature-length pose in a two-piece while two divers, ostensibly trying to find sunken treasure off the Corsican coast, fell to blows over the living prize. 'I took the part of an unclothed, wild little girl, as lacking in experience as the one in the first film. My acting seemed even worse – later I used to blush for shame at the thought of it. I was just a cheap little starlet hardly acting at all in a very mediocre film.'

Bardot now vaguely divined that she had two fights on her hands. She asked Vadim if she could give up her film career when they were married. He said no. The point first was to get married, however, and until then she could only see the opposition of Pilou. He kept on with his pedantry until the very end, making Brigitte hopping mad. It was certainly from him that she got her stubbornness. She tells the tale against both of them of how Pilou refused to let her consummate her marriage between the civil and religious ceremony which was to take place the next day.

The element of farce, which would somehow creep into all three of her weddings, had already been present at the *mairie* in the avenue Henri-Martin, where Daniel Gélin and his actress wife, Danièle Delorme, had acted as witnesses, all of them rather scruffily dressed à la Left Bank in Bogart-style trenchcoats. While the mayoress, who conducted the ceremony, pontificated about the significance of this Franco–Russian alliance, Papa Bardot fumed and blustered at the implication that his daughter was marrying a foreigner. The man had been born on French soil for goodness' sake. Anne-Marie tugged at his sleeve and begged him to keep quiet. Brigitte giggled. When they got home her father at last had his way. 'I have made a bed up for Vadim in the living room,' he said, allowing them exactly ten minutes by his watch to say goodnight before separating them at her bedside. Rationally she couldn't have expected anything else. The argument was another symbol of her revolt against men's expectations for her. It was only the sons and daughters of her own generation who would be given a packet of Pills and their parents' blessing and shown the way to the spare room with their lovers. M. and Mme Bardot were of the generation which wept to acknowledge their children's sexuality, even after it had the blessing of the Church.

That took place in Brigitte's case on 21 December at ten o'clock in the morning in the Catholic church of Notre Dame de Grâce in Passy, a large church with lots of parochial activities and the focal point of decent local Catholic society. Brigitte did not really seem to be enjoying the event, which was meticulously filmed in all its stages by Pilou who was only going to relinquish his charge very reluctantly. He tortured himself by being present at all the preparations. He snapped her buttoning herself up in her white dress with its high collar, covered buttons, and draped bustle, wearing a little pony tail as if she was just a child dressing up again and not preparing for the real event. Later she appeared quite petulant and sullen in the official photographs in a little white fur crescent of a hat, a neat kiss-curl well off her brow, an embroidered veil of tulle falling to her feet, a little white muff in her hands and surrounded by white lilac, freesias and Easter lilies in the family apartment. Her kiss for her sister combines smugness and resentment. Her more provocative kiss for Marc Allegret, who was Vadim's best man, shows that the film business brought out a different side in her at least. But the great beauty in the pictures is not Bardot at all but her mother with her much finer features and a life behind her – not a very long one, she was only forty-two – of largely refined experiences. Brigitte wore no make-up that day and only her fingernails were painted. Despite her corseted clothes, despite her sister's old-fashioned fur coat, and the establishment suit and tie of her bridegroom, Brigitte was a little girl still. Like every eighteen-year-old she had a lot of learn, but this particular little girl also had something to teach a whole lot of people.

6. Future Stars

Brigitte, who had laughed all through her civil marriage ceremony, started to cry the moment the reception was over. Vadim,
at the wheel of the car driving them south to an Alpine honeymoon, thought they were tears of happiness. 'I'm frightened,' she
said. They had only got as far as Fontainebleau.

It was a very real premonition. Though they had known each
other for nearly four years and all but exhausted their intimacy, in
some ways they had nothing in common at all. Brigitte thought
she wanted to be a housewife. Vadim did not take this the least bit
seriously.

At the beginning of 1953 Brigitte's entire world was Vadim.
She was only eighteen. Rather like a little girl who play-acts with a
doll's house at being a housewife, Brigitte set to in the flat her
parents had lent them in the rue Chardon-Lagache on the outskirts
of the sixteenth *arrondissement*. It was not too far from their own
home in the rue de la Pompe, yet far enough. It was a marvellous
respite after a courtship conducted in the full glare, if not of
publicity as would be the case with future courtships, at least of
parental opinion. At first there was a great deal to do because
though the couple had a roof over their heads they did not have
any furniture beneath it. That suited Vadim, who was a bohemian
at heart. They slept on a mattress on the floor and Brigitte
gradually accumulated furniture from cheap secondhand stores
and flea markets. She shopped for food and ran up curtains. She
has always been handy with a sewing machine and liked interior
decoration. She rearranged the furniture and planned little domestic surprises for her husband. It is something all women have to do
at some time during their lives and indeed enjoy doing when the
mood seizes them, whether they are intellectuals, sex-symbols,
mother-figures, or career women by preference most of the time.

The trouble was that Bardot had no other responsibility. Lots of actresses – Bette Davis, Marlene Dietrich, and Joan Collins among them – go over the top in their attempt to create the perfect domestic microcosm, conditioned by their profession to the idea that a private life can be effectively stage-managed. Marlene Dietrich's men were driven crazy by her brilliant impersonation of the *Hausfrau*. They wanted to be seen out on her arm, not sharing the delights of the late night news over a *Bockwurst* behind closed curtains. Brigitte's men would be no different. Even as a young girl Brigitte was happier staying in than going out, always provided she had someone to stay in with. Outside she feared public rape by millions of pairs of eyes and became basically agoraphobic. Worse still she feared she would be ignored. 'She would decide she wasn't pretty, spending hours in front of her mirror fiddling with her hair, changing her dress or blouse a dozen times and often collapsing in tears, leaving me to make excuses at the last minute,' says Vadim.

She did enjoy having friends round though the couple had very little money to spend on entertaining, but what she really liked best was the idea that she and Vadim now had their own love-nest, their own world, which nobody could invade. They had her mother's old Citroën to pootle around Paris when they wanted but best of all they had the pretty flat with a wrought-iron balcony overlooking the police station. They also had a caricature of a concierge who lived down three flights of stairs with her hoarse pet nightingale called Tino.

The brand-new housewife willingly dragged the dustbins up and down the stairs every day and tried to learn to cook. Vadim reluctantly tasted the dishes and escaped to his journalism. The snatched idylls in his bachelor pad at the quai d'Orléans began to seem like paradise to him now as he struggled to make his name in the world with a frivolous young wife, who was determined to be nothing but a wife, to support. He was terrified. He rarely handed out a compliment about anything domestic. Vadim says his minute attention to the detail of film sets is only matched by his complete indifference to his surroundings at home. He only ever remarks on the furnishings when he doesn't like them. This being so, as soon as he remarked on anything Brigitte immediately became defensive.

At first his indifference simply spurred Brigitte on to try harder. She became an obsessive housekeeper, studiously aware of the price of meat and dry-cleaning and reluctant to spend the money he gave her. 'Small things around the house still get her down easily,' he says. 'And yet she can be extremely generous about helping someone who is ill or saving a dog.'

Still, all was not yet lost between them. There were flashes of temperament, which excited him, beside the dogged will and self-interest to which he had already succumbed in the schoolgirl. There was a good deal of fighting in the early days and the result was often reminiscent of a French farce. Brigitte would throw things to make her point, she would scream and yell. That side of her was decidedly not premeditated or bourgeois. The memory of these scenes stayed with Vadim for twenty years and he has never minded reminiscing and laughing about them, or failed to appreciate the inherent drama which was just the sort of thing with which he planned to arouse an audience when the time came. 'After one big row she pretended to be OK and said, "Oh, would you be a darling and take the garbage downstairs now, Vadim?" The moment I was at the bottom of the stairs I heard the front door slam and the bolts go on. I was really mad. She had locked me out in my pyjamas.' Vadim says he battered the door down. 'She was scared like a mouse, running everywhere. It was such a small apartment, two rooms. There was no place to hide. I caught her and wanted to take her by the feet and beat her silly little head againt the wall. But that wouldn't have been very civilized. So I threw her on the floor and pulled the mattress over her and jumped up and down on that like Tarzan – no, like Tarzan's monkey. After that we made love beautifully, of course. A man must be strong with Brigitte. It is a fact, she has not had a strong man since me.' That sort of thing was a bit of a cliché for the woman who, according to her successor in the marital bed, Jane Fonda, would become the standard bearer of women's lib. But Brigitte was not consciously bearing any torch on behalf of a whole generation, attention to her own needs was what she liked best. It was much better than concentrating on her lonely disillusion while Vadim was out trying to get a break for them both.

Brigitte soon discovered she was hopeless at being alone. Even in their tiny two-room flat she got afraid after dark. If Vadim had to stay late at the magazine she used to wait outside in the car for him even in mid-winter, huddled in her overcoat. Vadim feared for her health and bought her a cocker spaniel to keep her company at home, the first of many dogs. She was delighted. She said he would protect her from monsters and called him Clown.

Like many a bride Brigitte rapidly discovered that marriage was not just about her physical charms. Vadim had been ensnared by her body but suddenly the same body didn't seem enough for him. She spent hours cinching in her waist in front of the mirror and throwing out her chest. The rue Chardon-Lagache, right under the spire of the church in which they were married, was no place to park a young eighteen-year-old with spirit. Its quiet tree-lined streets were quieter still than the rue de la Pompe, its landmarks a seminary, a clinic, and an institute of gerontology. Left to herself Brigitte was nagged by the thought that there was something terribly wrong with her. The domestic idyll was not pleasing the husband she had fought so hard to get. Her reasoning was quite simple, if fallacious. Her domestic aspirations must be right because from all she had seen, those were the very essence of a happy marriage. She must therefore be happy in hers. 'Our love was so marvellous and so reciprocal,' she tried to reassure herself. 'I used to wake up at night just so as I could look at him.' If she dreamed Vadim was angry with her, she would sulk and cry all day. She was in effect in the grip of a total fantasy.

It is in the gap between expectations and reality that everything goes wrong. Gradually the gap narrowed. First to go was Bardot the cook. Mrs Plemiannikov acknowledged she hated the kitchen stove and asked to be taken out every evening. The only way they could possibly afford this was for Bardot to work and this was the plan her husband had for her. In that first year of marriage she resumed her work as an *Elle* cover-girl. All through that summer she portrayed the sweet, fresh teenager in piqué, gingham, and petticoats, her accessories a fan, a basket, a kitten. In many ways she was that girl. 'A laughing, happy girl, full of practical jokes and enthusiasm', was how her mother wistfully described her. At home, however, that was not the image her husband was trying to perfect. While she threw open the curtains to let the sun in, he closed them. He was a much darker character and though he would never succeed in complicating his bride that much, he started to give her added dimensions. He set about vulgarizing her, modelling her on his footloose friends from the Café Flore, teaching her to use slang when she spoke and to eat with her fingers. He gave her a reading list which included Hemingway, Faulkner, Camus, Gide, the sexy Italian satirist Aretino, his old favourite, the Marquis de Sade, and other books which Pilou and Hattemer had failed to draw to her attention. He also set about making the girl on the pedestal accessible. He encouraged her to walk round the flat naked beneath his gaze, to be unashamed of her provocative walk and to pout, not grin. 'Whenever I walked, undressed, or ate breakfast, I always had the impression he was looking at me with someone else's eyes – and with everyone's eyes. Yet, I knew he was not seeing me but through me, his dream.' While she tried to tumble him into bed during these sessions, he made her concentrate on her work.

She had made a contract to obey him, so obey him she did as she had been brought up to, constantly refining her tantalizing act, auditioning, doing publicity shots and meeting anyone he advised. What he really wanted for her was an acting career because that was the one piece of magic that could lift a person right off the treadmill of ordinary life in those days before actors decided with one accord to be ordinary like everyone else. He saw plentiful evidence of that on the Left Bank among his ambitious, unorthodox friends. Simone Signoret had just been a secretary with the wrong taste in clothes even to play a bit part until she was spotted. Now she was Allegret's darling with a daughter by his brother. 'Vadim changed my mind about acting,' says Bardot. 'Vadim was the only man who was certain I had something special to offer on the screen. I marvelled at his confidence and laughed at his conceit. It was difficult not to listen to his arguments. "As long as I am here," he told me, "you need never be afraid of people or of life. I shall guide you to success. I love you and will make you succeed." His trust gave me fresh hope. I would do whatever he told me. He was both my teacher and master as well as my husband. I placed myself entirely in his hands. We went back to the beginning and he taught me how to speak, how to remember my lines and tried to show me how to act. Love was the driving force. The experience improved and rewarded me. He taught me what life was all about and the terrible effort it needs to grow up; I was very wild and he made me into a sociable being.' She worked hard for him and in the first two years of her marriage she made nine movies, often against her better judgement. 'Just learn,' Vadim kept telling her. 'It is not important at the start of a career what you do, so long as you are working.'

The surprise was that people seemed to want the new Brigitte, just as Vadim had said they would. She made one appearance opposite him in Les Dents Longues with Daniel Gélin and his wife Danièle Delorme, the couple who witnessed their civil wedding.

She moved on to *Le Portrait de son Père*, an unremarkable moral tale extolling the simple virtues of the countryside, and to act also in several costume dramas set in Versailles, Spain, and Ancient Rome. The role of cinema in those days was by no means the same as it is now and the sort of cinema Brigitte got her grounding in was more like the smaller world of television. The plots were more spelled out and they were slight and light. It is easy to forget too that the first films she made were black and white. Brigitte's parts were not large, but at least the rest of the credits were getting better. She acted in the same films as Sacha Guitry, Claudette Colbert, Jean-Pierre Aumont, Gérard Philipe, Jean-Louis Barrault, Edith Piaf, Orson Welles, Stanley Baker and Rosanna Podesta. She was directed by Robert Wise and, with American talent scouts all over Europe in those days, she landed a small part in *Act of Love*, produced by Anatole Litvak for United Artists with a script by Irwin Shaw. 'My head was on-screen for a couple of seconds, looking through a serving hatch. Mother sneezed and missed me.' Still, in those few seconds, directed by an international talent-spotter, she was one step nearer to Hollywood, which was the great goal of all little French starlets of the time.

Brigitte was beginning to acquire the trappings of a career. She had a portfolio and a list of credits. Vadim was quite methodical about his plans. One night he sat down and dictated a letter to be written in Brigitte's bold round hand. It was addressed to Olga Horstig-Primuz at her office on the Champs Élysées. A Yugoslav by birth, Olga had come to France when she was twelve and become a journalist. She got on extremely well with Michèle Morgan when she interviewed her and ended up by becoming her agent as well as her friend. Olga was well connected in the United States as well as France, where American producers were keen to offer patronage as part of the post-war effort in Europe. Even in those days Olga had the reputation of being ferociously protective and ambitious for her clients – her walls are papered with the photos of grateful performers from Morgan to Charlotte Rampling and Jane Birkin. Normally she wouldn't have wanted to represent a bit-part actress. Brigitte's letter, however, was dated 17 April 1953, a Friday. On the following Monday Brigitte would be in Cannes for the annual film festival. The letter the couple sent was endearingly naïve in view of the stunt Vadim was about to put into action. 'Madame,' it said, 'I would like to ask you to represent me and put me on your list. I would be so happy to

work with you . . . I will ring you tomorrow.' By the time Olga
had the leisure to answer a couple of weeks later she knew who
Brigitte Bardot was and she was convinced she was worth while,
'People turned their heads in the streets; she was absolutely
superb.'

It was hardly surprising that she turned heads in Rome, where
Olga accompanied her soon after she had put her on her books to
make two films in succession: *Tradita* and *Helen of Troy*. Apart
from the natural Italian delight in pretty girls, the Italian capital
was bubbling with star fever as one little girl after another went
into the gates of Cinecittà as a private citizen and came out public
property. Gina Lollobrigida and Pier Angeli had first turned
Italian, then American heads. Sophia Loren, Brigitte's exact
contemporary, was making her second film as the French girl
arrived. In *Helen*, a $6 million Technicolor extravaganza directed
by the American Robert Wise, Rosanna Podesta was to play the
Greek queen, Brigitte, as the mere beginner, her slave Andraste.
Wise was sufficiently impressed with the young girl to consider
seriously the maid swapping parts with the mistress. Alas for
Brigitte, preparations had gone too far. High hopes were attached
to this film in the international market and even with her small
part Brigitte attracted the attention of the Roman *paparazzi* as she
trolled up and down the via Veneto on her days off, provocatively
sucking at an ice cream. Vadim, who visited from Paris on an
assignment for Allegret called *Femina*, also attracted attention
when he accompanied her because, as often as not, he had not one
but two beautiful girls on his arm. The other was Ursula Andress.

Ursula, who made a name for herself ten years later by rising
out of the sea in a clinging wet Grecian costume in the James Bond
film *Dr No*, was seventeen at the time, two years younger than
Brigitte and at boarding school in Switzerland. At least she was
supposed to be at boarding school in Switzerland but she had run
away to be with Daniel Gélin, Vadim's friend who was making a
film called *Woman of Rome*. Having courted the little Swiss girl
Gélin proved less than permanently attentive and poor Ursula
moved into Brigitte's hotel room above the Spanish Steps, where
they shared a double bed. When Vadim arrived he was perfectly
happy to share it with both girls but he maintains in his autobiography that it was a completely innocent trio who breakfasted
every morning, albeit in the nude, in the sunshine on their
balcony, throwing rolls into the via Sistina on to passers-by.

Rome was very hot and the girls and Vadim took the opportunity of sleeping in the nude as well. 'I wonder how many saints would have been safe from eternal damnation had they found themselves in my position,' Vadim writes. 'And yet I did not allow myself one little kiss . . . the slightest dubious gesture.' The fact is Brigitte would not have allowed it.

Vadim occupied himself instead by telling the girls horror stories. Death still held a fascination for him and if Brigitte did not yet share that dark side of his character she certainly responded to the frisson of fear at the tales of vampires, incubi, and succubi, related in theatrical whispers late at night with the light out. Seven years later Vadim collected these tales in a book which was published first in Italy and then translated into English in the early sixties. One of the tales served as a base for his film *Mourir de Plaisir* in 1970.

Brigitte was beginning to gain the upper hand in their marriage. Vadim says he had already begun to feel that he was M. Bardot. If he didn't respond to her magnificent body three times a day, then she had now learned to flaunt it in front of others. She wasn't yet totally confident of betraying her husband, yet all the same the fire was being stoked and a backlog of dissatisfaction built up. She had begun to see that perhaps the fault did not lie entirely with herself.

Apart from anything else Brigitte started to suspect there were more than two people involved in her marriage. Not only was there Vadim as lover *and* Svengali, half of France, indeed half of Europe was being groomed by the steady drop of publicity on the printer's stone to see the young housewife as sex-star. Brigitte then realized that the other people were more important than the husband and wife. 'He was in part a father to me,' she said of Vadim. 'Or a brother. At the time I was enjoying myself, amused by what I thought his innocent eccentricities. I didn't realize myself how much he was playing with fire and even though he is cynical, he didn't either.'

It was not what Brigitte had expected from marriage and she could not reconcile her hopes with the reality. Having it repeatedly pointed out to her that she could attract other men, she began to take the suggestion seriously. Vadim was creating a monster. 'From the moment I liberated Brigitte, the moment I showed her how to be truly herself, our marriage was like a downhill racer,' he reflected afterwards. For, having embarked on the cult of self, Brigitte was determined to be the best Brigitte Bardot around.

Acclaim was coming from the most unlikely quarters to add nail after nail into the coffin of a marriage in which she had intended to take a back seat. She had even made a slight hit on the Paris stage in the Anouilh play, *l'Invitation au Château*, or *Ring Round the Moon* as it is in English, at least with Anouilh himself, who sent her a beautiful bouquet of flowers with a hand-written good-luck message which to this day is one of her treasures. 'You acted like an angel last night,' he enthused. 'I am certain you will have a great future. I won't be there to see you tonight because I'm going to drag my tired bones to the country.' He finished with a P.S.: 'I bring people luck.'

Anouilh, who is now seventy-four and fighting failing health in Switzerland, is touched that Bardot still has that note. He remembers the day they first met outside the Théâtre de l'Atelier in the place Charles Dullin. He and the director, André Barsacq, had seen the two small roles she had done in her first films and decided to give her a try in the leading role of Isabelle. Brigitte arrived at the rehearsal before them – she was still punctual in those days if she wanted something. She was standing outside, unsure what to do, when the playwright arrived for the audition. 'She was utterly charming, a complete beginner,' he says. She made the most of it. She stood on the stage and asked: 'Which way do you want me to face?' Anouilh burst out laughing. 'Why don't you face me?' he said. The part was hers and she did not lose it with the reading.

On the opening night Anouilh was not the only person to find her charming in a role, a leading one moreover, which was perfectly suited to her. The virginal, naïve Isabelle, a chorus girl at the Opera, is the surprise belle of the ball in the grand château thrown by the machiavellian Horace. Good triumphs over evil and everything ends up happily ever after. Even the critic Jean-Jacques Gautier, who had a reputation of terrifying actors, found complimentary things to say. Marcelle Capron in the French magazine *Combat* voiced the general opinion: 'Brigitte Bardot is less striking in the role than Dany Robin [who created it] but even her gaucheness is attractive. Her voice, which is still badly modulated and weak and becomes shrill when she pushes it, and her rather wooden gestures help Isabelle's character rather than destroying it.'

The memory of her performance is still vivid in Anouilh's mind after thirty years. 'The surprising thing about her, since she had never done any theatre, was that she played the role with a real actress's temperament,' he says. 'She certainly could have had a great career in the theatre but you know how it is, the cinema beckons, you get caught up in the whirlwind. It happens to all these stupid girls, they can't see further than the present.'

He also remembers that Brigitte was alone when she auditioned, without her mentor Vadim. 'When he heard that she'd got the part, he wanted a part in *Ring Round the Moon* himself,' says Anouilh. 'So he auditioned for us a week later. We didn't take him. He wasn't good enough,' he chuckles.

Vadim was condemned to write and what he wrote was the screenplay for *Futures Vedettes* from the novel by Vicky Baum, using his favourite character Sophie, who would be played by Brigitte. Marc Allegret would direct. By now Allegret had to agree. Brigitte looked better than she had in the screen test and this part was tailor-made for her. Vadim put down on paper many of the exact words which had passed between them, capturing her way of speaking exactly and highlighting her *joie de vivre*. 'She spoke and I wrote,' he says. 'The words in those first films, as in most of our films together, are really hers. They are written for her because she more or less wrote them.' And since the story takes place in the Vienna Conservatory, she could also make use of her feeling for music. The film shows her in her first real screen affair, demonstrating just how sensual she can be. Vadim, never one to underplay the gifts at his command, exhibits her nude in a bowl of Chinese goldfish. He was also able to pursue one of his favourite themes, the triangular love-affair, a popular fantasy of the rather cerebral French, and to illustrate in the two girls in the triangle the two sides of woman's nature, the Justine and Juliette of the Marquis de Sade. He had not yet lightened Brigitte's hair, still believing perhaps in some old-fashioned symbolism in which the bad girl was always dark.

It was no doubt a sign of those pre-liberation times that *Monthly Film Bulletin* preferred her co-star, Isabelle Pia, who played the ethereal student to Brigitte's passionate one. Yet it has to be said that in the energy Bardot brought to her performances she was finding a distinctive style all of her own. She wasn't a new Caron or a Martine Carol. Observers were not prepared at first for what they saw. Her trademark was utter charm, the word occurs again and again as people watched her on the screen and off, but they also used another word, 'superb', for the pride she had in her physical presence. It was a dangerous combination, charm and arrogance, so devastating that off-screen people didn't seem to trust her at all. They simply had not seen anything like it before. They wanted a girl who looked like that to be silly, vain, or a puppet and she *was* completely light-hearted, puppyish, healthy, a young girl in love with herself, with life and with one man, yet she was also careless, casual, *je m'enfou*, *désinvolte*. That made her a little threatening, like an animal which simply refused to be mastered. You could sniff that unbridled quality about her. It was frightening in a way which was difficult to define. Thirty years ago nice girls simply weren't like that, full of such animal vitality. They were coy. They knew their place.

Still, it excited intelligent men. It was charming, Anouilh says and still does. Anouilh was forty-three at the time, five years older than Arthur Miller. Brigitte was eighteen, eight years younger than Marilyn Monroe. The gap between them was too unwieldy, besides which Bardot was too recently married, but it is not difficult to imagine a Miller-Monroe attraction between this prince of French writers and his Continental showgirl. Anouilh, creator of two brilliant young girls' parts, the Lark and the resistance heroine Antigone, did not share the scepticism of younger observers. If his eyes too were drawn away from any cerebral content between the young lady's delicious ears by the pout and the bosom beneath, he had lived long enough to know that you cannot separate a girl's attractions. You must see them as a whole – and a charming whole is a unique thing in life. Brigitte, who was used to her father's gruff but comic ways, fully reciprocated his interest. And, despite their apparent culture gap, they had one thing in common apart from the traditional affection between the elder statesman and the young nymphet. Anouilh shared Bardot's growing mistrust of the French bourgeoisie. When he later moved to Switzerland, that symbolic citadel of the solid burgher in most people's minds, he told me that he found the Swiss attitude wholly relaxed, even sensual, as compared to the French. He has continued to live there ever since because he has found the Swiss completely nonchalant towards their neighbours where his native people are busybodies.

Myth has it that Anouilh even wrote a play for Bardot called *The Ginger Cat* but he denies this. There was a script, called simply *La Chatte*, about a cat-woman, half girl, half animal, 'hardly a very original notion, which she might have played, in fact it ended up on German television'. But Brigitte as cat was the idea of people who did not know her really well. She seemed the independent creature who walked alone because they were not used to anything like her but in reality she needed love like a little puppy. Brigitte herself says she is a hybrid, a 'cog or a dat, what a pity such a thing doesn't exist. You see I like the suppleness of cats but not their claws – I am not a person who scratches – and I like the affection of dogs but not their servility.'

Nothing further came of Brigitte's stage career, although for a while she was involved with the post-war issues that occupied stage people. The vehicle of the moment at the Sarah Bernhardt theatre was *The Crucible*, translated into French from Arthur Miller's original by Marcel Aymé because Sartre's secretary had turned it down on his behalf. ('That play has my name written all over it,' Sartre said when he saw it. 'Well, you should have more control over your staff,' said Simone Signoret who played the leading part.)

The Crucible was the story of Ethel and Julius Rosenberg, put into the mouths of John and Elizabeth Proctor, the seventeenth-century New England Puritan couple victimized as the Witches of Salem. The Rosenbergs, a Chicago couple arrested on spying charges in 1951, were due to be executed in 1953. The appeal verdict produced much opposition in the wake of McCarthyism and the Communist witch hunts of the forties in America. The case fired the imagination of liberals and intellectuals all over the world and was a leading cause campaigned by those film business idealists known as the Hollywood Ten. The Rosenbergs were ostensibly a decent, middle-class Jewish couple, the parents of two small boys, and their access to treacherous secrets was not proven to the majority of Americans. If they were being sent to the electric chair, it could only be a case of principle – a discouragement to the real traitors whom they refused to name. To many people, who were weary of war and destruction, it simply represented the victimization of those too powerless to defend themselves.

Miller, victimized himself by McCarthy's witch hunts (his passport had been confiscated and there was no question of him seeing the Paris production), wasted no time in getting these feelings down on paper and in agreeing to a French translation. By 1953 it was already in rehearsal in Paris with Yves Montand playing opposite his wife. It was perfect for the French mood on every level. It was about sex, metaphysics and social politics. Its political bias particularly pleased French intellectuals, who were fashionably pro-Communist after the war. Vadim and his immigrant friends spent hours drawing up petitions on behalf of the Rosenbergs, writing to the newspapers and filling exercise books with noble thoughts. Everything we know about Brigitte indicates she should have been too self-centred, too sensual, too middle-class, and too chauvinistic to care about such a cause. But care she did, precisely because she was feeling chauvinistic.

Brigitte was in England at the time, at Pinewood Studios making *Doctor at Sea*, her twelfth film. The English producer, Betty Box, had spotted her when she saw a roughcut of *Manina*. Unlike Papa Bardot she liked what she saw. Betty Box subscribed to French film magazines like *Cinémonde* and she hit on the idea of importing Continental talent to add another dimension to British films. Later she introduced Claudia Cardinale, Mylène Demongeot, and Sylva Koscina to English-speaking audiences. She had already tried to get the young Bardot for an earlier film called *A Day to Remember*. She was unsuccessful. With *Doctor at Sea*, however, Betty Box and the leading man, Dirk Bogarde, unwittingly took the right tack when they flew to Paris, ostensibly so he could cast his eye over his potential leading lady. Already Brigitte liked the mountain to come to Mahomet – in the future she would make many excuses for not leaving France, saying she loathed flying or that she could not speak English, but students of poker merely recognized she was perfecting a technique for which she had always had the strongest feeling.

As she sat in the bar of the Hôtel Meurice in the rue de Rivoli with Vadim she gave Bogarde a piece of advice. 'If you don't want to do something, never say, "I'm sorry, but . . . " just give them a straight no, that way they can't work on you.' Bogarde says he was very impressed. He recognized in the whisky-drinking girl – Vadim's course in hard living was paying off – not only someone who intended to succeed but who intended to do so on her terms. Already honing his literary career, he started to keep a diary about the filming, which was eventually published in *Playgoer* magazine and certainly helped to publicize the girl who had taken the role rejected by one of England's favourite actresses, Kay Kendall. 'She has a superb figure, long legs, flowing hair and gazelle-like grace,' he noted after their meeting. When she arrived in England without Vadim he wrote: 'She is like a breath of *Oklahoma* on the set every day. The kind of sex she suggests is warm, uninhibited, complete-

A well brought up young lady, aged five, in 1939
(John Hillelson Agency Ltd/Sygma)

Not the best looking seven-year-old in Hattemer, 1941.
Brigitte is the one in spectacles
(Rex Features Ltd)

Finding her feet for the first time:
Boris Kniazeff's ballet classes
(Popperfoto)

Aged eighteen: private
modelling tuition from fiancé
Roger Vadim
*(John Hillelson Agency Ltd/
Sygma)*

Summer 1952. Blossoming at
Louveciennes
(Rex Features Ltd)

Brigitte Bardot's first film,
Le Trou Normand, 1952.
Carried away by Bourvil
(*Kobal Collection*)

First trip to England – with
Dirk Bogarde in *Doctor at Sea*
(1955)
(*Kobal Collection*)

This pose with Louis Jourdain (in *The Bride is much too Beautiful*, 1956) is what fifties audiences expected . . . *(Kobal Collection)*

. . . and this, with Christian Marquand, is what Vadim gave them (in *And God Created Woman*, 1956) *(Kobal Collection)*

Bardot, now 'someone', in Picasso's studio above Cannes in 1956
(*John Hillelson Agency Ltd/Jerome Brière/Sygma*)

Off-duty with sister Mijanou and her boyfriend in a Paris café
(*Kobal Collection*)

Overleaf: Voulez-vous danser avec moi – the 'blonde gypsy' at her happiest
(*Kobal Collection*)

The film star was created
(Venice, 1958)
(*Keystone Press Agency
Ltd*)

And so was the recording
star. With Sacha Distel, the
same year
(*Keystone Press Agency
Ltd*)

ly natural . . . You see Brigitte takes the trouble to put across sex as an art. With many of our girls, it's a farce.'

The whole secret, as Betty Box had predicted, was that she was not one of our girls. The English Press lined up on the tarmac the very first day of her arrival to see what the French had sent us. Bardot played the French ding-a-ling to the hilt. 'I have brought with me a lot of nightdresses,' she said. 'I am hoping someone will ask me out.' The very next day the newspapers were full of pin-up photographs. Nothing like that happened in France where she was just – French. Pinewood's publicity department snapped her in a range of English situations, in a pub, drinking a pint of beer, that sort of thing. Brigitte played along charmingly. She was in England and she would give the English what they had always expected from French girls. She would be a floosie, a fly-by-night, a flibbertigibbet, the kind of girl who could get a decent British boy into trouble. She played the stereotype for all it was worth on the set and off. A foreigner could do things that no local girl could get away with. If she wanted to ruin her reputation, that was the problem of the French, not ours. The crew, colleagues, journalists loved the idea of an Anglo–French sparring match, it was a ready-made story and they all embroidered it as much as they dared. Rehearsing for a shower scene with scraps of sticking plaster on her nipples and over her pubic hair, Bardot tore these off and posed in front of the crew completely nude. It was a revolutionary gesture for 1955 in a world which had not yet seen the rise of *Playboy* magazine – when it did the pubic hair in the centrefold was air-brushed out. 'I found her an excessively frank girl,' says Ralph Thomas who directed the film, 'And she was very proud of her body.' When she left the set at night she left a series of alternative phone numbers where she might be reached – unless of course she was too occupied to take calls. And as an expert on sex, she fanned the flames of controversy by saying that British lads had no idea how to make her happy. 'What is the matter with British boys?' she asked. 'They can't make love.' They retorted exactly how they had been schooled – French girls ate too much garlic and smelled of unwashed knickers.

This year, thirty years later, the English were still crowing over a survey in the French magazine *Marie-France*, which reported that 50 per cent of the French never use a toothbrush and 10 per cent of their women wear the same underwear for days at a time. Richard Gordon, the doctor who wrote the 'Doctor' series and was a frequent visitor to the set to advise on the script, supported the story with his own biological theory. Brigitte's distinctive Parisian smell, which spelled irresponsible sex to anyone who had ever crossed the Channel on a teenage outing, was indeed the smell of sex, it was caused by over-active endocrine glands. In other words she was highly sexed. Gordon told Betty Box that, with all his medical experience, he had only ever smelled this overpowering muskiness before on women who shared Bardot's appetite for men. Quite apart from the way she looked, Nature had conspired in all departments to give her the built-in come-hither mechanism, which perfume manufacturers have been struggling for years to extract from flowers and animals.

The whispers about her sexual needs multiplied and they were helped along by the script, which was little more than a collection of mildly dirty jokes. Englishmen were agreed that here was the original naughty French girl, a challenge to them to prove themselves in the flesh and not just in the privacy of their bathrooms late at night over publicity stills or in their dreams.

In some cases the challenge became a threat to men, though not apparently to English girls. The Rank Charm School ladies, who had the opportunity to observe all this at Pinewood, looked on it with so much amusement. Susan Stephen, who is now married to England's most original director, Nic Roeg, was being groomed for stardom at the time along with Joan Collins and Diana Dors. She remembers Brigitte being perfectly charming to her when they were introduced in the canteen. She was sweet, simple, and straightforward, with none of the side that is regarded with deep suspicion in the film business. Susan did not find it difficult to take her part when rumours of an ugly incident went rushing round the set. 'Brigitte, who was obviously homesick, spent a lot of time on her own. She had one thing she loved to do. She had a record of a popular song and she used to sit all by herself in her dressing room, playing it over and over again. One day someone rushed in and said, "You know what's happened to Brigitte's record?" One of the men on the film, an assistant I think, had taken something sharp and had drawn a scratch right across it so she couldn't play it. She was very upset. She was a sweet girl.' Had the starlet rejected the assistant? 'I don't think so. It was a pure act of meanness. It was obvious to this man, indeed to us all, that Brigitte was about to be the next star and he couldn't take it.' The recording features Brigitte herself.

Once more it was apparent, if surprising, that women had more of an affinity for Brigitte than men, especially professional ones. They recognized that a lot of her attitudes were bravura and play-acting, the sort of sales-pitch you had to make as a woman to star in a man's world. It was plain to them, and to certain men – the ones that didn't make cheap passes – that she wasn't the dotty ding-a-ling of the public persona. Richard Gordon thought she was very bright indeed when he explained to her how to behave during an operation for one of the scenes in the film. 'I had the impression she could have gone ahead and taken a real appendix out all by herself,' he said. It was the insecure men and women who bitched about her. When the film was released Bogarde received about 500 letters accusing him of going off with 'that French hussy', so in the next Doctor film, *Doctor at Large*, the script arranged for him to fall in love with a 'nice' girl, Muriel Pavlow. Brigitte visited the two of them on the set when she came over for the Royal Film Performance. Though plenty of non-professional women would later malign her, she refused to retaliate. You will never hear any woman who had dealings with her accuse her of bitchiness. This is not because she was so confident she knew she had nothing to fear from other women, but rather the opposite. She knew the difficulties of being a woman.

The difficulties at Pinewood that year included the fact that the smutty script was not even written in straightforward English. It was naturally very colloquial. Her English nurse had not prepared her for this. Brigitte struggled along all alone, dictionary in hand. Vadim was in Paris and remained there. She telephoned him constantly, begging him to get on a plane and join her, but Vadim stayed firmly put. The husbands of starlets don't find the red carpet down for them when they hang around the set. Brigitte was just at the point when she needed to spread her wings professionally and he had it in mind for her to do so, besides which he had several more projects on the boil in France.

Though both of them had come to realize their marriage was not ideal, she did not give up easily. At times her loneliness was so bad she would go back to Paris just for a few hours. She was back at home between filming on 18 June 1953, when she threw herself into his interests which, in common with many other people in France that day, included the Rosenbergs. Vadim and his displaced friends sat up all night writing pamphlets, leaflets, and articles to distribute among their contacts in the Press in defence of the American couple. When Vadim drove Brigitte to the airport the next morning to send her back to the set she scattered from her handbag hundreds of slogans she had written, pleading for the lives of the condemned couple. She was on the Pinewood set when she heard that they had been executed. It was the first of many lost causes.

The most immediate lost cause was, however, closer at hand – her marriage. 'Doctor at Sea,' she said later, 'taught me I could get along by myself if I had to.' The film was obviously not destined for critical success but it did a lot for Bardot. It taught her English, which she speaks better than she admits, and it taught the English about her, which was the first step towards her becoming an international property. In England she excited the pens of the most enthusiastic entertainment writers this side of the Atlantic. Brigitte's 'humming bird personality had scored a triumph of sheer charm over a bad script', wrote Leonard Mosley, a writer who had been watching her for some time now, in the *Daily Express*. The old *Evening News* thought her 'bewitching', the *News Chronicle* 'delicious', the *Sunday Express* 'charming' – everyone's favourite adjective for Brigitte. Raymond Durgnat of *Films and Filming* said it was in the 'Doctor' film that she first emerged from the rank and file of starletry and even the Americans, who must have been bewildered by this example of parochial British comedy, called her 'pert' in the *New York Times* and 'visual proof that the beauties of France are not all geographic'.

Back in England Harold Conway in the *Daily Sketch* said she packed more sex-appeal into offering Dirk Bogarde a cup of coffee than Betty Grable got into an entire film. The new sex-symbol was beginning to be defined. It was not yet a blonde. Its measurements were 34–20–34. It was labelled a 'modern Venus de Milo', a 'twentieth-century Juno', the 'gorgeous Pekinese'. Her Pekinese profile was first remarked on by Kenneth Green, director of publicity at Pinewood. He it was who asked her at the end of the picture what she had learned in England during her stay. Her answer was quite simply, 'The meaning of infidelity'.

But whose infidelity? Everyone, including her husband, assumed she was talking about her own actions. 'I would prefer to have that kind of woman, knowing she is unfaithful to me, than to completely possess a little girl who just loves me and no one else and has no spirit, no *joie de vivre*, no appetites. I don't want a woman who is prepared to wait docilely, without curiosity, without hunger. That kind of woman scares me, I feel too trapped,' he said when she returned to him in Paris. 'If Brigitte had not asked me all the time to go to London, I would have been hurt and unhappy. She was honest and lonely. I knew what was happening . . . but I had important things to do in Paris. Important things for both of us.'

But whatever it looked like in retrospect, Brigitte's young girl's vows to Vadim had been taken totally seriously. He was the one who had not been satisfied with her as she was and had set about remodelling her. That dissatisfaction, she concluded, was a kind of infidelity. Vadim appeared to her to have no shame. He arranged to have Brigitte cast in a film called *La Lumière d'en Face*, which reflected this thinking. In it she played an over-sexed girl with an impotent husband. He went on to call the character in her next film, *Cette Sacrée Gamine*, by her own name, Brigitte. Art was imitating life and Brigitte was getting horribly confused because Vadim was not yet out of her system. They had both found out that you couldn't just invent romance the way it was in the movies.

She was young, nothing mattered much and she was, by most people's expectations, having a good time. The nudge nudge, wink wink school of thought, the men in shabby raincoats, the ones who were convinced that Bardot had loose elastic, salivated at the opportunity she had to have it off with whomever she liked in anonymous hotel rooms without ever having to own up to anyone because of the nature of her profession. But the reality of her profession was a great deal of loneliness away from the people she loved and who had always tried to manipulate her in one way or another. Young girls are not by nature promiscuous and Bardot wasn't yet a free spirit. Nor was any well brought up middle-class girl at the time when it suddenly became an acceptable pursuit. Later on, maybe, sex would become an indiscriminate gift but not at the beginning. Her looks had been given to her to satisfy just one man. Bardot was an old-fashioned romantic. Her man was Vadim, but he was not satisfied.

Bardot was not immoral, she knew that for sure. She was simply undone by love. Perhaps betrayed by love – it began to look very much like it. For what had love brought her? Her husband constantly engineered for her to be away from the home that she had so badly wanted. To begin with she was bewildered by this. 'Little by little the foundation of our love diminished. I was away from home much of the time filming. At first I missed Vadim terribly. Later, I became used to our separations.' The thought began to haunt her, if Vadim loved her so much, why had he wanted to change her? Why did he want other men to look at her in the way they did? To be the respectable married man's unattainable dream, as he put it. Wife-swapping, even in theory, was not part of the bourgeois morality she knew. Quite apart from anything else it was not part of her embryonic ego trip either. Far too much attention was being paid to the Bardot that was Vadim's creation rather than to Bardot herself. It might have been that she could never have been someone's little wife anyway but he had never allowed her to find that out. He simply gave her *carte blanche* to kick up her heels and try to find someone who did want Bardot herself, who felt something for the original model, who was possessive of her. Underneath the delicious dummy Vadim was creating a callous, insouciant, self-willed woman, who would go far beyond what he had in mind in order to find out just how desirable she was. Just as when she had been someone's daughter Bardot found she was not really living one life or another. She was still BB in waiting.

Coming back home after being away she could take stock of the situation. She *did* have an identity of her own. The great René Clair cast her in his first colour film, *Les Grandes Manoeuvres*, with two hot French stars of the moment, Gérard Philipe and Michèle Morgan. It was a delightful historical film, set in a provincial garrison town which Clair said reminded him of his boyhood in Versailles. Brigitte had grown up in exactly the same area and she could endorse his observations of the hypocrisies of bourgeois society. She wasn't called upon to do much more than look enchanting and move along the sub-plot but she was successful in that, the *New York Times* spotting her as 'the pretty object'.

Les Grandes Manoeuvres finished shooting in Boulogne just outside Paris on 8 July. By 11 July Brigitte was in Nice playing Olivia in *La Lumière d'en Face*, a film which seemed to mirror her married life. It was their story: 'a hot wife to a cold husband' said one French review. Vadim plugged his image as cradle-snatcher in the publicity notes for one of his films:

She is more advanced than the children of earlier generations. Along with this, she had blank spots. She knows Egyptian history down to the smallest detail but I had to teach her that rats don't lay eggs and that the moon always presents the same side to the earth.

'She cannot fry an egg but she covered the chairs and divans at home as well as a professional could. She drives her car in Paris with all the assurance of a taxi driver, but she fears spirits which become invisible monsters. It is to protect her from these monsters when I am working that I bought her the cocker spaniel Clown. Here, in order after Clown, is what Brigitte likes most in the world: other dogs, birds, the sun, money, the sea, flowers, period furniture, grass, kittens, and mice. I did not dare ask where she placed me, perhaps between the grass and the kittens.

There was something old-fashioned and gallant about the man who would later be called the Devil.

Yet he cast her in one provocative vehicle after another in which her sexuality sizzled. As Alan Brien wrote: 'She glows like an open stove.' The director used all the tricks of the trade available to him at the time. He lit her from the back standing in a thin nightdress, washing her legs under a tap, bending over in a loose blouse, bathing naked in a river. In England *La Lumière d'en Face* ran into trouble with local film censors in Bromley. It was more the feeling of Brigitte, of pent-up energy that scared people, which corresponded exactly to the feeling of the times. In *En Effeuillant la Marguerite* – 'Plucking the Daisy' – she seemed to offer herself to every man in the audience. In Italy the film was called 'offensive, immoral, shameless'. They preferred her in 'My Son Nero'. The French too loved this film and described it as a typical warm-hearted Roman folly, which they could see over and over again. It frankly disappointed the British audience, who were by now watching Brigitte for reasons other than comedy. 'Mlle Brigitte Bardot is a little out of her depth and class,' said *The Times*. They were referring to her bath in asses' milk. In a television interview at the time she appeared like a parody of Monroe, saying they had wanted it to be starch but she was afraid of coming out all stiff. In fact the starch had sunk to the bottom of the tub and left too much of Brigitte showing.

Roger Vadim had been working on this American image ever since the Cannes Festival of 1953. He planned to go there as soon as he heard that the American-financed *Act of Love* was going to be shown. It starred the thirty-seven-year-old Kirk Douglas and the young Dany Robin. Douglas had been good luck for several actresses in the past, like Pier Angeli who had become his girlfriend and gone to Hollywood. Vadim was leaving nothing to chance. He planned a Barnum and Bailey presentation of Brigitte on the American aircraft carrier the *Midway*, which was anchored in the bay. At the end of the festival the crew would host a party for stars and starlets. Gary Cooper was there and Edward G. Robinson, Mel Ferrer, Vittorio de Sica, Leslie Caron, Silvana Mangano, Raf Vallone, Lana Turner, and Olivia de Havilland. 'We were all conveyed by launch to the carrier as a friendly gesture to the Sixth Fleet,' Olivia told me recently. 'The crew gathered on the deck and one by one we were introduced to them in the expectation that we would come forth with words of encouragement and cheer.' Olivia returned to Cannes for the last time twelve years later as the first woman president of the jury, but then she was taking it easy, loving every minute of the razzmatazz of the festival fortnight, which was viewed with less cynicism then than it is now. For the American stars it was a first-class round trip from Los Angeles, all expenses paid. They were put up at the luxurious Carlton Hotel right on the promenade in the centre of town, the object of intense fascination for townspeople and film industry alike. The story goes that Brigitte, who had hardly starred in *Gone with the Wind*, was not in receipt of unlimited expenses. The photographers clubbed together to pay her hotel bill for the whole two weeks because she was so photogenic. The English newspaper photographers, however, do not remember having had to pay anything, so one can only imagine which photographers this story refers to – those of *Paris-Match*.

They were waiting on the aircraft carrier as Brigitte slipped aboard in, of all the unsuitable garments for April on the Riviera, a raincoat. *Paris-Match* reporter Raymond Cartier chronicled the event:

> Then the girl in the raincoat caught the photographers' eyes. The raincoat slipped from her shoulders. She emerged in a tight-fitting teenager's dress and with a toss of her head sent her ponytail flying. There was a second of silence, just enough for the electric charge to pass between the crowd of males and the figure in the floodlight. Then the *Midway* was engulfed in a

single shot of lightning and a crash of thunder: thousands of flashbulbs and shouts of admiration that exceeded in volume all the previous acclaims put together.

Pony-tail, teenager's dress, raincoat à la Humphrey Bogart, anyone who has ever been inside a cinema recognizes the derivations. Vadim was looking across the Atlantic and on the *Midway* he was playing to a captive American audience.

American studios had moulded people before into symbolic star material for their time but Brigitte's was rather a different story, a timely one too as the media started to expand just after the war. She was the vision of one man in league with the magazines and newspapers in a country, moreover, which had a very particular relationship with the printed word because of its strict libel laws. The law of personal privacy, which would in fact be further defined by Brigitte during her career, meant that stars who wanted the attention of the Press would be encouraged to enter into an agreement with the outlet of their choice, providing exclusive stories in return for a moratorium from litigation. Brigitte went along with this while it suited her. More than any other star before her, she was created by the Press rather than by the publicity machinery of her profession. This was entirely because of the accident of Vadim's affinity with *Match* and was also one of the reasons why theatre and cinema critics were so suspicious of her. To purists of the stage and screen she seemed a hybrid, a moving stills photograph, a cover-girl or a page-three phenomenon who had been thrust on their profession from the outside, not a genuine actress.

The person who has always taken the credit for getting her into the pages of the English-speaking Press was Leonard Mosley of the *Daily Express* who made her his very first story that year at Cannes, before the *Midway* stunt, calling her the little girl he found on the beach. 'She was a strip of sunburned, hoydenish girl lying on a Riviera beach and waiting for someone or something to turn up,' he explained. 'I turned up. So did a *Daily Express* photographer who snapped her – lean, schoolgirl limbs, wasp waist, adolescent bulges, long, uncombed hair. Thus was Brigitte Bardot discovered.' In his newspaper he wrote 'Watch what happens to this little French girl.'

Mosley recognized a sociological phenomenon when he saw one. After the event he wrote:

At that moment in the minds of men something snapped. Until that time a woman had always been a woman, and looked it. Brigitte Bardot showed that woman could also look and act like a tomboy. Nothing phoney about her. She became a symbol to the world – through her films and through her private life – of the happy girl who leaves the other soppy females and goes down to play with the gang of boys on the street corner. The first of the beatniks – that was Bardot. If she failed to make an uncombed head and an unpowdered face acceptable, she at least made them seem attractive. Older women may have said that she always looked as if she needed a wash and brush-up; most men were apt to reply, 'What does soap and water matter as long as she's friendly?' Bardot ushered in the era of the great unmade bed. And from the beaches of Saint-Tropez to the gang-infested alleyways of backstreet New York, she became the imaginary champion of females who accepted her looks and her attitudes as a way of life.

The rebellion started in 1953, the year Bardot returned from honeymoon. In England there was a queen on the throne again. In America Doris Day had just made *Calamity Jane*. The heroines of the rebellion were Heloïse, Joan of Arc, Eleanor of Acquitaine, Brett Ashley, Juliette Greco, Marlene Dietrich, Annie Oakley, the entire Land Army, Florence Nightingale – people who were fictional, dead, grandmothers maybe, but who would always be honorary 'girls', anyone who had ever bought the boys in the backroom a drink. These women were not mad at men, they loved them. They were mad at the girls who were spineless before them. They were envious of the freedom men had, which they couldn't actually use to the limit because of the lack of freedom for women. Something obviously had to be done by all those girls who had enjoyed climbing trees, riding bikes, and feeling the sun on their skin. These girls enjoyed their bodies – and didn't intend to suffer because of them, to stand cinched, bound, and gagged in decent society just because they were girls. They were determined to shed the bondage of their position and the artifice, not to bow on the screen to a Chaplin who was tying them to railway tracks, a Valentino who was lording it over them in the desert, an Abel Gance who was subjecting them to rape and pillage. They did not want to be Garbo who, every time she stepped out of line in *Flesh and the Devil* or *Anna Karenina*, was made to pay for her temerity.

It was all there in the symbolism of silent films – rain like tears would accompany their downfall. Vadim was looking for a new symbol, a new definition of women to turn the mid-century on.

One of the problems between the sexes, which he understood, was the need to keep alive the notion of passion for a member of the opposite sex, which is so opposite that in familiarity it needles, exasperates or bores. Vadim wondered what would happen if women became completely familiar, if they became the personi-fication of what men wanted in their wildest dreams, which was a companion who was physically perfect yet did not have to be left at home all the time, a psychological match for her man, utterly free and brave.

He struggled towards this definition for three years, moulding Brigitte on the closest existing sex-symbol, Marilyn Monroe, who had also been a cover-girl pictured in the surf and the wind, not dolled up in suspenders and mink. He saw the intrigue posed by blonde rather than dark hair, which would always make men wonder about the reality of their fantasies. (Bardot was always being asked what colour her pubic hair was.) But Bardot's blonde was not Marilyn's, which came out of a bottle. The sharp contours of the peroxide bob, which looked so dramatic on black and white film, yielded happily at this point to Bardot's tawny look, which worked so well on colour stock.

One of the American reporters who helped make Bardot's name after that first Cannes Festival remembers going with her to Le Cannet up above the town, where she threw herself into a wild impromptu dance for a photographer in the village square. 'She was like a blonde gypsy,' Margaret Gardener says now. It should have been a contradiction in terms, but that was Bardot's new classless look. All the potential of womanhood came together in her one person. The good and the bad, the earthy and the ice-cool – which blonde had meant. The sophistication of the blonde was changed for ever. Bardot's blonde came from the sun originally. It occurred to her and Vadim when they saw what happened to her on the beach. That is when she first unleashed it too, luxuriating, as the shy girl she was, in its protective covering. At the height of her career she would bleach it. Later hundreds of actresses – Jane Fonda, Julie Christie, Elke Sommer, and Susan George among them – would copy her style with more or less success. In the mid-fifties it was copied by all the girls in the street.

7. And God Created Woman

And God Created Woman is Vadim and Bardot's homage to the last superstar before her, Marilyn Monroe. The story speaks for itself. The heroine Juliette Hardy, played by Brigitte Bardot, is an orphan whose budding sexuality is too much for the children's home. Wherever she is fostered she unwittingly creates trouble. Men peep at her behind curtains, they jostle for a seat next to her on the bus. It is not conversation they have in mind but the involuntary pressure of her thighs against theirs when the vehicle lurches. A sympathetic older man devises the only plan he knows to take her off the open market. A suitable marriage partner must be found. The guy is good, sweet, protective, and truly loves her, but Juliette has discovered sex.

Juliette/Marilyn/Brigitte is not a bad girl. She is well-meaning and she tries to do the right thing. She suffers from the conflict between her conscience and her sexuality. Although she tries to make a go of her marriage, she is overcome by her instincts. The parallel between Brigitte and Vadim's story was actually enacted on the set. Instead of doing something, anything to stop the rot, the director/writer was transfixed by this parallel between art and life. It made Bardot a worthy successor in Vadim's mind to Monroe. The parallel between Monroe and Juliette is even more striking.

Eight years older than Bardot and a veteran of Hollywood since the age of seventeen, Marilyn was twenty-nine in 1956, the year *And God Created Woman* was made. In Hollywood she was making *Bus Stop*. She had just finished *The Seven Year Itch*. Behind her she had *Gentlemen Prefer Blondes* and *How to Marry a Millionaire*. She was at the height of her career. Her wonderful daffiness had been studiously copied by Bardot but she could not capture the sadness in the eye, the real vulnerability of the sex-symbol, a vulnerability she was, however, going to experience in her own life. Brigitte had in contrast to Monroe a brazenness about her which suggested that women could look after themselves and that they brought their own troubles on themselves.

Marilyn was to prove so vulnerable that she made the ultimate sacrifice, an overdose of pills and a lonely death with the plastic telephone in one hand her only company, a robot remote cry for help. But that was six years in the future. In the mid-fifties all you could see was her success story. The story of her life and her rise to stardom must have been floating round Paris among the star-struck young like a blueprint for their own success. It had storybook elements much more potent than the facts in Brigitte's life. Marilyn was the rich little poor girl, a Cinderella figure, product of an orphanage, fostered out to foster-parents whose own marriage seemed under threat as she became outrageously pubescent. No one tried to educate her, no one tried to make a decent girl out of her. With nothing much else to think about as she grew up, Marilyn seems to have felt herself a sexual being much earlier than Brigitte. She left the orphanage at eleven and was fostered into several families, never successfully. Thereafter she was taken in by her mother's best friend, Grace McKee. Unfortunately Grace had just got married to a man ten years younger than herself who had a roving eye. It looked as if the pubescent Norma Jean, as she was called, would have to go back to the orphanage. Grace's friend stepped in, however, and arranged a marriage with a former neighbour's son, Jim Dougher-ty. Norma Jean's husband made aeroplanes at the Lockheed factory in California. As Norman Mailer puts it in *Marilyn* he was 'a good-looking, practical adolescent . . . hopelessly entangled in the insane sexual musk which comes off a fifteen-year-old who talks to him with eyes as soft and luminous as a deer's' – the same insane sexual musk of the heroine of *Doctor at Sea*. Jim and Norma Jean married three weeks after her sixteenth birthday. She was over-ripe for her age, just like the brand-new Mrs Vadim, but just like Mrs Vadim and Juliette (whose future husband is a boat builder in St-Tropez) her husband was her first lover. She was married in white. At the reception she disgraced herself by picking up her veil, showing a leg and joining a conga line on-stage at the restaurant. It was 1942. In 1956 Juliette doesn't even bother to join the guests at her wedding breakfast but consummates her marriage within earshot of their eating and drinking. Put like that it sounds quite flagrant but of course there are mitigating circumstances which manipulate the sympathies of an audience. The nub of the matter is that they both discover something which is a dilemma for a full-blooded woman – that sex, an act of penetration which is enjoyable, is in conflict with their natural pride in themselves.

Neither of them has any patience with appearances but in some ways they are as dutiful as virgins. 'Norma Jean is ready for her first full assignment in acting – she throws herself into the part of the loving wife and works at keeping an immaculate apartment . . . the condition of housewife may actually possess attraction for her,' says Mailer. Again there are parallels between Brigitte on-screen and off. 'The "human being" is looking for security.' Her perfect performance around the house is marred one day when she takes pity on a shivering cow and invites it into her living room. Brigitte-Juliette owns a rabbit, a cat, a bird, and even Clown makes an appearance in the film to console her in a particularly vulnerable moment on the St-Tropez jetty. Marilyn, like Brigitte, is a diabolical cook. Vadim boasted that Brigitte could not fry an egg. Dougherty blames the break-up of his marriage on the fact that Marilyn used to serve only peas and carrots for the evening meal.

The parallels are endless. Marilyn called Dougherty 'a kind man', and 'a brother', she addressed him as 'daddy' in the notes she hid in his lunch-pail when he went to work, signing herself 'your Baby'. She was, according to him, physically 'a most responsive bride', and again like Brigitte she is bored without her husband. They even seem to have the same sort of fights as Brigitte and Vadim with Dougherty hurling Norma Jean fully clothed into the shower. They ended up laughing about that because Marilyn's dress was pre-shrunk. What is more Jim bought Norma Jean a dog to keep her company. Jim felt threatened by her sexuality, as Vadim might have done by Brigitte's, but he was taken away from the threat by the war. While he was away Norma Jean was spotted by a photographer and despite dark brown, too heavy hair, a bulbous nose, and an upper lip which is too short she became a hard-working successful cover-girl. She also became lonely and promiscuous but proud, her affections really quite unpredictable and capable of breaking spirits as much as hearts. Men did not seem to be able to strike her as deeply as she would like and her permanent friends were older women. Brigitte would discover this too in time.

Marilyn's foibles were not recorded in a book until four years later, in the biography by Maurice Zolotow, so the question remains, did Vadim build up the myth from current reports in newspapers and magazines consciously or was the connection between all these heroines even more interesting? Was he merely describing the perfect mid-twentieth-century sex-symbol, the naughty little good girl, when he wrote *And God Created Woman?* Was he, a man who had been dragged by the scruff of the neck into contact with the violent forces which shaped the times in which he lived, perfectly in tune with what this sex-symbol should be?

It is a perverse picture he paints in *And God Created Woman*. By all that is spontaneous, Christian and caring Juliette should be the most admired of women. She is kind, brave, honest with herself and other people, modest with strangers and loyal to friends, affectionate with children and animals, grateful to benefactors, she loves uncomplicated fun, she doesn't want to be the subject of barrack-room chat and above all she can't be bought. She should by rights be a saint - her initials are, symbolically, JC, Juliette Christiane - but the hypocritical majority of society sees her as a dangerous sinner. Just about a decade before women's lib Vadim spotted a problem of the future. If men can't buy women, their affections, their duty, their loyalty and chastity, all previous rules of society are broken. Men had a lot to fear from women. One uppity female could be labelled a whore, and paid for ostentatiously, but if women chose to rebel *en masse* and this became socially acceptable, no man could vouch for his own future. He might as well ejaculate into a void for all the control he would have over the investment of his sperm.

Raoul Levy, the film's producer, had little respect for society anyway. Born in Belgium, a fact he liked to keep quiet in France, he was a studio floor-sweeper turned producer and he had fought for himself every inch of the way. When he met Roger Vadim in the spring of 1956 he was not yet thirty and he had already been financially ruined five times. Vadim adored him on sight as an indefatigable spirit who could help him sustain his own high ambitions. Even his obvious faults seemed attractive to the film-maker and to practically everyone else he met for that matter. He was a series of fortuitous contradictions, a masochist and a tyrant, a charmer who could also strike people as physically repulsive. Most of all he was silver-tongued. And though he betrayed many people when it suited him, most remained loyal to him including Vadim who even these days swears undying love to his memory.

They met at the offices of the band leader Ray Ventura, now turned impresario, who had taken over an option on Brigitte's future projects on the death of Jacques Gauthier, producer of *La Lumière d'en Face*. Raoul was a quasi-diabolical creature of the sort much loved by the film industry on every continent. He lived far above his means in all the hot-spots of the time from the Riviera to Paris, talking himself into deals which temporarily supported a lifestyle of caviar and champagne, only to fall through when it became a question of boring tenacity. He was a brilliant gambler, a manic depressive, a person who always had to have a project in the air to replace the one that had gone down the drain in order to uphold his flagging spirits. His death by his own hand in 1967, outside the front door of a girl whom he would probably have lived to discount, was as typical of him as his life, and indeed of the sort of person who most attracted Vadim – the person to whom nothing, be it war, love, death, success, or poverty, mattered. You might say that Vadim had been in training to be this person ever since he was orphaned.

When Raoul met Vadim, who had a wife who was making a name for herself, he saw a way of capitalizing on her. He invented a project. Then he publicized it. Ray Ventura agreed to be co-producer and Vadim would write it. He knew what he wanted to say – he had lived through it all with Brigitte and he had dreamed about it all with Marilyn – but he did not have a plot as such. Levy mentioned a newspaper story about a crime in a remote village involving three brothers and a beautiful girl. Vadim started to write.

What happened after that was a series of poker moves. The players were Levy, Vadim, Brigitte, and her agent Olga Horstig, and each one challenged the next to raise the ante. Vadim, hooked on the wide screen of the American cinema, had infected Brigitte with the same enthusiasm. If *And God Created Woman* was Vadim's homage to Marilyn, it was Brigitte's to James Dean. At Cannes that year, where *East of Eden* was being shown, she developed a passion for Elia Kazan's brilliant wide-screen treatment of John Steinbeck's Cain and Abel saga. Like millions of other young girls it was due largely to her appreciation of its leading actor, dead before he had a chance to became a star. Small, heartbreakingly vulnerable and misunderstood, he was the go-between physically and psychologically betwen all sorts of hero-figures, perceived as heroes anyway by the cinema audience because they were larger than life on the screen. You could make a diagram of the things they shared. He was as frail as Sinatra, as gauche as Gary Cooper, as provocative as Brando and Presley with their cruder images which would endure into the sixties. He was one of the first screen anti-heroes.

Bardot was hardly a star-struck bobbysoxer. She says she has never been fascinated by people just because they were famous. She told Françoise Sagan when they were comparing their experiences that she had never seen the appeal of a Napoleon, a Joan of Arc or even a Mae West, and no box-office idol like Richard Burton ever came to her in her dreams. She had to identify with her heroes. She identified with Dean even though he was a man. There were many young girls like that in those days, washed in by the tide of the times, androgynous girls. There is also a genderless narcissism shared by stars. In America Jackie Curtis, the real-life transsexual who features in Lou Reed's 'Walk on the Wild Side', coined a phrase to describe the ambivalence of the times: 'Gary Cooper looked in the mirror and saw Greta Garbo, Greta Garbo looked in the mirror and saw James Dean.' Then too, Dean did have his feminine side, a bird-like quality with his fine features and full lips. He also shared character traits with Bardot. Like her he was branded evil and misunderstood, though both in life and in *East of Eden*, the film she so much admired, he was sincere, passionate, and affectionate. He could, it seemed, do no right. While fifties' mothers were warning their girls of the dangers of predatory males, Dean's uncanny beauty made girls feel predatory instead, yet it did him no good. Moody and abandoned, he watched at the door of the church on his motorbike while the girl in his life, Pier Angeli, an earlier discovery from the Cannes Film Festival, married someone else.

As Brigitte was making *Cette Sacrée Gamine* in Paris, James Dean crashed his racing Porsche near Salinas, California. He was killed on the spot and out of the strangely unblemished mass of metal rose a new Valentino myth. Dean had started the long drive from Sherman Oaks near Los Angeles where he lived to the Salinas race track on Brigitte's twenty-first birthday, Wednesday, 28 September 1955. She didn't fail to notice the significance of the date when the reports came in of his death. And the toss of the dice that day while she was celebrating her birthday which made Dean on another continent 6,000 miles away decide to drive himself, not be driven or flown up-state. He was due to compete in the Salinas races on the Saturday. But by 5.45 p.m. on Friday the last day of September he was dead, his neck broken in a highway collision with the negligent driver of an old Ford sedan. 'Live fast, die young and have a good-looking corpse,' Dean used to say, a line from *Knock on any Door* by Nicholas Ray who had directed him in *Rebel without a Cause*. He was twenty-four, just two years older than Bardot and he had always predicted that he would not live beyond thirty. His second name was a premonition of an early death: it was Byron.

That sort of attitude, linked with his extraordinary beauty, had not gone unnoticed by Bardot, who later patented the idea that men over thirty were 'ready for chrysanthemums', that is, the grave. It did not go unnoticed by Vadim with his ever-ready death-wish. It did not go unnoticed by the French in general. They awarded him the Crystal Star for the year's best foreign-language film for *East of Eden*. What is more they dedicated every September issue of the picture-goers' magazine, *Cinémonde*, to him for the next four years.

The French saw many messages for themselves in his life and death. While American critics were accusing Jean Cocteau of influencing West Coast teenagers in *Rebel without a Cause* to wild, nihilistic acts like his *enfants terribles* the French had nothing to fear from Cocteau, or Dean either, if he, the personification of the Rebel, was the fruit of Cocteau's imagination. French critics had known for a century that such *Weltschmerz* was an interesting Romantic tradition liable to set in among young people after wars and social cataclysms. Certain creative spirits believed, in a sort of parody of religious ecstasy, in rebirth through the vilest con-tamination they could imagine. Baudelaire's flowers of evil grew out of the gutter. Gide, whom Bardot had read with Vadim's guidance, carried the idea even further, by ridding even the worst crime of guilt if you simply took away any idea of motive. Jean Genet argued with his whole lifestyle for the purity of the anti-social stance. In a world that had been turned upside down by recent political events such ideas didn't make any less sense than anything else.

While these ideas were contained in books they had a naturally limited audience but once they were translated into the easy language of film they spread like a blaze in a pinewood to anyone who could afford a 1s.9d. ticket. François Truffaut, a contemporary of both Dean and Bardot, wrote about *Rebel without a Cause*:

> In James Dean, today's youth discovers itself. Less for the reasons usually advanced, sadism, hysteria, pessimism, cruelty and filth, than for others infinitely more simple and commonplace: modesty of feeling, continual fantasy life, moral purity without relation to everyday morality but all the more rigorous, eternal adolescent love tests and trials, intoxication, pride, and regret at feeling oneself 'outside' society, refusal and desire to become integrated and, finally, acceptance – or refusal – of the world as it is.

Albert Camus, another author on Bardot's crash course in culture, had written about this sort of feeling in *The Outsider* in 1944, a handbook of the fifties generation. Girls of that generation knew that its message was not only for men. Traditionally women had waited at home and wept while madcap male outsiders perpetrated Byronic acts. They watched the men flit from flower to flower, but their hearts still fluttered when they came in line for their attentions. They watched them snuff themselves out but they were imperturbable. Thackeray parodied their role in his Sorrows of Werther, who died for the love of a woman.

> Charlotte, having seen his body
> Borne before her on a shutter,
> Like a well-conducted person,
> Went on cutting bread and butter.

Women had always been the pillars of society, even those who were unwilling, but with Bardot for the first time a woman became the outsider.

Apart from any social symbols she could see in common with the rest of France, for Bardot the actress Dean's death was further proof of the uncanny way life and art have a habit of aping each other in her profession. In *Rebel without a Cause* he played a game of 'chicken' on the highway and won, in life he played and lost. She couldn't help identifying with him. He was the Warner Brothers' contract player she could so easily have become after her Cannes success; but she turned their contract down.

However important he was to French audiences the profession neglected *East of Eden* at the '56 Festival and the Grand Prix was won by the black-and-white film *Marty*. The convention was quite simple and still exists to a certain extent. To be meaningful a film was shot in black and white for a small screen. Technicolor and the wide screen, the latter albeit a French invention, were reserved for multi-million-dollar Hollywood productions and musical comedy, pure brash, bravura-type entertainment. Vadim wanted to do something different. He wanted to make an intimate little film in colour and to direct it himself. He knew he was being outrageous, pushing both form and content beyond the bounds of social and financial acceptability, but it was his only survival mechanism. He had to attract attention in any way he could. Truffaut had already suspected this when he harangued him for being pornographic without reason in 'Plucking The Daisy'. Only Levy took Vadim seriously.

At this point Olga Horstig entered the bidding. One of her better-known clients apart from Brigitte was Curt Jurgens. In 1955 he was forty-three and he had developed from being a German stage actor before the war to an international leading man on the screen. He had just made one of his best films, *An Eye for an Eye*. If Jurgens could be persuaded to lend his name to Vadim's venture Olga realized the film would capture a much larger market, which might lead Columbia Pictures to pump in the money for a Technicolor movie with world-wide distribution. It was well known that Jurgens had a weakness for beautiful young girls, so he did not object when Brigitte joined him and his agent for coffee after lunch at Fouquets across the Champs-Élysées from Olga's office. 'You don't mind, do you?' Olga began, 'I've invited Brigitte Bardot to join us.' She materialized as if on cue and Jurgens liked what he saw:

> First the walk – what the French call *la démarche*. Never again have I seen such a walk. As if she was carrying a basket of fruit on her head. The long neck surging up from the collar bone like a question mark. The features, the cheek-bones, the big, over-full mouth might belong to a coloured girl – like a trick picture Gauguin might have painted in Tahiti after waking from a dream of the Bretagne. For the skin is light, the hair blonde as wheat. How does she manage to be so attentive when her whole demeanour seems to say: 'These people talking – what's it to do

with me? Let me get back to my cosy bed or the sun and the beach!' She is tall, taller than most of the men who stop and stare . . .

Jurgens lost no time in writing this down after they met. Olga lost even less in handing over Vadim's script entitled *And God Created Woman* – which she just happened to have with her – and trying to persuade Jurgens to give the young film-makers just three weeks of his time. She made it sound attractive. It would be shot in St-Tropez, an idyllic village on the Riviera, in December when it was snowing in Bavaria. Jurgens couldn't take his eyes off Brigitte. 'You are very beautiful,' he said. 'I can well imagine that God thought of you when he created woman.' Brigitte thanked him and sealed some unspoken pact with her usual kiss on the cheek.

The only trouble was there was no obvious part for Jurgens in the script. The eldest of the three brothers was twenty-five and a cad. That wasn't the German's age, never mind his style. Vadim felt that Curt could hardly play a French fisherman with his German accent, moreover he had promised the part to his good-looking friend and ex-flatmate, Christian Marquand. One morning at eight o'clock Vadim was awoken by the telephone. It was Levy, who knew that if you wanted to clinch a deal in the film business you had to be on the spot. At 10.40 the two of them caught the Munich express from the Gare de l'Est. Brigitte waited at home in Paris for the outcome of the trip. Over lunch in the restaurant car Raoul persuaded Vadim to write the German actor the sort of part he could not refuse. The two of them then took a taxi to the best hotel in town, the Vier Jahreszeiten, where they took a suite and called Jurgens. The combination of events led to Jurgens agreeing to meet Levy and Vadim forty-eight hours later, although he didn't know either of them. Levy then set about imprisoning Vadim in the suite to do a sixty-page rewrite in the time available. He brought in caviar, smoked salmon, vodka and a well-rounded young lady called Maria so Vadim would want for nothing. 'Before I could even pull the top off my biro, Maria had undressed,' recounts Vadim. She got dressed immediately when he explained he had three weeks' work to do in two days and, according to him, it was Maria, the girl who had taken to hooking because of her weakness for fast expensive cars, who made the all-important suggestion that the Juliette character should show a fundamental disdain for money, which would make her sympathetic and innocent. It quickly led to the creation of the Jurgens part of a rich industrialist who had always been able to buy even the most correct women but who just could not find the key to unlock the heart of this over-sexed nymphet. Maria typed the script out perfectly – she would have been a typist, she said, if her mother had had her way – and then left. The result impressed Jurgens sufficiently for him to agree to do the film without seeing the final draft. In his autobiography Vadim is generous in his praise of the German actor who took a rare chance on an unknown director without any fuss or conditions attached. Brigitte too can't praise him enough for suggesting after the film was finished that they share the billing. 'He said it was my film and it wouldn't be fair otherwise. It was very chic of him,' she says.

It was indeed her film with all the elements of her future life laid down in it, and there are some transparent examples of the actress's spontaneous philosophy within the script. 'There's something stronger than me,' she says, 'which always makes me do stupid things. It's as if I was going to die tomorrow.' Juliette Hardy's suicidal tendencies are never acted upon as Bardot's would be, but they are clearly there. The suggestion is that she is doomed whatever she does. One character even says 'That girl was made to *lose* men.' For all her fantastic nubility that would be Brigitte's destiny. Meanwhile she loved the sea, the sand, the sun of St-Tropez, where the cast had stayed at the strangely named hotel L'Ail au Lit (it means garlic in bed, a pun on the name of the delicious Mediterranean garlic sauce aïoli). The fashionable Byblos, future haunt of film stars and hangers-on, was not yet built. Brigitte had found her home from home and all she needed was the money to invest in it.

Her other loves, as expressed both in the film and in real life, were food and music – Brazilian music as it happens. The music has the beat of the jungle to go with those lips, which Jurgens had spotted were not quite white lips. Camus the outsider was born in Algeria. The outsider as the black man in a white society was a theme which would be taken up by Mailer in *The White Negro*. At the time black music and black fashion were the alien ingredient which scared the middle classes half to death when they saw it taken up by their teenagers in revolt. They associated it with the one thing they feared from the negro race, indiscriminate propagation as a result of which they would take over half the world.

The black beat was present in Presley's music and in Mick Jagger's, and the main physical feature shared by this pedigree of new anti-heroes, with whom Brigitte shared her identity, was the over-generous fleshy mouth, which suggested the generosity of another orifice.

Brigitte was free with her favours during the making of *And God Created Woman*. It may not have been the first time since her marriage but it was the first time she did so with real passion. After hoping for so much from the relationship with Vadim, after watching her hopes crumble, after rationalizing her situation and finally admitting it was a lost cause, the new development was a great relief to her. The cards were now on the table and, moreover, she convinced herself that she was blameless – it was all Vadim's fault.

The first time he introduced her to her unknown co-star, Jean-Louis Trintignant, she was unimpressed. 'How do you expect me to play a love-scene with him?' she screamed. 'He's too small. He's ugly and he's not my type.' The weak part he plays in the film didn't help matters. It called for him to adore her and marry her, while she seduced and betrayed him despite herself. It was the story of her marriage to Vadim and Vadim says he knew before she did what she was feeling when she finally threw herself into the arms of another man.

Jean-Louis Trintignant has since played some fine parts; at the time he was known as the French James Dean, which might have influenced Brigitte, but the resemblance was not striking. There was very little sensuality in his face as a young man. He didn't look tortured or romantic. In fact he looked rather ordinary. None the less he had something which made Brigitte fall deeply in love and that was a passionate desire for her. Whenever Brigitte was feeling insecure, which was often, she had to acknowledge to herself that Vadim just did not flatter her ego in the way she longed for. His love took the form of letting her be, of allowing her to develop as a separate talent and person. She wanted to be dominated. She wanted insane jealousy on the part of a man in her life to convince her he loved her. That was why throughout her marriage she had flirted with other people, not because she intended to go beyond flirtation but because she wanted Vadim to react. It was not in Vadim to react. All he did was provoke her to even more outrageous behaviour as he coached her to be the average man's unobtainable dream. He made her strip, dance, flaunt herself, kiss, offer men her body. It was all a fiction to him even if it became more and more like fact to her. That summer Brigitte and Vadim had done the dancing, flaunting, and kissing, pushing that as far as it could go, yet it had not made them rich and famous. There remained only the ultimate sacrifice. Cast and crew on the film could tell something was about to happen. Bardot's eye might easily have lighted on Levy, as she and Vadim prowled round as if they were on heat, the one in anticipation of a fulfilled private life, the other of a film. Levy was the third in the beloved artistic triangle.

Even Bardot, who was not of a literary or philosophical bent, knew that would not spell real infidelity. The insult had to be more blatant. It had to be Trintignant, the virile actor that Vadim secretly wanted to be. And Vadim went along with it. Never before had Vadim actually made her consummate the act of love on-screen, even act the consummation as he did now. People on the set of *And God Created Woman* could never be quite certain that it was an act. Certainly when the director shouted, 'Cut', the couple carried blithely on with their clinches as if they couldn't bear to be apart for a minute. Still Vadim refused to feel jealousy. He never did, he said, when things were happening merely for the benefit of the camera. He was like a painter, or a pilot, or a racing driver in the grip of something cerebral or spiritual but never personal. He would repeat the same experience when he directed Jane Fonda in another man's arms.

At first Brigitte was only trying to provoke Vadim, but the man who was provoked was Trintignant. He was the complete opposite of the cool director. When he met Brigitte he didn't like her. He thought her too conceited, too devoted, as he said, to the single-minded pursuit of stardom. Once involved, however, once he had tasted her flesh – as she warns in the film to Jurgens, 'be careful, you will never be able to forget me' – the young man, infinitely suggestible, like all actors, became obsessive and possessive. 'She's too much in the public eye,' he said, 'I'd like her just to be a woman. I can't forget the millions of men who have looked at her in the cinema and would like to kiss her too.' The suggestion took about five weeks to mature in both their minds and it had come to a head by the time the cast and crew moved to the Victorine Studios at Nice to complete the indoor love scenes. Trintignant was married at the time, though separated from his beautiful wife, Stephane Audran, (she went on to marry the director Claude Chabrol), but when Brigitte went back with her husband to their suite at the Negresco Hotel it drove him crazy.

Compared to Vadim, Trintignant was a provincial, genuinely shy and stumbling. He came in real life from Provence, from the old Roman town of Nîmes, and went to the National Film School in Paris to try to lose his southern accent. Vadim thought his manners inelegant and found no excuse for them, even if he was in love with his wife. 'I granted him the excuse of his youth,' he says – in actual fact he was more or less the same age as Vadim and four years older than Brigitte. Trintignant demanded that she leave her husband or he would never see her again. Poor Brigitte wavered. Better the Devil she knew, but the flesh was stronger than her premonitions. She had a refined way of hurting both men because she insisted on telling both the truth. Vadim said that he really felt for her at this period. She unpacked her belongings in their room at least once after a showdown – engineered by her – and decided to stay with Vadim. She said, in a quote worthy of Monroe's character Sugar Kane, that it was the thirteenth of the month and although she wasn't superstitious, it was unlucky. The next day she left the set with Trintignant. Vadim felt a hollow inside him when he realized that his own little company, Brigitte and himself, would disband as well as cast and crew, at the end of the film. They had become a cottage industry together, yet they had enjoyed many tender moments and the huge experience of a first commitment. When he described passion as a boat containing two lovers carried along by the wayward elements towards a beckoning shore, Vadim was being emotional as well as philosophical. In their boat of passion, as in so many others, there was a hole which they barely noticed as they set sail. There seemed to be so much promise ahead on which Brigitte in particular focussed without ever taking time to shore up the growing leak. When she found her paradise island she had spent so much time daydreaming about it that there was inevitably something missing.

It was January 1956, and for Brigitte the start of a life of hollowing promiscuity.

8. Les Grandes Manoeuvres

All that summer Brigitte had it both ways. That is not to say she was unfaithful to Trintignant – yet. But after all those years of obeying Pilou, all those nights waiting for Vadim to come home, she was the sought after star both at home in bed with her lover and at the studios where her husband was working on the post-production of *And God Created Woman*. Without her they could not finish the film. She often kept them waiting to show that there were better things to be done, turning up two hours late if she felt like it. She was beginning to understand her own image of '*une femme un peu fatale*', as she put it. She completed the post-sync with Vadim without even referring to what had happened between them. Once, when they were dubbing the music, her eyes strayed to a dark-haired youth playing the guitar. He was Ray Ventura's nephew, an unknown musician called Sacha Distel.

Meanwhile Trintignant protested he couldn't live without her, which was just what she wanted to hear. So she went home to the new flat where she had installed him on the other side of the sixteenth *arrondissement* from the rue Chardon-Lagache. Its address, 71 avenue Paul Doumer, was just a stone's throw from her mother's home at its intersection with the rue de la Pompe. At first she simply devoted herself to a life of quiet domesticity of which Vadim had cheated her. 'There had been so many fights with him. He wanted to introduce me to everyone important. We went out every night to theatres, parties, restaurants and premières. So much activity bored me. Jean-Louis had other values.' Brigitte had liberated herself from the man who had liberated her from her bourgeois prison. At last she was writing her own script. When she came in front of a French reconciliation judge that April to discuss the matter of a divorce she defied all conventions by showing no regret for matrimony and announcing that the moment they discovered they could live without each other was the moment they no longer loved each other.

She felt she could do no wrong. She was 'somebody' and other people were ready to acknowledge it. Van Dongen had painted her, Picasso had already invited her to his home up above Cannes. Now the sculptor Aslan, well known at the time for his pin-up portraits, chose her as his model for the bust of Marianne, the symbol of virtue in the French Republic which stands in every town hall in the country. And on 2 June at the Victorine Studios she met Churchill, who was staying on Aristotle Onassis's yacht the *Christina* in the bay and making his own film deal about the history of the Second World War with the producer Jack le Vien. Churchill declared himself enchanted. Less than a week after that meeting everyone finally returned to Paris for the last time. The film and her marriage were over. Brigitte was learning to stand on her own two feet.

Alone in London making *Doctor at Sea* her loneliness had even overcome her shyness and she had learned to go out unescorted. Now Brigitte was invited back to London to the Royal Command Performance and once again she came alone. She stepped off the boat train at Victoria Station wearing a man's collar and tie as if to assert her new independence. Even without the publicity-conscious Vadim it was as if she had orchestrated the whole thing. Her luggage was lost and she had nothing to wear, thereby drawing immediate attention to herself. She went to the Savoy and lay low saying she had been too indiscreet in the past and that now she was going to meet the Queen it was a good time to keep quiet. Someone was sent for from Paris to bring her gown for the evening, a spangled Balmain with rather little above the waist.

She was, however, not the star of the evening. Not even the thirty-year-old monarch was the star. The honours went to Queen Elizabeth's exact contemporary, Marilyn Monroe. Brigitte didn't mind that at all. She was overcome with curiosity because after all without Marilyn she would not have become Brigitte. The line-up before the film was a good deal more thrilling to her than the film itself, which that year was *The Battle of the River Plate*. It looked horribly worthy and dull compared to the things she herself was doing on the screen. Willi Frischauer says he even caught a yawn, which might have been due to a late night but was probably a sigh of boredom.

During the film Bardot's thoughts strayed to Monroe, who had come to England with her husband, playwright Arthur Miller, to make *The Prince and the Showgirl* with Laurence Olivier. Bardot thought Monroe everything a woman should be. 'She was charming, incredibly beautiful, vulnerable, fragile.' On that day in 1956 Marilyn was smiling for the Queen and Princess Margaret, and Brigitte, positioned next to Ian Carmichael and Dana Andrews in the line-up, failed to notice just how vulnerable she was, doped to the eyeballs to get through the evening – though when it was all over and she was in her grave she thought she had prepared a special lesson in the dangers of the cinema just for her. While Brigitte was fixing her hair in a little ante-room which had been set aside for her she remembers Marilyn bursting in like a breath of fresh air. 'She looked as if she had just got out of bed. We had been told not to wear dresses that were too tight, well hers was. Someone wrote afterwards that she was so petrified she couldn't curtsey to the Queen. But she curtsied all right and there was no fear in her eyes.' Brigitte did notice a strange glint but she put it down to a magnificent arrogance and freedom which she envied. As Monroe became less and less able to deal with the star system and Hollywood became less and less enamoured with her, Bardot became obsessed with the easy way in which a superstar could fall from grace. You certainly paid your dues for the brief moment of glory and the ritzy lifestyle which went with it. Wherever she looked the vultures seemed poised and if you cheated them one way they would get you another. Carole Lombard had died in an air crash at thirty-four. Jean Harlow was only twenty-six when she died. Monroe was thirty-six when she died – the same age as Greta Garbo was on her retirement from the screen. Though it took Bardot four more years than those two in their various ways to retire, in the future it seemed to her like a magical age for decision-making.

For the moment there seemed to be no dangers at all. Brigitte hammed up her performance as the sexy little French girl who was now free to talk about every aspect of men and women's physiology since she had openly left her husband. The British Press, who knew Marilyn slept in Chanel No. 5, asked Brigitte what perfume she was wearing. Her reply in French confirmed Dr Richard Gordon's analysis: musk. Brigitte was proud to the point of provocation of herself as a sexual object, and demonstrated this in public not by Marilyn's wit and sadness, but by defiance, bravura and outrage when she felt cornered. In France she was already well known for this sort of thing and it was one of the aspects of her character which least appealed. It didn't always manifest itself in vulgarity, more a tactlessness which was so complete that people thought she must be trying to insult them.

On one occasion a Belgian showbusiness writer took her back to Brussels as a sort of trophy and put her on display in the evening at one of the capital's best restaurants with several other starlets. It was Brigitte who made the impact. She seemed to seek out the famous restaurateur personally and congratulated him on his unusual table centre which consisted of an extraordinary contraption for pouring water. When the party left after the meal the restaurateur who was overcome with admiration for her vitality insisted she take the water jug home as a souvenir. Brigitte's reaction left him smarting and in no doubt that he had been set up. 'I wouldn't dream of taking that ugly thing with me,' she exclaimed. Was she drunk, deliberately insulting, or was this a demonstration of her celebrated volte-face, her innocent desire not to be pinned down? Whatever the reason, there is no doubt that the single, uniting factor in all Brigitte's public performances was her desire to be noticed at all costs. A lack of false modesty would have been attractive, but a lack of respect, for herself as well as others, the one thing René Simon warned her about as a would-be performer, was extremely confusing.

Back in London the English Press pursued this aspect of her character. Logan Gourlay, writing in the *Daily Express*, asked her whether she was embarrassed by the stares and reactions of men. 'No, no, of course not. I am flattered. It would be sad if the men paid no attention to me,' she replied. He mentioned that a woman colleague at her press conference had observed that she had an air of innocent depravity, adding that she probably didn't know what the word depravity meant. 'It has something to do with sin, doesn't it?' said Bardot. 'I know what sin is.' She was proud to tell Gourley she had left her husband on the spur of the moment because she had fallen in love with another man. It wasn't the business of a popular newspaper to point out that the decision had in fact taken four years one way or another, or to disbelieve her when she said she would never marry again because she wanted to be free and not confined to one man. In 1956 the whiff of liberation excited the whole world, which had been working itself up to make this sort of public attitude acceptable. Bardot continually gave the quotes that were wanted to the people who were writing modern history in the pages of newspapers and magazines. 'It's better to be unfaithful than faithful without wanting to be.' 'I'm a girl from a good family who was very well brought up. One day I turned my back on it all and simply became a bohemian.' 'I like many types of men,' 'I do not care very much how they look. Except for the mouth. I like a man who has a big mouth. It shows he is generous. He doesn't have to be rich.'

At the time Trintignant had all the desired qualifications. He had the right physical attributes and he was a struggling actor about to be called up into the army. All through that summer, while she was working on *The Bride is much too Beautiful* at the studios in Paris, he was generous with his attentions and Brigitte basked in them. Again the film had a parallel to her own life, although it had been taken from a novel. It was the story of a nice girl who becomes a cover-girl and resorts to all sorts of jealous wiles to get her man, who happened in this case to be Louis Jourdan. The French thought the film sugary but they liked the idea of the chemistry between the leading players and, longing for history to repeat itself, they dwelled long on the exact role of this new film lover in Bardot's life. In essence they were right about Bardot's mood. When Trintignant was not there she quite simply resented him. She wanted to be free but as it turned out, whenever she had to meet a challenge on her own although she seemed fine at the time, afterwards she would go completely to pieces. It took less than two weeks after meeting the Queen, 'a terrible ordeal, dreadful protocol', for her to take to her bed in Louveciennes on doctor's orders. Her skin had erupted once more and she was covered in spots. Besides it was November and she felt like hibernating.

It was in December that this tiny prick in the bubble started to enlarge. It was Brigitte's first inkling that fame, as well as anonymity, can have its own see-saw motion. The vehicle for which she and Vadim had chanced so much, *And God Created Woman*, looked like being a dismal failure. 'Life spoils the script', is one of the favourite sayings of Joe Mankiewicz, the brilliant director of women, who had written such an endearing little part for Marilyn in *All About Eve*, and this was certainly not how Bardot had planned the outcome of her script. Shortly after her film opened on the Champs-Élysées an actor friend saw her looking mortally disappointed with 'a crumbling voice, her little dismal wound of a face.' The film had to be a success. Bardot had only been paid £6,000 for it and while that was a more generous sum in 1956 than now, it did not support a spoiled lifestyle for long. She had, moreover, taken all her irons out of the fire, thrown in her lot with another employee, an actor from the great bottomless pool of actors, all of which required financing and a script. She was not even as well off as she had been with Vadim, who had promised he would always look after her somehow. She could not possibly go creeping back to Vadim even if he would have her. She couldn't go back to her parents either. They were only waiting to tell her that this was what they had always tried to warn her about.

As for Levy, whose mouth was always where the money was, he had few good words to say about her. Like any producer who hits hard times he found it easiest to blame his human tools. He flatly refused to have her on his next project with Vadim, *Sait-on-Jamais* (*You Never Know*), which was going ahead in Venice. 'He was kind of upset when *And God Created Woman* was not an immediate success,' says Vadim. 'Brigitte was still not a star. She was a starlet, known because she was in the newspapers often. She was going to be a star – but she was not yet. The big star at this time was Françoise Arnoul. Brigitte would not bring him the money so he took Françoise Arnoul.' For Vadim what was about to happen was sadly ironic for the basis of *You Never Know* was the novel he had written as a young man, *The Wise Sophie*, with whom Brigitte had become so firmly identified in his mind.

For a while in 1956, which was to have been the year of her grand acclaim, it seemed to Brigitte that she was a victim of the sort of conspiracy women easily suspect when they have been exploited like footsoldiers to perish if necessary in the affray while the generals draw up new plans for success with new footsoldiers and scarcely a regret. The naughty boys were off to Venice together, the naughty girl was in Paris and she would soon be all alone in Paris because Trintignant was about to be called up into the French army.

Levy had banked everything on the idea that this scandalous film would attract huge attention and be sold for a fortune in the United States. He was originally very encouraged when the French censor went along with the plan, labelled Vadim 'Satan' and cut chunks out of it for home consumption. Producer and director gave it a gala première on 4 December at the Normandie cinema on the Champs-Élysées. But the reviews were lukewarm and such scandal as there was actually went against the picture at first. Vadim, who prides himself on being ahead of public opinion, says he has only ever been recognized after the critics have caught up with him. But it wasn't just the critics. Gary Cooper, who was one of the first to see the film at a private showing in Paris, reacted to the wedding night scene by saying, 'I guess I ought to put a sack over my face.' As so often happens the doyens of the profession, old men who knew other formulas for success, lagged far behind the prevailing mood of the public which is hungry for novelty. American distributors, terrified of the Puritan backbone of the country which had forced Mae West out of work and Marlene Dietrich to change her image, were just not confident society had grown up enough for this sort of thing. Levy was so discouraged that he was offering the North American rights for a mere $200,000 cash – £75,000 at the time. Less than 1 million Americans in a country of 200 million would have to see it to make the deal worth while for them. On the Champs-Élysées that December, a big selling season in the calendar of motion pictures, receipts went just over £50,000. With his usual flair Levy described this as 'a pimple on the top of my overdraft'. Suddenly, as Bardot carefully noted, the tide began to turn. It happened in 1957.

In London Matt White of the *Daily Sketch* had the same reaction as Gary Cooper but, contrary to expectations, it was to work in the film's favour. 'She had me blushing in the nervous darkness of the cinema,' he wrote. Donald Zec, the famous *Daily Mirror* correspondent, said, 'It is the most suggestive, near the knuckle picture I have ever seen anywhere.' At this time Britain was actually ahead in breaking the taboos surrounding sex in the cinema. The receipts for *Doctor at Sea* had proved that a foreigner could get away with things. So in 1955 we repeated the trick of starring a foreign actress by casting the American Julie Harris – James Dean's partner in *East of Eden* – in *I am a Camera*. Later remade for the screen in even more startling form as *Cabaret*, Christopher Isherwood's story of the amoral girl in pre-war Berlin openly, even frivolously broached the subject of abortion and had an altogether smart-ass attitude to sex, illustrated by the line: 'What shall we do first, have a drink or go to bed?' It was chosen for the Royal Film Performance.

As soon as Levy realized what he had on his hands his attitude changed. The receipts from Tokyo and Hong Kong, from the

Middle East and from northern Europe showed that these audiences had none of the reservations of the French. Fans had to be restrained by the police and they mutilated themselves to prove their undying love. In Britain a wife was granted a divorce – when her husband refused to sleep with her because he preferred watching Bardot films. Her picture was even pinned up in Moscow, selling for a fortune on the black market, and in London cinema managers had to lock up their posters and chain their cardboard cut-outs to the foyers. Levy decided to spend some of the incoming receipts on a legendary reception at the Venice Film Festival, which would create even more business. He hired three planes to draw BB's initials in the skies and threw a lavish seven-course banquet for 250 guests in a medieval palazzo on the Grand Canal. These were the bonuses of showbusiness that he liked best when the performance climbed down from the screen and he was the mastermind all the way along, vying with himself to present the public and the profession with an occasion which would become part of history. He was to host another such occasion the following year at the same festival, arriving this time in his own plane marked BB. The public responded beautifully, cheering Brigitte as she was propelled by gondoliers up and down the waterways, but it was noted by the Italian Parliament that it had cost the country 12 million lire to entertain the French star. Italian stars like Gina Lollobrigida simply stayed away.

But the biggest windfall for the three of them naturally came from the United States where Levy had had the last-minute good sense not to lose all control of the rights. Remembering the tactics that had financed the picture in the first place, he made it his business to get what he wanted. He simply took the reels of the film in a suitcase, scraped together his last old francs and went to New York.

When the picture opened in Times Square in October 1957 the cinema was dominated by a huge, semi-naked cut-out of its star. The film was a sensation. A year after its opening it had taken not $200,000 but $2 million. The Americans, who were accustomed to the idea that they had invented the sex-symbol, immediately started drumming up a feud between their latest incarnation, Marilyn Monroe, and the usurper Brigitte. 'War to the last wiggle!' screamed the headlines. Marilyn, who was making *Some Like It Hot* at the time, had her own problems, needing forty-seven takes to say 'It's me, Sugar,' correctly. Red-eyed and half doped from sleeping pills, she had everything to fear from a rival.

It was the Americans who coined the phrase, 'Bardolatry', and wrote reams trying to analyse this new affront to society. 'Obviously a petulant young face and a beautiful bottom cannot entirely explain such success,' wrote Toni Howard in an article reprinted from America in the old *Evening News*.

> Although Bardolatry is not a revolutionary doctrine, it is a dialectically sound combination of two very old and sure-fire appeals, those of the ingenue and the vamp. Certainly the *enfante terrible* is nothing new in French cinema. From Danielle Darrieux to Daniele Delorme, the *enfante terrible* has gambolled and pouted and mugged her way through countless films, wearing her adolescent innocence like a pure-food-and-drug label.
>
> Nor is there anything new about the *femme fatale*, that artificial erotic image whose voluptuous movements and artfully offhand nudity have been a trade-mark of French movies for decades.
>
> It is in combining the two, mixing innocence and sensuality with an equally liberal hand that the French professional mythmakers have come up with the film phenomenon that is Brigitte Bardot.

Vadim observed that it was the very first time the American cinema-going public had had the opportunity of seeing the female nude on screen as a work of art. To a puritanical nation it was an extraordinary message that love so portrayed was no longer a sin. It didn't sink in all at once, but it did mean that art houses on the two coasts especially could open up and show French films to audiences who were prepared to look before they judged. Eight million Americans went to see *And God Created Woman*, and though to Vadim's chagrin very few saw the unadulterated version, mutilated as it was by women's leagues and local censors, today they still recognize his name and his association with it.

They could scarcely forget the scandal which the Church itself, particularly the Roman Catholic one, who had already been victorious in the matter of Mae West and Dietrich, managed to create while seeking exactly the opposite. In Lake Placid, New York, that winter Monsignor James T. Lyng obviously had not yet realized that a media generation had arrived where there is no such thing as bad publicity. As soon as James McLaughlin, the manager of the Palace theatre, put up the posters for his forthcoming attraction, *And God Created Woman*, the Monsignor picked up his skirts and rushed across the street to ask him to take them down. He offered to give him £250 of his own money, more than enough for his plane fare to New York, to pick up an alternative film. Naturally enough all this made McLaughlin even more greedy. He was doing nothing wrong as the New York state censors had passed the picture for mature viewing.

Monsignor Lyng reacted by asking his parishioners to boycott the theatre. He asked Catholic shopkeepers to refuse to display any of its bills. It being 1957 they did, and they were joined by the Protestants. McLaughlin went on showing the film and though his trade was adversely affected by the campaign it was his second most successful film at the box office that year.

In downtown Philadelphia the film was shown at two cinemas, the Studio and the World. Philadelphia, city of brotherly love and cradle of the American constitution, had abolished film censorship but this did not deter the district attorney who invoked a law against obscene publications and spectacles. Six detectives were dispatched to the cinema. They confiscated the film and arrested the managers, who in their turn retaliated in a way which proved totally to their advantage. Released on $500 bail they got a court order to return the films and naturally they did not spare the publicity machine. They were aided along the way by the unscrupulous nature of American politics. For Philadelphia's Democratic mayor took the opportunity of accusing the district attorney of acting as he had in order to get the votes of prim Republican ladies. While they fought it out between them the public went to the cinemas.

In Cleveland, Ohio, cinema managers were arrested. In Providence, Massachusetts, three local judges went to the cinema in full ceremonial rig to pronounce their verdict on the film. In Memphis, Tennessee, in the Bible Belt where there was still censorship the picture was quite simply banned. But the cinema manager quietly took the film over the Mississippi River to West Memphis which was under Arkansas laws. Instead of hanging back, as judges and church leaders were trying to insist, the public now decided it had come of age and would go and see the films it

wanted to see. Memphis was after all the home town of Elvis
Presley, who was just ahead of Bardot in turning them on to his
energetic brand of sex with the film *Love Me Tender* the year
before.

There was a difference of course. Presley was a man, Bardot
was a woman. Something quite extraordinary was happening if
the taboos attached to civilized sexual behaviour were being
thrown out of the window by women. You couldn't even talk
about a reversion to primitivism. Primitive societies had codes of
behaviour which placed motherhood on a higher plane of duty
than abstinence, it is true, but most of those even insisted on a
certain ritual modesty preceding actually coupling. You couldn't
even really draw parallels between the spontaneous behaviour
Bardot professed to encourage and that of animals. Their rutting
was triggered by overpowering and irresistible smells. The naked
desire of the females to receive a male was quite embarrassing
anywhere else but the farmyard, but then again it was motherhood they craved, not the constant stimulus of the male organ.
They were happy in the company of the harem. None of this was
Bardot's scene. Her impetus to couple with any number of the
opposite sex with no responsibility was that of a man. Insiders in
Hollywood knew that this behaviour was not very different from
that of many other women, especially actresses whose electric
energy stemmed from an over-developed sex-drive. Marilyn
herself was supposed not to have gone for a single week without
the comfort of male flesh and to have compared their performances as lovers when she was among friends and to have had as
many as twelve abortions since she was given to spontaneity. The
difference was that it made her unhappy whereas Bardot said it
made her happy. She also boasted about it openly. The Americans
compelled the French with multiple dollars to explain to them
what it was all about, commissioning articles from the most
unlikely sources to defend the new child-woman, which they
aptly christened jail-bait, but Vadim intellectualized as being the
personification of the psychosis of the post-war generation. André
Maurois, writing in *Playboy*, asked what a man was to make of
Brigitte?

A vamp? No, men just returned from five years of war were no
longer disposed to be taken in by the obvious wiles of a
social-climber, a gold-digger or a female spy. A young virgin, a

lascivious child, a nymphet, a Lolita? But that wasn't Brigitte at all, she was a true woman. Very young, yes. Perverse, wicked, not exactly. Rather audacious, immodest, but with the innocence of a young animal. There lay the secret of reaching the most blasé spectator: so much sheer naturalness simply could not be ignored.

The woman in the street could sense that all this spelled trouble for her because she didn't have the same weapons as a Marilyn or a Bardot. She wanted to stick to the old rules. Simone de Beauvoir tried to persuade them that the new rules were better. Bardot was a way of women getting their own back on men, she explained.

Her eroticism is not magical, but aggressive. In the game of love, she is as much a hunter as she is a prey. The male is an object to her, just as she is to him. And that is precisely what wounds masculine pride. In the Latin countries, where men cling to the myth of 'the woman as object' BB's naturalness seems to them more perverse than any possible sophistication. To spurn jewels and cosmetics and high heels and girdles is to refuse to transform oneself into a remote idol . . . the male feels uncomfortable if, instead of a doll of flesh and blood, he holds in his arms a conscious being who is sizing him up. A free woman is the very contrary of a loose woman.

De Beauvoir's elegant little booklet explaining the innocence of Bardot drove the Americans with their thirst for culture and their strange Puritanism even more insane for the French star. De Beauvoir had good reason to hope that women could be as free as men at the time, for she had fallen insanely in love with the Chicago novelist Nelson Algren as she relates in *The Mandarins*.

Brigitte's champions ranged themselves and they included her fair share of formidable women. De Beauvoir, Horstig, Gouze-Renal, Marguerite Yourcenar, the sole French woman academician, now American-based, had one thing in common apart from brain cells – they were not seductive and sylph-like. If they resented that, they also inherited with their physiques a certain freedom which Brigitte never had. Unfair as it may be, a formidable woman can have sex freely without ruining her reputation, but a beautiful woman arouses possessiveness and therefore requires the protection of men.

9. Girl without a Veil

Looked at now *And God Created Woman* is barely a *divertissement*. The plot seems simple and dull and you can feel nothing for the characters apart from Jurgens perhaps, who as the true profession-al in the bunch, does have a tender touch. Even the beauties of St-Tropez are scarcely shown to their best advantage. A wire fence, a boatyard and a suburban backyard would not persuade most people to go there for their holidays. It is a cheap movie with no titillation even for the voyeur since Bardot's passion on screen is not for her real-life lover. Moreover such love-making as appears between Bardot and Jean-Louis Trintignant on the one hand and Bardot and Christian Marquand on the other is badly truncated in the final cut. This is not entirely Vadim's fault. The censor cut out about twenty minutes and this is what Brigitte has to say about it. 'I didn't time it but there were certainly a lot of cuts, which was a pity. For example there was a long scene on the beach where Christian Marquand slipped my dress off as he caressed me. It was not offensive because it was beautiful.' Today's audience would certainly want Marquand to explore thoroughly on their behalf the extraordinary body of the girl that had driven him and them crazy throughout the entire story.

From our standpoint the film is frustrating for another reason. For the appeal of that body is strangely intellectual. Juliette is so perverse, so sullen, so full of teenage self-opinion, that only a mother could love her, or a frustrated lover, or a society in itself so frustrated that it is about to break all the rules. One must give Vadim the benefit of the doubt and assume the film was not merely intended to titillate. Vadim wanted to put a natural energy on-screen, to replace stuffy old middle-class values, which sup-pressed a young girl's joy in life, with natural animal excitement. The whole point of sex in the cinema or any other art is its excitement value. Good sex doesn't just produce a cockstand which withers on gratification, it vibrates the whole being and

136

lingers before and after consummation. To be explicit is not always the secret of excitement, as Jean Genet had shown a couple of years earlier in an erotic film which triumphed in its understated sex. Bardot herself didn't know this. She was not a cinema-goer and was fond of saying that though she admired Garbo she had never seen a single one of her movies and she had only ever seen Dietrich in stills. Vadim on the other hand knew exactly what was going on in the fringe and the mainstream of his profession. He paid homage to Alfred Hitchcock by appearing briefly in one scene in *And God Created Woman* as a passenger on a bus, just as he had appeared briefly the year before in 'Plucking the Daisy'.

What Vadim had put on the screen was a whole philosophy. When he had said to Madame Bardot ten years previously that it would be fun to take a girl like Brigitte and make her go off the rails he was not drawing on his imagination alone but that of the Marquis de Sade. Now he declared his sources by making Brigitte Juliette, the personification of vice rewarded, sister of the Marquis's Justine, innocence reviled. Vadim had spotted something that the world had known for a while, though he was the first to show it to a mass audience. He had recognized the voyeuristic nature of the cinema, which for obvious reasons has always been shown in the dark. The theatre, in contrast, had its roots in daytime performances. An audience in the light is enjoying a social occasion. Whereas an audience in the dark is having a private experience and its thoughts don't have to stray very far to turn to masturbation or heavy petting. None the less passion has to be passionate to excite rather than deprave. It also has to exist in contrast to a less passionate experience if it is to be meaningful. In later years Bardot, who liked to be stimulated as much as anyone, was to discover a strong streak of bourgeois modesty, or as the French say *pudeur* with its coy overtones, to protect her from the apathy induced by sexual overdoses. Vadim's film has a sort of innocence which future film-makers lacked though it was to point them on towards the next commercial direction. Before *And God Created Woman* only 350 British cinemas screened foreign-language movies, and most of them were X-rated. Afterwards the figure jumped to 4,000, which in terms of today's declining outlets for all sorts of films seems an incredible luxury. The success of Bardot, of Vadim, of *And God Created Woman*, and of St-Tropez were out of all proportion to the reality of any one of them. It was all a question of timing.

It is a popular idea that before Bardot bought La Madrague (the local word for a Provençal fishing net and the name of several restaurants in the region) in June 1958 St-Tropez was a sleepy fishing village. Certainly her reputation is in part responsible for what it is today, a port with 6,000 inhabitants and an annual influx of 25,000 voyeurs. But even before the war – Brigitte was just five at the time – the novelist Colette was complaining that she had to sell her house, La Treille Muscate, which is in exactly the same part of the peninsula. Every summer even in those days campers would try to pitch their tents in the garden and autograph hunters would arrive on the doorstep. The Riviera was not yet the province of package tourists but the writing was on the wall.

The idle life in the South of France, which Brigitte Bardot enjoys these days more than anything else, was made famous by the super-rich and pioneered by royalty. They lured the artistes there to make their lives more interesting. In fact Queen Victoria used to winter there at a hotel at Cimiez up above Nice. Queen Victoria, who didn't have nude bathing on her mind, did not mind staying miles from the sea. All that changed in the twenties. In the ten years before Bardot was born European and American talent poured into the area. Picasso, Braque, Derain, Bakst mixed with Léger, Hemingway, and Fitzgerald. The visual artists all worked for the Diaghilev ballet and were followed with semi-professional interest by Madame Bardot, who put her daughter into ballet class. 'The Diaghilev ballet was the focal point of the whole modern movement in the arts,' said Gerald Murphy, the friendly patron who appears as Dick Diver in Fitzgerald's 1934 novel *Tender is the Night*. Ballet was a frivolity in the nineteenth century and ballet dancers were the first chorus girls, the play-things of married men. In the hands of the legendary geniuses of the French theatre and music world, sponsored on the Riviera by the last aristocrats of Europe, it built a bridge between popular and serious thought, a combination which is the trademark of the egalitarian twentieth century. Brigitte's first theatrical love started a movement on the brink of the media age with long-lasting repercussions which, among other things, could put a *bonne bourgeoise* into the erotic spotlight and let her feel proud of it as well as out of her depth sometimes. While Brigitte was still taking her holidays on the Atlantic coast, the celebrities filled up the lower slopes of the Alpes-Maritimes and then they pushed along the coast in their quest for privacy, for these are the people with whom the public forges its most exacting contract.

Colette sold her little four-roomed house, with its terrace covered with wisteria, its pine wood and fig trees and its bottomless well, fifteen years before Bardot moved in to the area. She left behind her tortoise-shell cats to go wild in the undergrowth and Brigitte started to feed their descendants.

For a lover of nature as she had been since childhood, it was an inspired haven with its overwhelming scents, the constant, comforting drone of the insects, the dense colours, the dark shade in the savage thickets and the highlights on the sparkling sea. Brigitte, bruised by love-affairs or simply the irritant imperfections of people in general, has often spoken of its healing qualities. Her friend, the novelist Françoise Parturier, says that first and foremost celebrities come to St-Tropez for its sheer physical beauty.

In fact it was M. and Mme Bardot who invested in the place before Brigitte. They had bought an apartment in the area when it was quite undeveloped because they were not rich enough to buy one in Cannes. It was one of the reasons why Levy and Vadim, who first visited St-Tropez in 1955, had been drawn there. In those days it was a very innocent place compared to what it is now. Under the influence of the sun and of history every inhibition has now been shed in the belief that just round the corner lives the actress who made such behaviour permissible and gained the full approval of her times. According to Mme Parturier the Roman centurion who gave the place his name was washed up on the beach with his head severed from his body, and that is as good a symbol as any for what the place has since become. If there is any intellectual activity it is not very visible. The physical activity is taking place right on the beach if need be, in full view of the children of package tourists. Bardot herself hates this, not because of the public nature of the physical activity itself but because the bodies are not necessarily beautiful. At twenty, she says, she revelled in taking her clothes off, at fifty she would be well advised to keep them on and the 'fondant-pink tourists' even more so. They don't heed the warning. Whatever shape or size they are they all want to behave like BB at her nubile best.

Even today when Bardot is fifty most people who get off the plane at Nice secretly harbour the dream that they will bump into her and that in a flash it will be made plain to them what sex-appeal is all about. Whatever it is, its curiosity value is not confined to the working man and woman. Some people take their luxury yachts perilously close to her private beach in the happy anticipation that she will be walking her dogs for their enjoyment without a stitch on. Others have even been known to hire helicopters to inspect the property and its owner from above. Bardot-watching is an obsessive sport with just a hint of danger attached but success is unlikely especially in the summer months. Bardot moves north.

Colette's experience was a foretaste of what was to become Brigitte's insoluble problem. Instead of being seductive, the flesh has become insulting, the mood violent. It spreads right through every class. French hoodlums who want to have a good time head down to the south of France on their motorbikes to live it up. People dare not leave their holiday homes empty for fear of finding not only the television stolen, an expensive item in France, but the mass-produced garden furniture as well. Bardot was once having dinner at a local restaurant and came out to find her jeep stolen. She hitched home. That was not difficult. It was difficult, however, to find the vehicle since she had forgotten the number.

Over the years La Madrague itself has been burgled but the hauls have only had erotic value – a pair of black panties, two pairs of stockings, a pair of jeans, and three photographs of herself in bikinis. Whether from wisdom or as a symptom of her legendary frugality, she has not filled the house with any stunning valuables.

She has also been very protective of it, agitating against new housing estates which would undermine her peace of mind and that of her neighbours. On the camp sites there is drug abuse and even murder. One very well-known member of the community has had the bathrooms and changing rooms throughout his house fitted with one-way glass so he can watch the girls at their ablutions. He likes nothing better than to get them so ripped on drugs and the pink local wine that he can spread their legs and hold them down while a photographer rapes them with his camera. He doesn't understand why a woman with the ego of Bardot doesn't want to join in these activities since other girls are lining up for the privilege. The same sort of thing used to happen at the court of Tiberius in Capri. If they don't throw bodies into the sea around St-Tropez one feels it is only because of the absence of high rocks. Writers, artists, and actresses have always enjoyed a certain liberty in their behaviour and morals but the locals are now worried about what happens when immorality undermines the behaviour of the man in the street. He, the person Bardot turned on in her heyday, the ordinary person she needed to make her extraordinary, is the blot on the landscape who tries her patience yet is wedded to her existence. For actors, by the very nature of their chosen profession, have to be visible flesh and blood to their audience. Even when they are retired or resting, the high profile and the desire to be centre stage is the mainspring and motivation of their life, unlike other people who seek anonymity. Writers and directors hide away in the hinterland of St-Tropez, vulnerable only as the land shrinks, but the place Brigitte chose as her haven is also vulnerable from the sea.

In 1958 La Madrague was just a boathouse on an outlying piece of land in the baie des Canoubiers. The St-Tropez regulars did include Françoise Sagan, who had gone there to find the simple life, but there were no other celebrities lounging in the red chairs at Sénéquier and the long white beaches were empty. At l'Escale you could take your customary evening drink in peace and at Chez Palmyre you could dance practically unobserved to the barrel-organ and the accordion – practically. The French newspapers and magazines had continual copy about the antics in the place which included pitched soda-siphon battles which they somehow made sound more sinful than childish. St-Tropez had invented the bikini and it never looked back. If it didn't exactly invent ethnic clothes it certainly took the suggestion of peasant appeal from Brigitte's film and set out to become a fashion mecca due to the industry of local needlewomen. Sam White, the *Evening Standard*'s correspondent in France, said aptly that St-Tropez set its stamp on the fifties as a phenomenon of the times as surely as the Charleston did on the twenties. This was the place the rich came to slum just as they had on the Left Bank in Paris. Once there they simply defied the law of France and took their clothes off. The voyeurs were bound to follow.

It was a glorious dream that Bardot would be able to get away from it all in the sun and perhaps not that important if she didn't. She was twenty-four. La Madrague was her present to herself from the proceeds of her most famous film to date. Her other present to herself, Jean-Louis Trintignant, was to prove less durable. When he went away for military service it seemed like a personal betrayal. Her passion for him could not survive the empty nights in which he was too far away to tell her he loved her. Brigitte had no immediate replacement in mind. She put up reed fences round her property and extended it to accommodate at least five couples, who would usually include in the future her ex-husband and the current companion of his choice. Even that first summer Vadim was not far away in a rented Provençal house in the village. Nor was he far away when he decided to marry again, the ceremony being performed by le Comte de Lausse, commander of the Free French Forces and mayor of the St-Tropez region.

For some time now, ever since the success of *And God Created Woman*, Brigitte had been drawn again into Vadim's circle. Raoul Levy had signed four non-exclusive contracts with her escalating from £12,000 to £15,000 to £30,000 and finally £40,000 per vehicle. Brigitte was in a highly confident mood, having just made *Une Parisienne* with the legendary French heart-throb Charles Boyer who was quite beguiled by her and repeated once again the views of people inside rather than outside the profession. 'In my opinion she will become a very good actress,' he said. 'She is lively and impulsive and she learns her parts quickly. She doesn't run around nude. She undresses very nicely when the script calls for it. She is a very likeable young woman who makes it easy on her co-stars. Her secret is always to behave like a girl of eighteen, but to be natural about it, not contrived.'

What is more this time she had attracted very encouraging notices. Michel Capdenac in *Les Lettres Françaises* noted her range of performance which lifted her above the popular notion of her as woman as object. He was quite carried away. 'She is surrounded by a halo of breath-taking eroticism,' he wrote. 'Neither truly mischievous, innocent or perverse she is always in control of herself, wiggling, billing and cooing by the way she looks at you and flaunts her cataract of hair. She is enjoying growing into her mythical personality.' Even *Le Figaro*, delight of delights, had mentioned her and the idol Marilyn in the same breath. 'A little m̶a̶s̶ter-piece,' they called her, 'A ravishing doll with all the ̶a̶t̶t̶r̶i̶butes of a grown-up'. They were saying that one day she might be the French equivalent of Marilyn, the essential living doll: 'We are not quite there, but I do think she is sounding better and better.'

The Bardot myth included the supposition that there wasn't an artificial bone in her body. Everything about her was supposed to be natural. She was also said to hate acting. Things came to such a head that the April after she bought her villa she simply refused to go to the big party at that year's Cannes Film Festival, extending her own invitation to anyone who wanted to shed the usual trappings of glamour and dance in the near nude *chez* Brigitte. The Cannes front was deserted.

Mindful of Raoul's mistrust of her only months before and bargaining on the strength of this street popularity and of their film's latest success at the American box office, she now negotiated herself 5 per cent of the profits of the next film they suggested, *Les Bijoutiers du Clair de Lune* (*Heaven Fell That Night*), if it was ever made – and 25 per cent of the two films that came after that. 'Percentages are why I am rich,' she boasted to a sceptical film business, which knows just how difficult it is to get any money to filter through after distribution.

Les Bijoutiers du Clair de Lune was already second best. When Raoul Levy saw the success of *And God Created Woman* in America he conceived one of his grandiose plans. He wanted to unite Bardot and Sinatra. He got as far as the title, *Paris by Night*. He claimed it would be the greatest chemical fusion since nitroglycerine. As described by Bardot herself, it was not going to be sexy like her other films. She would sleep in the bath and he would kill himself in her car. To get to this state of affairs Sinatra would play a down-and-out impresario, drinking himself to death in Paris. Bardot would rescue him from himself and take him home with her. There would be music by Cole Porter.

It sounds like the best thing Sinatra ever turned down from his point of view. In 1957 he was riding high and he had absolutely no intention of ever again being in his pre-*From Here to Eternity* position when he was neither the most popular singer in the world any more nor the most popular actor. The films which had taken him right to the top of the charts again since his Academy Award in 1953 sound like a list of the best of Hollywood – *The Tender Trap*, *The Man with the Golden Arm*, *Around the World in Eighty Days*, *Guys and Dolls*, *High Society*, and *Pal Joey*. He reeked power coupled with a sweet physical vulnerability, which was heady for the French.

Once he had an idea Levy did not waste time. At midday he told Vadim about it. By six that evening they had an outline for a screenplay. The next morning they took a plane to Miami where they had just arranged to meet Sinatra who was playing the superstar twenty-four hours a day at the garish Fontainebleau Hotel. Vadim describes the meeting: 'Frank Sinatra got up at four o'clock in the afternoon. He met us in his suite for the first

143

whisky, dressed in bright orange lamé overalls and flanked by two curvaceous redheads.' Vadim was to find there was really no seducing Sinatra. He was suspicious of flattery and intolerant of contradiction. Sentimentality veils an iron will and judgement. He took Levy and Vadim to a Chianti and spaghetti dinner in a little local restaurant. As it turned out he was in business with the owner. Then they listened to Ella Fitzgerald in the Fontainebleau nightclub. Raoul, who picked up the wife of an Italian boxer, was forced to take the first plane out of town. When they all re-met in Chicago Sinatra impressed the Europeans no end with his noisy police escort. Vadim concluded from all this that the film would be made and started to work with an American writer. The problem lay in getting Brigitte and Sinatra together. They were both stars, nervous of stepping out of their own environment. 'I've had that location bit,' Sinatra said after he had made *The Pride and The Passion* in Europe, 'too many idiots standing around watching' – and terrified of being eclipsed by each other.

Brigitte was a star and one who was afraid of flying and didn't want to leave her lover. She refused to audition by appearing for Sinatra in America. Sinatra was damned if he was going to audition in front of her in Paris. Both Trintignant and Lauren Bacall, who was involved with Sinatra at the time, seemed, perhaps not surprisingly, to want to preserve the distance between them. So nothing happened. When Sinatra went to Paris he simply did not look Brigitte up. Levy tried to get the project off the ground for nearly two years and even resorted to considering a very different chemical formula – Brigitte and Danny Kaye, who had just made *The Court Jester* with Glynis Johns. It might have worked as a comedy, which was Brigitte's forte, but no one really wanted a comedy from her at that time. Remembering her grounding in dance he also thought of Fred Astaire. Gene Kelly too remembers some talk of Bardot teaming up with him. He had met her already when she was very young with Vadim, hanging around the studios in Paris and he was to meet her again when he was making the mawkish comedy *Gigot* with Jackie Gleason in the early sixties when she was on the next sound-stage making *Vie Privée*. Nothing came of the suggestion that they should work together, however, and he puts it down to her fear of speaking English.

Despite all these big names and shrewd in-fighters who had planned and gambled their way to the top in the toughest town in the world, there was another factor to consider. Bardot in 1957 appropriately embodied the threat posed by both children and animals on a picture. No leading man, dependent on his own attractions, wanted to work with her in case she stole the show. It happened again and again. The Italian Rossano Brazzi said: 'I do not want to commit professional suicide. Leading men in her pictures spend most of the time just looking at her. So does the audience.' Even David Niven, suave enough one might imagine to deflect any suggestion of competition and not strictly a sex-symbol, turned Brigitte down.

Levy subsequently turned his sights to the big names in French theatre, Edwige Feuillère and Jean Gabin, for the film *En Cas de Malheur* ('In Case of Adversity'), only to have the same reaction. 'What, work with that thing that always goes around naked!' Gabin said. Though he of all people had an eye for a pretty woman – he had been Michèle Morgan's lover, infatuated with Ginger Rogers, and the long-time companion of Marlene Dietrich – who smothered him with her spaghetti and pot au feu – he tried everything he knew to get out of his contract. The battle went on till the very last moment with the film delayed for two weeks by the vagaries of Bardot's love life. The film was eventually made by the experienced director Claude Autant-Lara, and the result was that Bardot gained at least two clever fans in France, which was rapidly reassessing its wayward daughter – Gabin himself and François Truffaut who said 'More than an actress, she is a person – unique.'

Still most people persisted in thinking of her as a giant-killer, an ill-starred Carmen or an Eva as the similar character is called in the novel *The Woman and the Puppet* by Pierre Louys, which was to be her next role. Don Mateo, a wealthy bull-breeder, falls in love with the student Eva at the Seville Feria and leaves everything for her, including his invalid wife. Eva is not all she seems and the Don embarks on a series of humiliations as he finds out the truth. Von Sternberg had chosen the story for his last, brilliantly successful film with Dietrich made in 1935, *The Devil is a Woman*. It had also been remade in Mexico in 1950. The Bardot version was beset with jealousies and inadequacies right from the start when both Fernando Lamas and Tyrone Power had the usual reaction to starring with her. Instead the Spanish star Antonio Vilar was cast and both principals suffered: first Brigitte, whose jaw became dislocated when he slapped her too enthusiastically, then Vilar, who slipped a disc while cavorting in a four-poster bed. Brigitte had decided that if she was a star she might as well behave like one, which meant she refused to see the Hollywood columnist Hedda Hopper, who might have been a helpful ally in the circumstances which were developing where she just could not get the formula right. The film did not work at all, being called vulgar, unpleasant, and indigestible on both sides of the Atlantic.

In June 1957 Levy, Vadim, and Bardot had taken off for Spain where she met up with the British actor Stephen Boyd, who had been enjoying some success on screen – but not so much that he refused the assignment – ever since he had been spotted as a cinema usher in Leicester Square. Erotic content was still the name of the game in *Les Bijoutiers du Clair de Lune*. Brigitte runs off with Boyd, who has murdered her uncle in a vendetta, and holes up with him for a week of violent sado-masochistic sex in the Spanish mountains. Off the emotional hook from Vadim, Brigitte started to be reliably unreliable about her work. The unit was installed in Torremolinos on the south coast which was then relatively unspoiled. However little these package tour resorts have going for them now since the advent of millions of tourists and billions of tons of concrete, they usually have sun. Not in 1957. It rained. Boyd was not sexually drawn to his co-star and on-screen both tried to upstage the other. 'When I'm trying to play serious love scenes with her, she is busy positioning her bottom for the best angle shots,' he complained. Boyd didn't understand Bardot's moods, nor did he pretend to. Most of these centred round the fact that Annette Stroyberg, the Danish au pair, who had followed Vadim to Venice when he was making *Sait-on-Jamais*, had just found out she was pregnant by him. From Brigitte's point of view, she didn't have the delicacy to keep away from the set. It was all more than she could bear and she had no one to run to because Trintignant was in the army.

Not for the first time Brigitte solicited the affection of animals but it was the first time she became wildly sentimental and indiscriminate about them. First there was a stray dog Guapa, whom she decided she needed to befriend her spaniel Clown. Then she found herself a donkey, which she presented ostentatiously to some local children who couldn't have cared less about donkeys, and finally she pretended to fight a baby bull. In the company of the radiant Stroyberg she became obsessed with her looks, which were marred by the usual nervous skin rash.

Determined not to go over budget on the home straight to success, Vadim and Levy tried not to take any notice. Vadim, who had seen most of these moods at least once before when Pilou had refused his permission for them to marry, knew she would stop at nothing. If a nervous breakdown didn't work she would try something worse, which would hardly benefit any of them, and the beauty of her position in all this was that she simply didn't care. That, at least, was what she always pretended. She had never wanted to be an actress and she didn't want to be one now. Vadim's own slightly romantic *maladie du siècle* had turned in her into the most negative sort of contemporary existentialism, or even worse than that, manipulative nihilism, very much the weapon of the next generation glutted on welfare and drugs. Bardot was a pioneer in hypochondria. She now summoned any number of doctors until they agreed she had to have a rest and go home to Paris, and the arms of Trintignant. When Trintignant returned to the army, she returned to Spain, this time to the arms of Gustavo Rojo, a Spanish actor. She was trying to find oblivion. She also discovered another passion which, unlike any single man, would actually last a lifetime – Flamenco dancing which she said was like having sex.

The trouble was that while Bardot was trying to manipulate events, her wild behaviour and her inability to sustain any pattern of moves usually ended up with her being manipulated, just as Vadim had predicted when he described the 'new' woman and when he wrote *And God Created Woman*. Rojo may have enjoyed her favours but he also enjoyed the publicity they could bring him. Before whisking her away for a dirty weekend he notified the Press. Trintignant, reading his newspaper in barracks, demanded an explanation. Bardot denied she had ever been anywhere for the weekend and said she was going to marry him. Trintignant regretted that this was not possible because his wife would not give him a divorce. Brigitte then went back to Rojo and told him she had never had any intention of marrying Jean-Louis. Rojo said that was just as well because he was going to marry her himself. Somehow the film was finished and Bardot eluded both of them to concentrate on the singer, Gilbert Bécaud, to whom she was introduced by her music teacher, Claude Bolling.

It was no doubt these tales from her private life which accounted for the fact that by the end of 1957, 47 per cent of French conversation was said to be about her. The French had never had a star who let it be known that she behaved like this. Not all of the talk was good. One magazine – not *Match* this time but *Cinémonde* – calculated that her photograph had appeared over 29,000 times in their pages alone. In opinion polls between Continental film fans she easily beat all the European stars who at the time included Gina Lollobrigida. Elizabeth Taylor and even Marilyn Monroe were left trailing way behind.

The ensuing sequence of events was totally tragic and was to prove one thing to Brigitte, that, like Juliette, and despite everything in her favour, she was destined to lose men. On 6 December 1957, just five years after the marriage she had once wanted so much, the First Chamber of the Civil Tribunal of the Seine granted a divorce to Vadim and Bardot on the colourful and accurate grounds that they had seriously insulted one another. The day before Annette Stroyberg had given him a daughter, Nathalie. 'Brigitte never wanted a child,' says Vadim, 'and it is too much of a responsibility to persuade a woman to become a mother when she doesn't want to.' Their ties were well and truly cut. Trintignant, irritated by Bécaud when he came back on Christmas leave, preferred even the imprisonment of the army to the web Bardot was trying to weave around both of them. Bécaud, probably trying to preserve his marriage, pilloried her in public when she followed him to Geneva. He called a press conference and told the reporters, who up to now had gallantly kept quiet about his little fling, that she was annoying him. It was all too much for Bardot, who, remembering that such things had worked with Pilou and Vadim, seems to have threatened another suicide attempt. It shamed her immediately and she has not referred to it since. As soon as it was all over she called it food–poisoning, a case of too many sewage-ridden mussels. Even she was finding herself an object of ridicule and her life a mess.

10. The Bride is too Beautiful

Stars in the limelight become everyone's quarry. Sacha Distel had not forgotten his meeting with Brigitte. She was the friend of his uncle Ray Ventura, he was Juliette Greco's accompanist and Juliette was Bardot's friend. He had escorted Annette Stroyberg and his father was a Russian emigré just like Vadim's. There were at least four points at which their lives intertwined which persuaded him she would not refuse an invitation to his birthday party at L'Esquinade, the St-Tropez night-spot, in the summer of 1958.

There was only one reason why she accepted: Sacha himself. He was dark, extremely attractive and under thirty, just how she liked them. She took one look at him and they danced barefoot and in casual dress till the place closed in the early hours of the morning and everyone else had left. Stars have to behave as is required of them. They went home to La Madrague.

It was an idyllic summer holiday. Sacha taught Brigitte to play the guitar. Brigitte, who had already embarked on her singing career, was a responsive pupil. Sacha also taught Brigitte to become a woman rather than the androgynous shock-machine which Vadim had sought to promote. She was heard to say that she wanted a baby and to whisper how beautiful marriage actually was if you found the right man. By day they lazed around and swam, by night they went out to local restaurants. The world was kept at bay and the house run by a secretary called Allain Carré.

Like all attractive women who weary from time to time of the opposite sex, Brigitte has had her friendships with men who pose no threat to her. Allain seemed to be one of these. But he turned out to be more jealous of his hold over her than she could ever have hoped from a lover. He was aware that she had flopped from bed to bed with one attractive man after another since the days of Jean-Louis Trintignant. He knew about her affairs with perfectly formed playboy tennis stars like Jean-Noel Grinda, but they had somehow always liberated Brigitte to spend time with Allain in the end. Sacha was something else though – all-absorbing.

Brigitte had high hopes of the affair with Sacha. For the first time she was not motivated by revenge on the past when she chose him. It was the high point of her life. She was nearly twenty-four. The sun shone all through that heady summer while one of the most beautiful couples in the world made love inside La Madrague on the Provençal counterpanes under the whitewash and rafters and outside under the bougainvillea bushes. The heat made Brigitte feel beautiful where the cold pinched her and brought out her spots. Her skin tanned easily, her nose freckled lightly and her hair lightened naturally. Her body, alternately speckled with salt and sand or burnished with oil, felt healthier than it ever had done before.

For followers of the affair in the pages of the world's Press sun-worship, with its odour of idleness, its memories of the Tahitian morals of the maidens of Gauguin, its obvious associa-tion with nudity, its evocation of strange primitive fertility rites, rapidly replaced the kohled eyes and exhumed night-club pallor of Juliette Greco as one of the seven deadly sins. Bardot, moreover, was guilty of both of them, wearing too much make-up and too few clothes. Only a decade before, when Claudette Colbert was the sweet-natured French pin-up, girls who came to the Mediterranean wore ample one-piece swimsuits and rubber bath-ing caps covered their hair. Now in 1958 all over Europe girls painted provocative little freckles on their noses and bared their navels, to the delight of their menfolk and the distress of older women. They unleashed their hair and streaked it to get the summer look. They became *sportif* as never before. Feeling their limbs kissed by the elements and provoked by pleasurable exercise they also began to think of making love like Bardot, with some exotic youth always on hand to gratify the itch set up by the sun.

There was a slight cloud on the horizon apart from Allain Carré, who had not yet disclosed his hand, in the form of the magazine photographers who were always to be found perched up Brigitte's trees trying to snap the loving couple *in flagrante* or any other way. She called them the fruit of her orchard, a slur on their masculinity. Sacha tried not to notice that the telephone rang every five minutes but ring it did and one call was from Ed Sullivan in America who invited both Brigitte and Sacha on his show. Brigitte refused point blank. She turned down $50,000 for a single appearance, having been assured she would only have to say hello. But Sacha, an ambitious young man, at twenty-five already older than Brigitte but unlike her with no great professional hits under his belt, thought twice about the offer when he was asked. Neither of them was earning any money as they whiled their lives away on one of the most expensive coasts in France. It was obvious their idyll could not last. An insuperable problem started to nag Sacha which allowed itself to be dispelled only temporarily in a haze of summer wine, guitar sounds and love. The summer was going to end.

When he flew to New York he discovered an even worse problem. In Paris and the South of France he had a slight reputation as *chanteur* and guitarist. In the United States he was simply the new Mr Bardot. Ed Sullivan didn't give a damn that he thought he was a musician, he billed him as the most envied man in the world and Sacha felt more naked than he had ever done in Brigitte's bed. When he finally sang 'Parlez-Moi d'Amour' on the show, he realized at once both the acclaim that could be his as a performer in his own right and the absolute impossibility of tying himself to Brigitte's apron strings. He wasn't the first to acknowledge this – Vadim had already called himself Mr Bardot when his relatively unknown young bride had first attracted the stares of men in the street. Distel was certainly not going to be the last. As recently as 1983 the same thing happened when Alain Bougrain-Dubourg quarrelled with her after she had trusted him to make a television film of her life. Though Distel went on basking in his friendship with Bardot for a while, writing little songs about her 'Brigitte, Brigitte, Pouting or smiling, Angel or Devil, which is your true face?' and flying to New York to record them, he had begun to feel his own muscles. He embarked on a recording career which spanned two continents. Brigitte, who hated to be alone, continued to praise his manliness, but she had started to ache for the limelight again herself.

Things were not over between them yet, however, for Brigitte as always was proving a tenacious lover, totally incapable of using any subtlety where male psychology was concerned. She had never had to. From Pilou to Vadim she had had just what she wanted. Despite the way he had exploited her physical attractions Vadim had taken his obligations as protector – to himself as well as her – seriously. But when she threw both these men up for the thrill of the chase in full glare of publicity, she proved one thing that her admirers would take a little longer to experience – that a girl, most girls that is, not just Brigitte, could get any man, but they could not necessarily keep them. Therein lay the trick which Brigitte never bothered to perfect since there was always another man on the horizon drawn by the challenge of her body. Only recently Sacha Distel, now happily married for years, analysed what went wrong between them. It sounded strangely familiar. 'Brigitte was somebody who needed the man she was in love with to be with her constantly. To do the things she wanted to do. To take second place. And that was not what I had in mind at all. I was working very hard to become Sacha Distel, successful singer, not Mr Bardot. If Brigitte had felt like it she could have been Mrs Distel. There was never any doubt in my mind that anybody I married would have to be Mrs Distel.'

Brigitte did want to be Mrs Distel, but on her terms. All through 1958 she behaved immensely badly. When Sacha was concentrating on his work she always had her employee, Allain Carré, to fall back upon. Carré had already acted as escort and go-between when he took her to the theatre and introduced her backstage to Raf Vallone. Now the two of them went to see another young star, who Brigitte had already noticed with Sacha in the cinema when the two of them had gone one night to see *Les Tricheurs* at the Marignan. His name was Jacques Charrier. This time he was treading the boards opposite Pascale Audret in *The Diary of Anne Frank*. Brigitte had a good excuse to get to know him. She was looking for a new co-star and Sacha had made it clear he was not interested.

The third film in Levy's scheme of things was going to be *Babette Goes to War*. Was it because of the difficulty of getting co-stars to compete with her assets that Levy decided this time Brigitte was going to cover herself up? Bardot, who was not quite ready to break with Levy, went along with it. She said she was tired of flaunting everything she had and wanted to make a film which any sixteen-year-old could see. She was going to play a French refugee in England who is parachuted back to France in full Tommy outfit to kidnap a German general. Once again life imitated art in the most peculiar way, prompting the suggestible breed of actors with their next moves so that they never bother to put any effort into reality. Charrier was the son of a famous French military family. He had grown up in French garrisons in

Germany, France, and North Africa and his father was a colonel in the artillery. His three brothers had gone into the army and were serving in Algeria. Charrier fell hook, line, and sinker for the girl in the fatigues. He was three years younger than her, a debutant actor with perfect features and a shy personality and unlike Sacha he had absolutely no misgivings about an affair with Brigitte ruining his own career. Within weeks he made it plain that he had none of the macho reservations of Distel. Charrier was putty in Brigitte's hands and she moulded him in her mind into the perfect suitor.

It was a very confused little girl who went to the *mairie* once more on 18 June 1959 to get married. All through the winter months making *Babette* she had hesitated between Sacha and Jacques. The trouble is there was no hesitation in either of their minds. One did not want to marry her, the other would do so if that is what it took to make her happy. With the help of Allain Carré and of events which took Sacha on a singing tour to Portugal and kept Charrier working on two films at once, she had been able to see a lot of both of them, at the same time letting just enough information trickle back to the other to enable them to crystallize their positions. When the man of her choice wouldn't do what she wanted she broke with him publicly, getting Allain Carré to deal with the Press: 'Mlle Bardot has asked me to announce that she has severed all relations with M. Sacha Distel,' he announced. If such a declaration was supposed to provoke a response from the singer, it was unsuccessful. Distel merely remarked that the main lesson Bardot had taught him was that actresses were not to be trusted and went on his way. He explored the truth of this theory briefly with Annette Stroyberg, who had also been put in front of the cameras by Vadim, and then went on to marry his ski champion Francine Bréaud.

Charrier, on the other hand, was much impressed by the formal announcement. It made him feel better to have things down in black and white because he had just found out that he was going to be a father. Brigitte had leapt prematurely into pregnancy just as Annette Stroyberg had with Vadim. According to Carré she phoned him in the middle of the night immediately after returning from location in England at RAF Abingdon to confide that in between parachute jumps she and Charrier had made a baby.

It sounds as if Brigitte, motivated by frustration with Sacha, may have been using the most innocent of lives to get her own way and restore her self-respect. But on paper Charrier had a good deal in common with her. At the time she was convinced of his qualifications. 'I have not always loved wisely, but I was young,' she said. 'Vadim revealed me to myself, Trintignant seduced me. Rojo fired my passion. Sacha gave me tenderness with every word, with every kiss. But Jacques stole my heart. Jacques changed my life. There will be no more after this.' She desperately wanted to believe what she said. His background in a correct middle-class family, to whom he was a bit of a mystery, was the same as her own. In a way they were two orphans from respectability who had found each other and would now find their own respectability together. He experienced just as much resistance to his marriage with Bardot as she had to hers with Vadim. But with this choice of a devoted and suitable man who just happened to share her profession, she now had high hopes of putting this resistance behind her. The two of them worked at a sickly domestic image, supported in full by the Press and the public, who were enchanted by what they saw. Brigitte and Charrier in the kitchen making ratatouille – or rather Charrier making it and Brigitte, who had always loathed home-cooking, flirtatiously refusing to taste – Brigitte and Charrier in loafers, in shirtsleeves, in aprons, in gingham, in Paisley, in denim, in dirndls, in every possible fabric, pose, and guise of informality. Brigitte and Charrier barefoot in each other's arms in the sun. Even her wedding dress, painfully nipped in to disguise her hastiness, was simple peasant gingham. Three thousand copies of it were made and sold in a Paris chain-store. All this virginal appeal was a demure apology for her mistakes and a way of starting afresh. It brought Brigitte back to the family which had given her such a blinkered upbringing. When it came to the point, this second marriage was orchestrated just as much as the first had been by the proud father of the bride, Pilou.

This time it was decided that a secret ceremony should be held in the village town hall at Louveciennes, a couple of hundred yards from Grandmother Mucel's house, which the Bardots had inherited. Anne-Marie Bardot carefully told the Press that the couple had already been married on 5 June while going ahead with her preparations for the great day. Louveciennes, the home of Madame Du Barry, Louis XV's mistress who was guillotined during the French Revolution, had the advantage of lying about twenty miles outside the capital right in the country, hopefully inaccessible to all but the keenest fans. The *mairie* was a particularly delightful, non-official-looking building in the shadow of Louis XIV's great aqueduct, like a country house topped with the tricolor, the perfect setting for a June wedding. But Charrier in particular had not realized, despite all the photo sessions he had endured, just how keen a Bardot fan could be. He expected a quiet family gathering, captured informally under the cedar trees in the garden for the family album by Pilou's camera alone.

When the happy couple set out for the wedding, not from the rue Général Le Clerc just down the road in the Yvelines, but from La Madrague in St-Tropez nearly 1,000 miles away, he should have had some idea what it was all about, particularly when they left the house in separate cars, both lying down in the back seat behind their respective drivers. They were reunited at Toulon where they took the Blue Train together overnight to the Gare d'Orléans in Paris. Then at 11.10 a.m. a convoy of cars, headed by a light grey Dauphine, arrived at the town hall in Louveciennes carrying Brigitte, her sister Mijanou, their parents, her habitual stand-in Maggy (she had become a good friend), Colonel Charrier, and his son. When Jacques tried to take his place next to the bride he was turned away by policemen trying to control a howling mob of photographers and onlookers who had been waiting outside the doors since seven in the morning. They had been tipped off about the day of the wedding by the town hall staff.

Once more the element of farce swept through the ceremony. Pilou became blustering and irate. Brigitte, still a bewildering mixture of dutiful daughter and outrageous hussy, threatened to call the whole thing off until she remembered what condition she was in.

As with her first marriage the difficulties which began before the ceremony continued afterwards. First they were all garrisoned in the family chalet down the road for a brief reception at which the police were loath to open the doors for long enough even to admit the wedding cake. Then almost immediately the couple returned to La Madrague, the house haunted with memories of the previous carefree summer with Sacha. All of a sudden the omens did not seem so good as they had previously. The holiday home too was besieged by photographers. Within a week Charrier was in hospital with appendicitis. Within a month Brigitte had to report to the Victorine Studios in Nice to make her third film with

Michel Boisrond, *Voulez-Vous Danser Avec Moi.*

To avoid the photographers and the drive along the coast, which would have been impossible to do each morning in those days, Brigitte and Charrier took a little house, La Tour Margot, in the Haut-de-Cagnes, where Renoir used to paint, about ten miles from Nice. The house was fortified by a high wall and a palm-tree screen, which no one actually managed to penetrate, but the photographers soon stationed themselves outside all the same. What is more, the magazine *Cinémonde* was soon announcing to the world Brigitte's intention to get married again, this time to the star of the film, Henri Vidal, whose marriage to Michèle Morgan had suffered from his persistent misuse of hard drugs. The film was to be a light-hearted thriller in which Brigitte's performance would afterwards be acclaimed as worthy of Danielle Darrieux, but it was dogged by the sort of tragedy which seemed quite ominous to Brigitte in her condition. After only a few days' shooting one of the actresses, Sylva Lopez, fell ill and died, like Kay Kendall that same year, of leukaemia. Brigitte had taken Kay's place in *Doctor at Sea*, now Sylva's was taken by Dawn Addams, the girl whose life seems to have inspired the quintessential liberation picture *Darling* with the Brigitte look-alike Julie Christie. Later that summer Henri Vidal died. Then, when Charrier like Trintignant had to leave Brigitte to do his military service in the autumn, he fell ill again. Life in the barracks of the 11th Lancers at Orange in the South of France showed him what other men thought of Brigitte – most of them were working on curing their adolescent spots with the aid of any one of 30,000 pictures cut from the magazines. It was too much for a sensitive child-bridegroom, who imagined their fantasies becoming reality in Brigitte's bed during his absence.

Charrier was pulled in one direction and then another, not least by Brigitte who blamed him repeatedly for making her go through the ordeal of pregnancy on her own and had her doctors sign multiple requests for compassionate leave. Once at her side he was immediately assailed by guilt when questions were asked in the French Parliament about these leaves of absence. Finally he had a complete nervous breakdown in the military hospital of Val de Grâce and was given a temporary discharge with what was aptly called a heart condition. The fact that Brigitte's husband was unfit for service was the subject of a good deal of lurid ridicule from the French Press. And for the son of a military family at a period when soldiering was remembered to have saved the free world and its virtues had in no way yet been called into question, it was a terrible time. As the fifties drew to a close and history was about to be rewritten, it was pointed out over and over that even Elvis Presley, who was otherwise completely beyond the pale, had had the decency and the guts to serve his country.

Alongside the child-bridegroom was a child-bride, even though she was going through it all for the second time around. At this time in her life Brigitte was calling everything into question, behaving more like an adolescent than she had done in her teens. She hated her career and was beginning to see nothing but disadvantages to it. 'I am not really interested in the cinema,' she said. 'I loathed it when I started it six years ago and to tell the truth, I don't enjoy it even now as one ought to enjoy one's work. If this fame, which people call my lucky break, were to stop tomorrow I shouldn't care. When you find yourself in this strange position of semi-goddess, which is so unnatural anyway, publicity takes its revenge on you. People are forever finding something wrong with you. If you hit back you are being difficult. If you give the wrong answers – and it's not always easy to give the right ones – the words sound dreadful. The film world is an absurd world. I am not reacting against it just to be difficult but because I am determined to live my life as I am, not as others make me. I am all right when I work. I am not superficial and I am not ungrateful. But the life of Brigitte Bardot, film star, and the life of Brigitte Bardot, just one of millions of other Parisians, are not compatible. I have to live with both my selves as best I may.'

Great good sense it sounds now, but at the time nobody gave her her just deserts because no one could be quite sure where the truth lay. She had been billed by her own husband, Vadim, as a natural phenomenon. 'Brigitte does not act, she exists,' he had said, what you saw on screen was 'the real Bardot, all animality, sensuality and femininity unfolded'. No wonder she could not get away from herself. Nobody seemed to be able to get the whole thing in perspective at the turn of the decade and women were feeling particularly edgy when it became apparent that Brigitte was not awaiting the common destiny of womanhood, the birth of her child, with anything like the traditional pleasure. 'I never do anything by chance,' she said and assured them that this pregnancy was no exception. 'But I am not finding pregnancy much of a joy. Of course I am afraid of childbirth, but I am afraid I can't find a way of avoiding it.' This was Brigitte grounded by life as generations of women before her and honestly hating it. Though Brigitte was only twenty-six she was not a healthy prima gravida, taking to her bed for bouts of torpor and self-pity. Beautiful women are not always grateful for pregnancy, feeling their whole being undermined by an unknown intruder who bloats them out of shape, minimizes their sex-drive, or saddles them with guilt whenever they make love, destroys their everyday energy, and their courage. Pregnancy, it seemed to Brigitte, was like being strapped into an aeroplane, a thing which she hated and which was inevitably bound to come to earth one way or another. The flight lasted nine months, which gave her a lot of time to contemplate life and death.

The child may have been conceived in a flurry of wilfulness but it has to be said on Brigitte's behalf that she was committed to carrying it. Many a less maligned woman was not and indeed many made a point of making this attitude public. Ten years later there was a public petition to legalize abortion in France signed unashamedly by such friends, fans, or contemporaries of Brigitte as Jeanne Moreau, Françoise Sagan, Catherine Deneuve, and Simone de Beauvoir. 'A million women have abortions every year in France,' they wrote, and then in defiance of the law, which could make them liable to a heavy fine if not imprisonment, 'I declare that I am one of them.' Brigitte agreed to support the movement financially but she would not sign. Even in 1960 it was not difficult to get an abortion in France, certainly not for someone with the connections and the ready money of a screen actress. She could easily have aborted her baby rather than marry Charrier, but she did not.

11. Contempt

Bébé's baby gave her no pleasure at all. Whereas her mother had wanted a boy, Brigitte would have been better off with a girl for she was becoming very suspicious of the opposite sex. Brigitte held the newborn at arm's length, installed him not only in a room of his own but a flat of his own next door to that of his parents. She refused to feed him herself, insisting he would be bottlefed. At first she kept up a good pretence, mouthing all the usual clichés. He was the most beautiful baby in the world, she had always known he would be a boy, she had already chosen his name – Nicolas – she had never given a single thought to girls' names, she had *his* nursery and *his* wardrobe prepared.

It was a pastiche of a nursery which recalled her own, this time with pale blue walls, white woolly carpet and blue-and-white curtains. There was a white crib on wheels with a frilly organza canopy. There was even the Second Empire birdcage with which she had grown up, full now to bursting with the toy animals from her childhood and much later. She has not stopped collecting them. There was everything a baby could need till he was out of babyhood – and much more: a white high-chair, a white playpen, and a white chest of drawers stuffed with precocious little outfits that befitted the son of a star, miniature duffle coats and hooded towelling bathrobes. Brigitte distributed fifty similar layettes to fifty other Parisian babies who shared Nicolas's birthday. She posed coyly for the cameras like a teenager with a teddy, in flowered nighties with her hair in ribbons and bunches, her sleeping son oblivious for the moment of his extraordinary birthright.

Charrier, the dupe of newsmen, posed for the cameras immediately after the birth with someone else's baby son, also called Nicolas, downstairs in the Café Royale in the avenue Paul Doumer. Charrier revealed that his Nicolas had inherited his own dimples, that he and Brigitte, who was already recovering from a painless birth, had given him the instant nickname, Dimples, and that Brigitte had just two words to say when she heard it was a boy: '*Chic, alors.*'

Charrier had changed since his illness and Brigitte and he had not been getting on for a long time. They seemed to bring out the worst in each other. Brigitte seemed compelled to tease him, which Charrier could not bear. Aware of his weakness, he tried to be physically tough which Brigitte hated, indeed feared. She was thirsting for caresses. Once discharged from the army, Charrier's dilemma was by no means over. Towards the end of Brigitte's pregnancy the couple were imprisoned like a pair of animals in the flat. 'It was inhuman what they did to me,' she says now. 'I couldn't go for a walk, I couldn't go out, I couldn't even go to my doctor. I lived like a nun for three months, I couldn't move. I needed an X-ray but I couldn't go out for it. Nicolas's birth was a terrible time for me and people treated me like savages.' Brigitte became so nervous that she refused to take any telephone calls and would not even speak to her mother. She set lawyers on anyone who tried to write about her as a film star. She was trying very hard to come to terms with her new role as wife and mother and to wrest some dignity for herself from the vulgar baying of the media. They in turn were determined that she should pay her dues to them who had made her Brigitte Bardot. Outside the thirties block, where the Charriers occupied the balcony floor, 250 newsmen were camped day and night. They all knew that the first picture of Bébé with baby would be worth a fortune and they stood on each other's shoulders and toes to try to get it. They pointed their cameras at blank windows and into thin air. They paid high prices to rent rooms which overlooked every conceivable corner of her flat. The results were published all over the Press, minimizing coverage of legitimate news items like the Algerian war. Society-watchers discussed the significance of the birth in the most intimate terms, some even advocating a Caesarean operation so that the baby would not weaken those muscles which had proved more evocative and valuable to France than the virginity of Joan of Arc.

Until then Brigitte had planned to have the baby in one of the smart clinics of the sixteenth *arrondissement*, but it gradually became plain that, as with the marriage, a leak could not be avoided and that, in this case, if things were not handled properly a tragedy might ensue. Clinic staff were already being bribed to let photographers in on the birth or immediately after and Brigitte was not even confined yet. From time to time at the very end of her pregnancy she ran the gauntlet of admirers and detractors alike, who gathered outside on the avenue for a glimpse of the sex-symbol fleshed out by maternity. Charrier made one last field trip, back to the family home in the country to ask a local doctor to deliver the baby at home in Paris. After that he refused to leave the marital flat. He suffered from agoraphobia outside and claustrophobia within. At night he dreamed he was confined in an army cell. He lost forty pounds in weight and became pitifully thin. Finally he took to his bed. Brigitte coped more or less alone and when at eight months pregnant she fell up the stairs to the flat and he was photographed coming to her aid in pyjamas in the middle of the day, his low self-esteem was complete.

Nevertheless he was pleased with his son and proud of him. 'It's a boy and it's as big as this,' he demonstrated like a fisherman with a catch. The photographers made him repeat the gesture thirty times. He said his son weighed 7lb 4oz. He had added his own name of Jacques to Brigitte's first choice. He said the baby was healthy and strong with a powerful tenor voice. It was 3 a.m. on 11 January 1960. The long wait was over at last. Wearing the serious horn-rimmed glasses of a responsible father figure he bought champagne all round for the Press and looked forward to resuming a normal life.

By now, despite herself, Brigitte's idea of a normal life was inside a cinema studio and it was to the Joinville Studios in Paris that she went the minute she was mobile after the birth, about ten days later. The film was to be *La Vérité*, directed by Henri Clouzot, a story of a gypsy bohemian girl who seduces her sister's lover and then kills him. Clouzot had been working on the script during Brigitte's advancing pregnancy with no help at all from the actress, who was absorbed in perfecting her performance as a reluctant mother-to-be. But despite his reputation as the brilliant writer-director of *The Wages of Fear* and *Les Diaboliques* Clouzot did need her help. The film would not start shooting until May but first there was the usual tricky problem of auditioning leading men. Bardot started two weeks after the arrival of Nicolas Jacques Charrier and she made it quite clear when she did so that his father was not up for the part. Since life was in her case so prone to imitate art, onlookers, including Jacques himself, concluded that she was also auditioning for a replacement off-screen.

Brigitte had not quite made up her mind about that, but she did know she was fed up for the time being with playing the fat Mrs Charrier. As for her attitude to Nicolas, a woman does not decide all at once what kind of mother she is going to be. She tries out her new role and it either absorbs her or leaves her indifferent or worse and guilty to be so. Years later, when Nicolas was twelve, Brigitte told Peter Evans: 'I am very sad to have had that baby. What will be his life? People who are making babies and families now are mad. It is such a bad world.' But when he was first born the state of the world did not worry her so much as the state of her figure. She was very afraid that she might have lost the magic that had made her into Bébé, the nation's baby, the adored, spoiled woman-child, that she had been usurped like millions of women before her by the new, younger generation, in her case by the new little Charrier, child of a man she wasn't absolutely certain she respected. She set out almost immediately to try to reverse these forces of nature. In her mood of post-natal insecurity, paymistress of an extended household of three, it made great good sense to ask for Jean-Louis Trintignant to play opposite her in her new film, the man with whom she had made music which had resounded right round the world.

It was at this time, right at the start of the sixties, that Brigitte's life began to be something of an anachronism, which was ironic since she had done so much to herald the mood of the coming decade. Her failure to adjust to such a universal experience as childbirth left her a marked woman in the eyes of other women who had adjusted. It was a very difficult time for her because she was not insensitive to the liberated mood of the young, which she had done as much as anyone to create, and she was aware of her responsibilities. She knew she liked children in principle, just as she liked animals. But she knew also that a woman with a child is never free and that her bondage was much more complete than anything she had suffered as a child herself. She felt that the only way out was to make a clean break at the very beginning. The practical solution was not easy to find. Her mother would have loved the late opportunity of caring for a boy but she had no experience of one. Brigitte could also not quite forget that she had made her extremely unhappy as a child. Her parents-in-law may have disapproved of her but they were familiar with sons. They were Charriers and there was a sense in which Brigitte thought

Child bride with second husband, Jacques Charrier, in 1958
(*Rex Features Ltd*)

BB with baby Nicolas, his father Jacques, and godmother Christine Gouze-Renal
(*Rex Features Ltd*)

Screen testing for a leading
man in *The Truth* (1960) –
with Sami Frey
(Keystone Press Agency Ltd)

Suicide scene from *The Truth*,
narrowly avoided in real life
(Rex Features Ltd)

Before her conservation days. In the mid-sixties Brigitte's main interest was Bob Zaguri: here she is watching him play basket-ball and, below, they attend a gala occasion
(Left: Popperfoto. Below: Kobal Collection)

On *Viva Maria* (1965) Jeanne Moreau seemed to be the professional actress, Bardot the
wide-eyed little girl. But Bardot was the professional publicist – Jeanne stayed at home
when the film opened in America (below)
(Both photographs: Rex Features Ltd)

The high life in Gunther Sachs's private jet. He was her third husband and they married in 1966
(Keystone Press Agency Ltd)

In *Tales of Mystery and Imagination* (1967), directed by Louis Malle
(Rex Features Ltd)

Some of the young men in Brigitte's life: Mike Sarne
(top left), Luigi Rizzi (bottom left), Christian Kalt (top
right), and Patrick Gilles (bottom right)
(All photographs: Rex Features Ltd)

Teaching the BB pout to Vanessa, daughter of Jane Fonda and Roger Vadim
(*John Hillelson Agency Ltd/L. de Raemy/Sygma*)

Don Juan, 1973. Vadim is directing Bardot and Jane Birkin
(*John Hillelson Agency Ltd/L. de Raemy/Sygma*)

only a Charrier could bring up a Charrier, a mysteriously disappointing creature, who appeared on the face of it to have all the virtues but who somehow danced to a tamer drum than a Bardot. And yet the wild drums had not made Brigitte happy. Therefore when she and Charrier were divorced when young Nicolas was only two, she allowed the father to keep custody of the child. 'I was just a child myself, I couldn't look after myself even, I was no good for anyone else. I needed a mother, a support, a shoulder to cry on, I needed roots. I couldn't give anyone else roots if I was completely rootless myself. I was unbalanced, lost and I couldn't lean on a little newborn baby. I would have made his life hell. I spent all my time in tears and I went out with anybody and everybody anywhere just to get out when I felt the walls closing round me. I don't care what anybody else thought. I felt I was in prison and that was no life for a child.'

The whole period took the most terrible and nearly fatal toll of her for the strong whiff of self-disgust was accompanied by the overwhelming disapproval of others. 'I think it was at that time that France really turned against Brigitte,' says a friend who was close to her. 'It wasn't inevitable. They were prepared to adopt her and the baby as Madonna and child. They adored her. But Brigitte saw what they expected next. They expected her to put the child on a pedestal. To devote herself to it. In the future actresses were always being photographed with their children at airports or on the set. It was part of their image. They littered them like little animals, married or not. But Brigitte grew up in old-fashioned times when you couldn't have it both ways. You did not bare the breast to passion that suckled the child. She had always been terrified of being bored. She was terrified of being penniless. Now she was terrified of being bored, penniless and responsible for another human being. More than that, she hated to do what was expected.'

Bardot's statements on the matter seem outrageous even twenty-five years later. 'I am no mother and I won't be one,' she said. The public felt she should have thought about that nine months earlier and labelled her the witch of the century. In this era of planned parenthood she would probably get even shorter shrift. At the time Bardot, who has always maintained that she voluntarily chose to become a mother, showed an abject lack of interest in Nicolas's daily progress. 'I suppose he is all right, he is well looked after,' she said tossing her irresponsible head. There was an

163

aura of bravura about her carelessness, of giving the people once more what they expected, because whenever it came to the crunch she was never very far away from the boy. True she visited him rather rarely and in a rather artificial way, always bringing gifts of toys for him to cuddle to exonerate her from the duty. Whenever she came back from a trip she would spend a day with him but not much more. But the two parents kept in contact and whenever she was not working Nicolas would shuffle over from his father's home in St-Tropez to La Madrague to swim in his mother's pool. Otherwise he lived with his father and stepmother, the daughter of a wealthy banking family, who seems to have enjoyed his company. It can't have been an easy life for the boy, for he lost this stepmother too when his father divorced for the second time. This time he was sent to live in a house outside Paris with Jacques' sister who had several children of her own. His mother kept the exact address a secret to make certain he wasn't pestered to give interviews. He was a shy boy, who constitutionally favoured the Charriers, and as a result Brigitte was careful not to expose him to too much of the publicized madness surrounding her activities. He was sent to an expensive private school where there would be no pressures on him. She was quite determined that he wouldn't go into showbusiness and she told people he wanted to go to university and had set his heart on becoming a lawyer.

As he grew older she might have exploited him as an escort but she did not. Onlookers said she did not like him enough, that he reminded her of his father and painful episodes in their married life together. But she never ostracized Nicolas from her circle. He had in fact decided on a musical career and she was well able to give him some helpful introductions including one to Eddy Barclay. Recently when he needed a job because he was planning to marry a young Norwegian blonde who looked very much like the teenage Brigitte, she invited him to work as music coordinator on the film of her life made for French television. 'Now our relationship is different,' she says, 'He knows how to get by in the world and I can rely on him if necessary, because after all he is my only living relative apart from my sister. And if necessary he can even rely on me.'

In truth he always could. Right at the outset Brigitte bought a country estate just outside Paris and not very far from her grandmother's house in Louveciennes where he would be within visiting distance of the entire family yet was hidden by a moat of farmland enclosed by a twelve-foot wall from the prying eyes of photographers, or the curious public, or worse as it turned out. When the boy was only a year old the Organisation de l'Armée Secrète (OAS), who were carrying on a blackmail campaign against French celebrities to further their Algerian ambitions, threatened to kidnap him. In those disturbed days of the early 1960s, when tempers were running high over the death of the French colonial empire, it was by no means an idle threat. At least one similar blackmail victim was injured by an OAS *bombe plastique* at the time. And always in the mind of any superstar is the horrible kidnap of the Lindbergh baby. The French were especially aware of that because Lindbergh had landed *The Spirit of St Louis* in France. Bardot did as any other French citizen and mother would do and appealed for police protection when she received this letter, but unlike any other *citoyenne* she didn't get it. The French police believed it was a publicity stunt and her plea fell on deaf ears. At this point she showed herself quite resourceful enough to play both mother tiger and police chief if need be and hired her own armed guards to take young Nicolas and his nurse out of harm's way to Switzerland.

What was really courageous about the incident was her insistence on sending the letter demanding 50,000 francs to her friend, Jean-Jacques Servan-Schreiber, at the magazine *L'Express*, a move which had been strictly forbidden by the blackmailers. Bardot has always tried to achieve her aims by the most direct methods. The magazine published the letter, a xeroxed sheet headed with Brigitte's name and address and signed by one J. Lenoir, head of financial services, on behalf of Général Raoul Salan, commander-in-chief of the OAS. She gave him his answer in public: 'I won't pay a centime because I have no wish to live in a Nazi country.' The public, including presumably the boys at the *préfecture*, said that she always had been careful with her money. De Gaulle himself, however, was much impressed and said, 'This young woman seems to have sterling qualities.'

Having failed to corral Trintignant back into her orbit after Nicolas's birth – the actor was recovering from a leg broken in a skiing accident which would not mend in time for the producer – she now embarked on a series of tests with a staggering line-up of male pulchritude to find another co-star. This was certainly not what the public expected from a brand-new mother. Opening their papers in the morning, they found her cradled by some of the most erotic biceps in France. One after another they were summoned to the studios by Clouzot to audition with her beneath the covers of an enormous four-poster bed, starting with Jean-Paul Belmondo and Laurent Terzieff who had been with her husband in the film *Les Tricheurs*. Whatever frail sanity Charrier had regained with fatherhood now went out of the window. Like many husbands would, he became wildly jealous and when it was announced that her new leading man would be Sami Frey, Clouzot had to dissuade Charrier from haunting the studio. Brigitte's professional life had to take precedence over her husband's feelings. 'He is such a problem,' she grieved. 'He is so jealous, especially about my love scenes, and all Henri Clouzot wants is to make them more and more real.' Clouzot found her easy to direct. 'She loves to excite men,' he explained – during the tests she had been unflagging. 'However exhausted, she would resume whenever a new potential partner was produced.'

Jealousy had been just what she had asked of Vadim, now she could not bear it in Charrier, who showed his insecurity by punctuating Brigitte's mannish behaviour with grand attempts at self-destruction. Convinced her love scenes were too authentic, he first tried to hang himself and then slashed his wrists and was confined once more to the clinic. Meanwhile Vera Clouzot was confined to another clinic, convinced apparently that her middle-aged husband had also succumbed to the charms of his star. But she was ill and she was to die that year aged only thirty-nine. Vera, with her Portuguese blood, had always had the reputation of being a difficult wife and Clouzot was delighted when she was gainfully occupied on one of his films. 'She was funny, unbearable, generous, crazy, unhappy, and capable of making others unhappy,' says Simone Signoret, who worked with her on *Les Diaboliques*, and these not unnaturally included her husband's leading actresses. Now her illness put an extra strain on Clouzot, who was himself a difficult husband. A Clouzot film was a drama in itself and everyone both on- and off-set felt constrained to push it to its most illogical conclusions, particularly Clouzot who wrote his own scripts. Where Brigitte was concerned he teased the whole thing along. 'I am only interested in her for aesthetic reasons,' he said. 'I am a pipe-smoking old man.' If it had not seemed so tragic to the principals, it would have been the stuff of high comedy.

Meanwhile the young men kept coming – all of them had the generous American-style lips, the tousled dark hair, the informal, boyish manner which Bardot liked best. There was Gérard Blain, Charles Belmont, Jean-Pierre Cassel, Marc Michel, Jean-Marc Bory, Hugues Aufrey. The winner, Frey, who is now the companion of Delphine Seyrig, was engaged to be married to Pascale Audret at the time. She was the actress who had been starring with Charrier on-stage when Bardot spotted him and married him. Even though the auditioning was over, such coincidences just seemed to add to his feelings of jealousy and hurt. He stuck close to Brigitte throughout the filming, driving her to the studio every morning and waiting for her to finish shooting in the canteen if necessary if Clouzot wouldn't have him on the set. He had no work of his own to take his mind off whatever Brigitte was doing or to provide him with the dignity of an independent income. 'He has to come to me for the money if he wants to buy a packet of cigarettes,' his father observed bitterly and spoke for the whole nation when he maintained that no woman had the right to undermine a man in the way his daughter-in-law was doing.

Pascale Audret, who thought she spotted the signs of infatuation in Sami Frey, claimed Bardot had literally bewitched her fiancé. Brigitte added fuel to the flame by insisting she was 'just a woman with two eyes, two ears, a nose and a mouth. I have feelings and thoughts and I am a wife and a mother above all else.' They were sure she was protesting too much. All this was far too rich for the now bearded and haggard Charrier who was still in hospital.

The truth was that no one knew the truth, and that included Bardot who had not given up on her marriage nearly as abruptly as the public assumed. It was as involved a piece of fiction as ever delights those people who love the film business. The more brilliant the director, the more tricky the games that are played to explore the similarities between the real and the supposed world. You have to have strong nerves to enjoy it and neither Brigitte or Jacques were feeling particularly strong at the time. She seemed to be fighting for her life on all fronts both as Brigitte Bardot and as Dominique Marceau, the anti-heroine in the film who finally ends up committing suicide.

As Brigitte first and foremost, no matter how fit she appeared, there was the physical and psychological drain of new motherhood. There was the challenge to her as breadwinner and, in the circumstances of her invalid husband, virtual single parent. On the set she was hiding from her husband, at home she was hiding from the public. She dared not open the curtains let alone the windows because of the photographers on the roof opposite. There was the rift with her in-laws and the deep gulf that fame had hollowed out between her and her own very ordinary family. How to sustain on her own the position she had created as first lady of France became the burning question. During her pregnancy she had spotted for the first time with the aid of her advisors the law as the single woman's friend. She had tried to copyright her reputation because she saw she could not build on it for ever. With Nicolas hungry in the cradle she started to explore this position further, launching a law-suit against the bottlers of table water for their advertising campaign *Bébé aime Perrier?*, which she claimed cast doubt on the solidity of her marriage. And in July she had an adversary in the shape of Allain Carré who, peeved perhaps at her marriage, had sold his account of life with Brigitte to a national magazine.

Carré used to arrive at the avenue Paul Doumer at nine o'clock in the morning to do the mail while she was at the studios. But one day in June 1960 she was at home waiting for him. The Sunday newspapers were full of completely accurate accounts of Brigitte's fiery relationships with one young man after another. Worse than that, he went into intimate detail about her penny-pinching, which he described as legendary. Carré subsequently tried to defend himself by saying he had not really been malicious, merely stupid. He had been strung along by the reporter who had wheedled things out of him which he hadn't meant to say and which sounded much worse in print. Brigitte was implacable. Other people in her entourage were always getting offers from the newspapers – her make-up woman, Odette Beroyer, says she was offered 50 million francs to betray her – Carré had accepted the money. Brigitte didn't even ask him why. She just asked him *whether*. 'I took the keys from his hand, kicked him up the backside and slammed the door in his face.' Allain went skidding across the landing and practically fell over the banisters. 'Afterwards I wondered what I had done. I was completely dependent on Allain. He was my whole life, my family, he was a nurse for Nicolas, and for me when I was ill, he cooked for me, he did the housework, the washing-up and the mail, he drove my car and held my hand when I was depressed. He took me to restaurants when I felt like going out. I couldn't do a thing about what he had written because it was true.'

In her work there was the challenge of making a film with a director who had an artistic reputation way above her own, coupled with the inevitable attachment she would develop for him as mentor and friend. For a virtually untutored girl, who allowed herself, however, to be tutored by men, Henri Clouzot was a fascinating proposition. Even in middle-age he devoured life. He had the knack of being able to read a book about some skill it would take others a lifetime to learn and then to take a crack at it himself with all the flair of a teenager. He learned to play cards that way, to read a score, to paint and to bullfight, which he tried out in Spain *chez* Luis Dominguin. At forty-five he decided to learn to swim in the pool at the Eden Roc Hôtel in the South of France. A week later he was in the Mediterranean, which creams around jagged rocks at this point, swimming underwater with an aqualung. The temporary passions of the film set, which may or may not find carnal expression, are one of the tools of the job, but it is hard for anyone on the outside to understand this. Clouzot, with his lust for life, drove Bardot to the limits of her physical endurance, trying to make an actress out of her to enhance his film. In the end he was perhaps justified by earning Brigitte some of the best notices of her career and an Oscar at least in Brazil where they had already dedicated a rumba to her. But what a vulnerable position she had to put herself in to achieve a couple of nice words in print, picked out in detail in the spotlight and torn to analytical shreds. At the time she thought Clouzot was a devil, 'diabolic, destructive, negative, bizarre, yet brimming with talent'. If he wanted to heighten an actress's performance he would resort to physical violence. One day, when he slapped her across the face, she hit him back. But in Clouzot the Devil's work had truly met her match.

If tranquillizers were necessary in the circumstances she resorted to them and she was by no means the first to do so. In Los Angeles her one-time idol Marilyn Monroe had just two years to live. At night, with her head racing with conflicting notions, she didn't go to bed but instead went out on the town. One Saturday night in September she was out with Sami Frey when they were challenged in a Left Bank night-club called La Rhumerie by Jacques Charrier, whose jealous scenes were becoming the only reliable thing about him. Charrier hit Frey and Frey hit Charrier. Brigitte screamed and the photographers pounced. Only afterwards did anyone ask themselves if the whole thing hadn't been staged by the manipulative producer Raoul Levy, who was for ever fanning the flames by saying how hysterical Bardot was, how sick or beside herself, as if to prove she was indeed a film star. It didn't take much for Bardot to believe this piece of publicity too. 'I must chase away from my hall the intruder who has the name of BB,' she exclaimed on television in a fit of almost religious fervour as if she really was possessed. 'I want to say: BB is no more. Long live Brigitte! My soul is not my own any more, I cannot live like I want to. I am going to give up films!' She cancelled one in which she was due to appear with her husband and flew to the South of France, which had always offered her sanity.

Considering the misunderstandings between herself and the father of her child it is not surprising she did not go home to La Madrague where he could find her. By going to stay with her friends the racing driver Jean-Claude Simon and his wife Mercedes who had been Sophia Loren's secretary, she also hoped to avoid the Press. Charrier himself, meanwhile, was trying to soothe his nerves on a motoring holiday on the Basque coast. Little Nicolas was in Bazoches at the farm near Paris.

The Simons had a little village house near Monte Carlo at Cabrolle. Christine Gouze-Renal, who visited Brigitte there, knew instinctively that she would find it depressing before long. It was way off the beaten track at the end of a dark ravine but for the time being it was exactly what she thought she wanted. Wrapped in the gentle embrace of the Riviera, the sea in front of her, the Alps behind, Brigitte tried to relax. Even the Simons' maid was not told her identity so that she would be left in peace. She would have to have been blind, deaf, and dumb not to have recognized her, but for a while she kept up the pretence.

It was mid-September in the Alpes-Maritimes when the place is preparing to shut up for the winter and only the real residents are left behind. The sun gets up slowly at this time of year and the nights are chill but the days are golden, made for walking, which is still one of Brigitte's favourite sports. On her walks she contemplated her twenty-sixth birthday which was looming up at the end of the month. Birthdays have always been milestones for Brigitte, more than for most people.

Brigitte had more or less successfully prolonged the illusion of her teens by giving herself over to the passions that a girl feels more strongly than ever in her early twenties. But motherhood at twenty-five had brought an abrupt awareness of mortality.

Twenty-five is the end of official youth. Brigitte had lived for a quarter of a century, more than a third of an average lifespan. It is certainly time for looking forward but it is also already a time for looking back. As Brigitte did her accounts that autumn she was not too sure about the way things were balancing out. 'Fame has brought me so much unhappiness,' she wailed. 'If only every man who sees my films did not get the impression he can make love to me, I would be a lot happier.' The truth of the matter was that she had forged no alliances to sustain her. She was all alone. Her family could not help her in the sophisticated circles she had chosen and she had split with the man who could have because he had seemed to have a heart of stone. Brigitte thrashed around wildly, looking for someone to blame for her isolation. Charrier had proved himself sentimental to the point of nonsense, yet she had started out with such high hopes of him. 'I am sure he had a fantastic career ahead of him which I quite simply ruined by being me,' she says. 'We had to go through too much in too short a time and we had no track record as a couple to deal with it. Anyway there was nothing concrete to deal with because everything was distorted by the Press.' She wondered whether Sami Frey would prove a more durable lover under the same circumstances. She even wondered about Clouzot. 'I am tired and worn out, I cannot make up my mind about anything.' That day outside the villa she saw the photographers.

They were there again at the birthday lunch she celebrated with Henri Clouzot at the Colombe d'Or. All the same she was very gay during the meal. Being at the lovely old timbered hotel run by the Roux family who were used to the behaviour of film stars – Yves Montand has virtually lived there most of his professional life – was like being among her own family. After all they had been through together on behalf of the film she had grown fond of Clouzot. It was the sort of fondness that rarely outlasts the job and it did not this time. Moreover Clouzot, who might in other circumstances have been a guiding hand in future years, was about to fall on difficult times himself after his wife's premature death, confined to a sanatorium with failing eyesight and ill-health. Suddenly Brigitte seemed to have a premonition of all this and to see in stark relief that she was completely adrift. She realized that they had only really been close when she was Dominique Marceau and that Dominique was dead. 'I have no private life any more,' she said to Henri over the dessert. 'I have no life to speak of at all. I am a hunted woman. I can't take a step without being surrounded and questioned. I am being tortured. I would so much like to be a woman just like everyone else.' She drove back to the little house where she was staying perplexed by the irony that in the most popular heights of their career the famous are often alone.

The next day she was alone again. She went for lunch as usual in a restaurant on the coast at Cap-Martin. Paul Vaille, the owner, was used to seeing her arrive in time to take a swim in the sea before eating. After the meal she would take her siesta on a lilo. Afterwards he remembered that Brigitte had been in a curious mood. 'She wasn't the same person that Wednesday. She arrived at midday as usual wearing purple jeans and a very tight white top and she sat at her usual table next to the barbecue. She seemed to have cheered up by the time she left at four o'clock and she gave me a nice smile. But at the beginning she was very preoccupied and sad. She just stared at the trout I was grilling for her. A few minutes later I plucked up my courage – I had been trying to do it for a long time – to ask her permission to take her photo. She said, "I beg you to leave me alone, monsieur. Anyway I am going to die." I am telling you, that really upset me.'

Not as much as it upset Bardot. At eight o'clock that evening she still hadn't come out of her room and Mercedes Simon realized she wasn't in the house at all. She was alerted by some neighbours, Antoine Valette and a thirteen-year-old boy, Jean-Louis Bournos, who had heard a noise near the well at the bottom of the adjoining sloping gardens. Mercedes Simon's houseguest was lying there unconscious, her wrists slashed. Later they discovered she had also taken an overdose of barbiturates. In the house they found a note in her big, round, childish handwriting. It was unpunctuated, incoherent, but the message was plain. 'I am completely fed up,' it said. 'I am desperately unhappy I am going to change things one way or another I am suffering so much I might as well have a reason to suffer See you soon B'.

Brigitte never says *au revoir* but it was nevertheless her valediction to her foolish youth.

12. Private Life

The end of the fifties was the end of the pioneer youth movement and Bardot gave her place up to its adoption by the masses. The attempted suicide certainly changed matters for her and for the rest of her world. It seemed to take the guilt away. However she lived from now on, on borrowed time, she felt justified. If she wanted to have men she would and no one who had not paid the same dues as she had would ever make her suffer for it again. As for the world, it had let her do it. So that was the sort of girl she was after all. She wasn't a virgin, fallen despite herself, her magnificent body violated by harsh life, she was nothing to shed tears over, she was simply an actress. The world seemed to give up its struggle to believe in the potential for purity, for order, for goodness, for all the things for which it had fought during the bloody war, and to settle down to a well earned period of hedonism, no holds barred. Her mistakes set everyone else free and whenever they needed a scapegoat there she was. She was fair game. She had been bad and she had survived. You didn't have to like her for it. In fact many people didn't like her at all. The whole saga was a disappointment in a way, a proof that there was no such thing as God after all, or if there was, that Bardot had not been created by Him but was indeed the Devil's work. But it was also a vindication. People could behave passionately and vulgarly without restraint, and they could get away with it. They could have everything. No other legend had got away with it. With Rudolph Valentino, with James Dean, the deaths had magnified the lies, and had done two things. They had made the stars immortal and they had proved that the wages of sin, of lust, of daring, of venality, of pride, of too much beauty, of too much of everything were indeed death. But Bardot was not immortal. She was human flesh and blood. It was all dazzling popular proof of the new philosophy of the here, the now, the tangible, the crass, the manipulative. Myth-making was history, the fucking years had begun.

Bardot was indeed flesh and blood. With her stomach pumped out she was a mess, pale, hung-over, and at death's door. Everyone converged on Nice like vultures at the bier of the sweet, vulnerable, conscience-stricken child they hoped lay inside in a private room at the St François Clinic in the town. Up in the hills at the scene of the attempt the fans ripped the blood-stained tiles from the fountain base as souvenirs. No one seemed to have any idea how to behave. The ambulancemen who were called to the scene of Brigitte's near suicide were sceptical about it. One local newspaperman was so appalled by the sight of so much blood in the garden that he felt certain she had to die. 'Nah,' said the stretcher-bearer. 'Think what a mess a pint of milk makes. She has got seven more pints.'

Mme Bardot, installed at the Hotel Negresco on the sea-front, put on her best, tragic stage-mother performance as the begetter of a national symbol. 'I am addressing you as a Mummy,' she said. 'Brigitte Bardot is public property. You have helped her and she has not forgotten it. But today it is her life that is at stake. I am asking you as a Mummy to give her some breathing space: give it to her until her next film. Give my daughter the time to heal.' Then, in a personal message to all French mothers she said: 'Don't buy newspapers which print pictures of my daughter's face on the cover. Please boycott them!'

They all blamed each other for what had happened. Mme Bardot blamed the Press, so did Henri Clouzot. The Press in turn blamed Clouzot for wringing her most splendid performance out of her by cruel, inhuman means and Bardot for staging another publicity coup. 'Film stars do not kill themselves for receiving too much publicity,' wrote Leslie Mallory in the old *News Chronicle*. Some people noted with cynicism that life had once more imitated the script, this time of *La Vérité*. Even the poor manipulated public had their suspicions and when Brigitte was recovering she found many hate letters in her mail-bag suggesting more efficient ways of killing herself. 'Next time why not jump off the Eiffel Tower,' one woman wrote. 'That way you will be sure to succeed and there will be one less slut on this earth.' Everyone blamed the rat-race, the pressure that showbusiness was now under with increasing expenses and huge, hungry audiences to distort actresses' psyches by pushing them further and further out on a limb of dissolution. It all went to feed the new movement in which performers would feel justified in openly taking what they wanted from the advantages of the profession and would forego the pressures of glamour to behave as they wished.

The memory of that time still lingers with Brigitte when she is feeling lonely and perplexed. No matter who you are, what you have done, or what people imagine you have done, it is not easy to read spiteful letters or to understand that other people, who normally have to be jolted out of apathy, genuinely wish you ill. Brigitte still remembers a particularly ugly incident which occurred when she was in a lift at the rue Nicolo clinic in Paris going to the fourth floor to visit her stand-in who had been operated on for appendicitis. An orderly, a middle-aged married woman, stepped in with a tray for another patient. As they rode upwards together, with no means of escape, the woman tried to stab her with a fork. The woman was irrational, hysterical. Her boy had been killed fighting for France, she screamed. She was a patriot while Brigitte was undermining the moral fibre of the country. She was going to kill her on behalf of all the women in France who had ever lost their husbands to younger, more beautiful, more brazen, more hopeful mistresses. On second thoughts death was too good for her, she would deface her with the fork, she would draw its prongs through the vulnerable flesh of Brigitte's cheek and when her corrupting beauty was in shreds France would be saved. Such a small rearrangement of her features would make such a difference to the world. She knew those features not because she knew the actress's films, she wouldn't debase herself by going to them, but you could not avoid the face on the front of magazines. The lift, one of those stately old nineteenth-century vehicles, progressed extremely slowly towards its destination. The woman, who had worked herself into a frenzy with her own words, lifted her arm and wielded the fork like a stiletto. Brigitte raised her elbow to defend herself and the fork stuck in her sleeve. The grandiose gesture foundered once again in farce. The experience was, however, so powerful that the scene was included in Louis Malle's biographical film about Brigitte the following year, *Vie Privée*.

Brigitte claims that she has never knowingly taken another woman's man. Pascale Audret, for one, dreaming that summer of 1960 of her wedding with Sami Frey which would now never take place, didn't agree with her as he rushed to Brigitte's side. If this sort of morals were to be let loose on the world and openly condoned no one would ever feel safe again about forging lasting contracts in their private lives. This, of course, is what happened very soon. If Bardot had died, as she still says she sincerely wished she had, these things might have been resisted. She says she felt even more of a failure for failing her suicide. 'I planned it extremely carefully. It should have happened. I don't want to go into it in detail but I was supposed to die and if I didn't it was only because of a combination of miracles.' To die or not to die was of international importance. She could have died to save all our reputations as well as her own. She lived.

Only three days later, reincarnated with some new meaning for the world, she left the St François Clinic in Nice on the arm of Francis Cosne, who had been one of the visitors to her bedside. She was still deathly pale, wearing a headscarf, sunglasses, a long pullover à la Juliette Greco, tight spotted pants, and flesh-coloured dressings on her wrists, but she was also carrying a red rose like an article of faith in the future. Cosne was to be the producer of her next picture. He and Vadim had driven straight to her bedside when they heard her life was in the balance. Bardot was bankable and Cosne was extremely worried about his investment.

It is important to realize, if you are tempted to adopt a cynical attitude to this whole scenario and comment, quite rightly, that this sort of thing is not a proper measure of genuine feelings in Surbiton, Iowa, or indeed Aix-en-Provence, that people in the entertainment business have amazing powers of recuperation.

Whether the situation was really a matter of life or death has no importance because it seemed at the time to all concerned to be important. Plea for help or whatever, through it Bardot changed her life, just as she had said in the note she would. I have got to die sometime so why not now, she reasoned, and one part of her did die, the guilt-ridden little girl who was straddling two cultures.

Brigitte, her mother and father and a carload of toy animals made it back to La Madrague in early October, escorted by a police motorcade. In the company of her family and friends, who included Mercedes Simon and Vadim, she nursed herself back to health. Charrier was out of her life for good. The army made an attempt to recall him to Algiers, having first ordered that all pin-ups of Brigitte be taken down in the barracks. He was plainly not suited for the military life, however, and after another spell in a psychiatric hospital they discharged him for good to resume an adequate film career. Whenever he has been asked about his marriage to Brigitte he has been extremely gallant. He has said he would do it all over again even though it was a mistake at the time. He has always praised her beauty and her talent, refused to acknowledge that she was the Pygmalion of Vadim and, like Vadim before him, said that she was quite good enough to make it on her own without being moulded by any man.

With both Vadim and Brigitte now free and in St-Tropez together, some people even thought they might get married again. 'He is my best friend,' Brigitte kept reiterating, 'I owe everything to him.' But marriage was where it had all gone wrong – twice – and it was very far from her mind. She was going to do away with any concept of duty from now on, apart from the duty to enjoy herself. She began to install a series of pliant lovers in La Madrague, starting with Jicky Dussart who would be her personal photographer and friend long after their affair ended and who bequeathed her a semi-permanent guardian in the form of his Alsatian puppy.

As autumn turned to winter, Brigitte turned again to Sami Frey. They cuddled, kissed, shopped and walked around St-Tropez but it was a very subdued little community which watched rather than ogled Brigitte's return to health. For decency's sake some of them speculated that she was planning to convert to Judaism to marry Sami but Brigitte did not need to change her religion to come to terms with herself. She had and still has a general, not a specific faith. She did not think, even at the worst times, that all was wrong with the universe, only with her part of it. She never thought God would blame her for being free and feeling good, that was the attitude of hypocritical society, and she has never given up the idea that she will have to account to Him for everything she has done, if only on the principle of the philosopher Pascal that you have nothing to lose by believing in God.

In St-Tropez, out of season, the evidence of His favour is overwhelming. Under the clear skies, nourished by good food and cheap, robust wine she took stock of her situation and realized that when she did as she wanted and not what other people had in mind for her she was much better off. She decided to invest her money instead of spending it so she could be in control of her career and she bought several properties including the chalet Le Chouan at Meribel. A Bank of France director who met her in this mood said he was astounded by the interest she took in the stock market.

She decided too that if she was going to go back into the film business to pay for the leisure she enjoyed, it would be on her terms. She would set the seal on her sanity. In fact she would take a hand in the production of the light comedy *La Bride sur le Cou*, which she started shooting in January the next year.

She knew the director, Jean Aurel, already from *Une Parisienne* earlier in her career, which he had co-written, but within a week of the start of shooting she had asked him to leave the set. Vadim replaced him. Aurel had his supporters, who included François Truffaut who had graduated by this time from chief French film fan in the pages of the intellectual review *Cahiers du Cinéma*, to one of the much acclaimed 'new wave' directors. While Brigitte was making *Babette*, he had been making *The Four Hundred Blows*, choosing as his little star Jean-Pierre Léaud, the child in the Cocteau film of the same year *Testament d'Orphée* in which Brigitte made a brief appearance along with a dazzling array of names including Cocteau himself, Picasso, Dominguin, and Françoise Sagan.

Neither Truffaut's budding reputation nor their myriad connections were to any avail. Aurel was fired and it very much looked as though Vadim and Brigitte had engineered this, their professional rematch, during the long winter evenings by the open fire at La Madrague. For Brigitte it was the gentlest way of returning to the screen, working with the person she knew best of all. The scant, frothy plot could not have been further removed from the tortuous story of *La Verité*. Vadim virtually threw the script away and coaxed the sort of impromptu performance they both understood from the old days. To make things even easier for her he called the character she played – a model who resorts to amazing deceits to attract the man she loves – by his old pet-name for her, Sophie. He also created a dance sequence to boost her self-confidence. It was a little personal tribute to their past, modelled on the slapstick American comedies the French love and for which Louis Bardot had a particular passion. Though it was never a great success, Vadim felt he was breaking new ground for French audiences by attempting a home-grown version of one of their favourite genres. The English-speaking critics unanimously hated it, using inappropriately vicious words – contemptible, clumsy, prurient, appalling, processed, odourless, sexless – for something which had a place they didn't comprehend in the affections of a much more naïve French cinema-going public.

To the English and the Americans and indeed the Germans and the Japanese the whole point of Bardot was sex. Vadim did plan to tease this audience along by allowing them, as he had so often done in the past, to believe they were seeing her completely in the nude in one scene – in fact she was wearing a bodystocking – but in the end the scene was removed by the English censor. The story, the character, and the treatment were all very familiar stuff, even down to the censor's cut. But with that cut something new happened as well. Brigitte, who naturally objected to it, just as she had always objected to any interference with her intentions, started to talk about a new morality which was the invention of the times. Instead of the revelation of the body being beautiful yet provocative and heathen, she now proclaimed it as the only evidence of sanity and railed against censorship as dangerous. 'It is not a good thing to ban anything,' she said. 'It just encourages curiosity and increases temptation. You don't stop children from smoking by banning it – they just react by smoking in secret. It is much better to discourage them. Offer them a cigar or a pipe and they won't want to go on smoking after the first puff. It's the same with the cinema. I have never taken drugs, but if I had been tempted to do so, just seeing a film about drug addiction would have cured me of it.'

All this preoccupation with children and morality had one source – much as she had tried to deny it, Brigitte was a mother now. When she got back to St-Tropez after the film she brought the builders into La Madrague and extended the house to make plenty of room for little Nicolas when he came to visit. As a mother she began for the first time to understand her own parents and their concerns for her, which had looked so unreasonable in the past. As she watched her father spoonfeeding his grandson, who was quickly nicknamed after him and called Petit-Pilou, her heart went out to both of them. And Pilou, who had only been waiting for an expression of her affection and forgiveness, redoubled his attentions to her. He looked so awkward, a frail man with wire-rimmed glasses getting on for seventy, escorting a beautiful blonde in the mini-skirted uniform of the sixties, but he was very proud of her. He even brought out a book of sentimental poems for her, which left her in little doubt as to who was the talented one in the family but touched her all the same. Pilou evidently saw her as Marie-Antoinette, an Arcadian shepherdess at heart, high handed just because she was so special, never evil, just naïve:

179

Dear little shepherdess,
Why do you carry on like this?
Baby, husband, lover will not do,
You crave some other kiss.
Next kiss will be for keeps
That's what you say,
Yet still you run around the town
Just having your own way.

The idea of the shepherdess came from Bazoches, which was an eighteenth-century sheepfold converted into a farm. Watching her in the long flowery print frocks she favoured, her hair blowing free, barefoot on the lawn, running down to the little boating lake, planting extravagant kisses on the noses of lambs and kids – and keeping a healthy distance from her own offspring – she must indeed have seemed like the unfortunate queen who had played her own rustic games just a few miles away at Versailles only to be guillotined by the masses. Brigitte had survived her games, but only just. Pilou obviously knew her well but this was all much gentler stuff than in the past, tinged with wry affection and humour and fully reciprocated by her. The year 1961 rolled away in an aura of mutual pleasure. For the first time she and Mme Bardot could enjoy doing the simple, domestic things together that Anne-Marie had envisaged when she first knew she had a daughter. Brigitte and she were in and out of each other's houses. 'You should see her when she visits us. She kisses everybody including the maids and dogs. She always has some funny story to tell us and acts it out until she has us all in stitches.' She could be like a bomb on a short fuse, her mother acknowledged, but her temper tantrums were over almost as soon as they had begun. 'She is not really temperamental,' Anne-Marie said, 'that's all false. At heart she is still the little *bourgeoise* she always was.'

The first question she would ask was usually a domestic one. 'Mama, have you got the pink sheets back from the laundry yet?'

'Really, Brigitte,' her mother would jibe, 'Haven't you got anything else on your mind but sheets?'

She was even getting on quite well with her younger sister Mijanou, who had given up the cinema in disgust when only twenty-one. None of this had stopped Mijanou wanting to marry an actor, Patrick Bauchan, whose ambition was to be a director like Vadim. He had often thought of trying to make history repeat itself by moulding Mijanou into a second Bardot. As a young girl it had seemed inevitable that she should make a couple of films. Directors pursued the name. Brigitte made the introductions and Mijanou was cast first in *Club des Femmes* as co-star of a white pussy cat called Felix, which she inherited after the production, and then in *Jusqu'au Dernier* (*Up Till Now*). The film was about a travelling gypsy circus and Mijanou, who was a very good little horsewoman, played the part of the bareback rider. Unlike Brigitte she had also taken up the offer of going to Hollywood to play in a film called *Sexpot Goes to College* and she had come back full of warnings that Brigitte had already predicted. 'In America they all wanted to make me into a sexy actress as if it was the only possible thing for a girl with my surname to be.' She hated the experience and preferred to forget her films which she called her mistakes. If people remarked on the fact that with such a dislike for the profession it was surprising she should choose an actor for a bridegroom, she would simply burst out laughing. 'Patrick – I met him through some friends who have nothing at all to do with the cinema. His career was a complete piece of chance. Have you ever heard of a good marriage growing in front of the cameras?' Mijanou could corroborate everything Brigitte had to say about the unsavoury nature of the film business.

Everyone seemed inclined to give Brigitte the benefit of the doubt and that released her more than anything from her prison – off-screen. Mijanou would even ask her to become the godmother of her little daughter, Camille, who was a couple of years younger than Nicolas, and Brigitte would accept. The two children would spend their holidays together with their maternal grandmother. When they were in St-Tropez in the summer they would both come over from Anne-Marie's house to visit Brigitte. Everything was in place to prove to her that the concepts of family, duty, private happiness, and responsibility were not beyond her after all. Now all she had to do was to reconcile them with her work.

One of the ways she saw of doing this was to go back to her first love, music and movement. She had already released one record after *And God Created Woman* in which she narrated the story of the film and introduced the soundtrack. (It was while she was making this with Ray Ventura's band that she had run across his nephew Sacha Distel.) She would also release the song 'Sidonie' from *Vie Privée*, two or three songs from her later films *Viva Maria* and *Boulevard du Rhum*, and 'To Each His Man' from *Les*

Novices. She now decided she could have an independent musical career. Coached by the pianist and music-hall artist Claude Bolling she did find a style which echoed the light-hearted charm of her very first film performances. In this vein she recorded such songs as 'La Madrague', a tribute to the sunshine life on the Riviera, Peter Skellern's 'You're A Lady', perennials like 'It's A Bossa Nova' and 'Everybody Loves My Baby', and four songs whose titles illustrate the themes of her life: 'Mister Sun', 'Nude In The Sunshine', 'The End of Summer', and 'I Dance Therefore I Am'. It was a style which did not tax either her or her audiences, which was all her own and, like all her public persona, was innovative and even prophetic. Her exotic costumes and the narrative treatment of songs like 'Bonnie And Clyde' on television with Serge Gainsbourg seem very like today's video music, which, not entirely by coincidence perhaps, is about to stage its own annual festival in St-Tropez starting in 1985. Brigitte enjoyed making this sort of music so much that she would stay up all night if necessary after filming all day. Her annual New Year's Eve cabaret slot became as popular with French television audiences in its time as de Gaulle's annual pep talk to the nation on the same day. 'Like ripe pheasant and the youngest Beaujolais' was how the *Evening Standard*'s Sam White would describe the double act in 1967. Brigitte was of course still the Beaujolais. 'Having seen Bardot's performance privately screened, there is no danger of French TV viewers sharing the British disappointment with the Beatles,' wrote Sam.

> This is the best of the four or five New Year's Eve shows she has so far given. This time she has chosen as partner the singer Serge Gainsbourg, whose sad, unconventional looks act as a perfect foil to her own sexy, kittenish image. She is naked or half naked a good deal of the time, first as a kind of modern motorbike-riding Lady Godiva, then she is transformed into a fur-clad panther of a woman. Then again she is Salome, dressed in diamonds and then a kind of Superwoman with long straight brown hair, pink tights and a heavy chain around her hips.

Other incarnations included a hussar in front of Buckingham Palace, singing like Maurice Chevalier without any initial aitches, a nymphet lamenting the lost summer in St-Tropez and Brigitte as herself inside La Madrague, 'an interior of great charm and simplicity'. Sam White concluded:

> One of her best songs is titled 'I Feel Strange Desires Creeping Up The Back Of My Kidneys'. It is done with enormous charm and talent. In fact one recognises Brigitte's talent as an actress much more vividly in these sketches than one does in any of her films. It makes one regret that she has never had a film role worthy of really testing her.

In the film studios Brigitte remained busy. First she made the Agnes Bernauer segment in the new Boisrond film *Les Amours Célèbres*. It was based on a very popular French comic strip and united the two top box-office draws, Alain Delon and Brigitte Bardot, rather to the latter's advantage. In still photographs the couple looked stunning but rumours quickly circulated that the chemistry just didn't work on-screen. At the Billancourt Studios in Paris wrestlers were employed as bodyguards to keep newsmen at bay, but, mysteriously there were none. It was not just that they had all taken the lesson of the near suicide to heart and did not want to ruffle the star. A much more mysterious exchange was happening between fact and fiction. Brigitte at peace with herself could not engender the same sparks or carve for herself the same devotion, especially at a time when the public was taking the lesson to heart that anyone, however banal, middle-class, malproportioned, or unhappy could make themselves into a star if they did not mind the consequences. None the less the French liked Agnes Bernauer but not the English-speaking market, which had never been able to see Brigitte, the epitome of the modern girl, in historical roles.

They saw the point of Louis Malle's *Vie Privée*, but they didn't much like that either, perhaps because the idea was based on one of England's own pet properties, the original *Private Lives* by Noël Coward. The idea of casting Brigitte Bardot in old-fashioned comedy in the Gertrude Lawrence role came originally from her friend Christine Gouze-Renal. Ostensibly the two actresses could not have been more different. The thin, beaky Gertrude was not much to look at in close-up, yet her acknowledged talent for stage comedy was such that the lights of the West End were dimmed when she died in 1952. Bardot says she would never dare return to the stage, but we have Anouilh's testimony that she could if she wished, moreover Louis Malle tells me he has always had the greatest respect for Bardot as a light comedienne.

In the event she was required to be more of a tragedienne. *Vie Privée*, a piece of faction which reflected the timely preoccupation with the thin dividing line between art and reality, is about the perils of being Brigitte. Malle, just two years older than Brigitte, had graduated from being Jacques Cousteau's underwater camera-man to one of the most acclaimed of the 'new wave' directors. He had had great success with *The Lovers* and *Zazie dans le Métro* and he wrote the script for *Vie Privée* as well as directing it. (His assistant director was the young Volker Schloendorff.) This film again, however, was doomed to failure, possibly because it unwittingly brought out the farcical side of her life rather than the tragic. The public, who had hounded her nearly to death, simply could not sympathize with the undignified demise of the character in the picture, who accidentally falls off a roof, albeit because of hounding similar to that Brigitte had experienced.

Malle himself always said that the ending was the best thing about the film. He thought the French didn't like it because everyone in France had their own picture of what Brigitte was really like and they were waiting to see it confirmed on screen. He couldn't please them all. 'It might have been more interesting to make a film strictly on Bardot herself,' he said, 'but that would have required someone other than her in the part.'

Abroad the film was released just after the death of Monroe and this irony was not wasted on audiences, who were stinging with guilt about her end. Again the public wagged the finger at the media, accusing them of the murder this time of the little girl who had never got on their wrong side. Marilyn was just dazzlingly dotty to her public, an innocent at large, however much she alienated other actors such as Laurence Olivier. Bardot, whose performance in *And God Created Woman* was based on Monroe's early life, now seemed to have based a further film on her death. It could hardly have been good enough in the circumstances whatev-er it was like and Bosley Crowther in the *New York Times* probably understood this when he wrote: 'The unspoken irony of this picture is that an actress who is so poor at her job should be the representation of the bitterness of fame in such a film.'

The frisson Brigitte used to create was just not working. Leading men were now quite easy to cast, as if they sensed they had nothing to fear from her. They were bound to out-act her and this was a problem in itself. Marcello Mastroianni, her co-star in *Vie Privée*, was completely uninterested in her, both on and off the set. 'They were supposed to be lovers but they wouldn't speak to each other,' Malle despaired. The last thing Mastroianni would admit to feeling was threatened. With blustering Italian humour he said, 'Can you really see me telephoning Fellini and saying, "Papa I can't make a go of it, I've bumped into a girl with a bust!" ' To anyone who had ever seen the maestro's preoccupation with ladies of grotesque dimensions this was a particularly intelligent thing to say. In the future Mastroianni was to prove that he did like some French girls very much – he spent a long time with Catherine Deneuve – but with this particular French girl he seemed to be able to put an infallible finger on the problem, which no one else had quite identified. First he saw that it needed a peculiarly frustrated type of man to fall in love with her. The man had to be unconfident through youth or age, poverty or disorientation and inclined to be macho, which was superficially attractive to her, out of weakness rather than strength. He had to see her – the challenge which no one else could quite take on and remain sane – with the tenderness of the gigolo. He had to see the vulnerability of strong women. He had to be given to gambling rather than hard slog, to imagine that the magic of stardom would somehow rub off on his member in the act of possessing her. He had in short to be a maelstrom of contradictions, which he had hitherto been unable to resolve in order to liberate himself as a traditional male. Mastroianni said he was very sorry for the schizophrenic actress whose two personalities terrorized each other. He was also sorry that he had ever made the film. He didn't go to the première and he didn't want to be associated with the publicity. He went further and said he never intended to make another film outside Italy. As for BB? What did he think of her? She was simply pleasant. It was a very anodyne description.

Mastroianni spotted what was wrong in 1961, that, unfair as it might be, the stable private life dulled the image on-screen. As one of the weathercocks of the century, Bardot had been buffeted nearly to death. That was her Faustian contract. The deal was that in return she had her beauty, her wealth, and her pleasures, and at the very least an interested public. Now she had reformed, becoming a regular old victim like the rest of her gender, a veritable Gretchen, a mere pawn in someone else's contract.

Not unnaturally Bardot hated the position she found herself in and started to talk about retirement. She had made twenty-six films in ten years, she had her nest-egg and she had quite enough to do, she said, without being the butt of the critics' venom. 'I'm the man of the house. I have to do everything myself. I look after the child, the cooking, the housekeeping, I pay the taxes, I still have to look good and do my job. I don't care a jot what other people think about me. Those who like me will go on doing so and those who don't, too bad. I have always been the same person at heart, I have no principles in life and I am open about it. *Vie Privée* should have been a good film but I don't think it will be a turning-point in my career. I've seen enough turning-points anyway – *Ring Round The Moon, And God Created Woman, In Case of Adversity, La Verité* – I'd like a turning-point in real life, which has become absolutely impossible. There is too big a gap between what I am and what people think I am.'

Still she agreed to make one more film with Francis Cosne and Vadim, *Warrior's Rest*, in recognition of the first aid they had rendered after her suicide attempt. For Vadim it was second best. For a long time now he had wanted to make a modern production of the Marquis de Sade's *Le Vice et la Virtu*. He saw Brigitte once more as Juliette, vice rewarded, and had opened the bidding three or four years before by asking her to star opposite Annette Stroyberg as Justine or virtue punished. Annette had indeed shown that virtue has its own snags. She could not sustain the role of perfect little wife that Vadim required of her and she in turn became a parody of Brigitte, abandoning her child to its father, quite apart from adopting her predecessor's hairstyles and her profession. It all went to show something that Vadim had always suspected, that it probably didn't matter all that much how you lived your life since there would be both good and bad consequences in the sort of reverse measure you had not necessarily anticipated. In fact you could go a long way to eliminate pain by doing away with the perverse invention of the soul and listening only to the voice of nature. As de Sade's dying man says to the priest who has come to confess him, 'Renounce the idea of another world, there is not one. But do not renounce the pleasure of being happy or causing happiness in this world. That is the only way Nature has to offer you of doubling or lengthening your life.'

Stroyberg had abandoned Vadim and now he had a new Justine in mind, Catherine Deneuve. Deneuve, just like Annette, just like Brigitte for that matter, had put all her faith in a domestic relationship with Vadim. Disappointed by his vacillation between a new life with her and the old one with Annette she had quite simply organized her life for herself. She had become the mother of his son, mistress of her own very comfortable home and the most acclaimed French cinema star of her generation, the only one who is still talked about in Paris as being reliably bankable. So, whichever approach you adopted, the virtuous one or not, it seemed to Vadim the wheel would come full circle in the end, and as if to prove it here was Brigitte/Juliette telling the world she was going to become good again, that she was never going to make another film, that she was going to retire from public life and take up interior decorating. She was planning to become Juliette's good sister Justine.

In the meantime he had taught Juliette a lot about how to enjoy herself and one of the things that didn't come into that category was sharing the limelight with Vadim's other women. She had said no to Stroyberg and now she said no to Deneuve. Brigitte would not play vice to Deneuve's virtue and that was that. Instead she had another plot in mind, taken from the novel *Warrior's Rest* by Christiane Rochfort who had worked on the script of *La Verité*. Rochfort's novel was generally acclaimed to be brilliant by all except Mme de Gaulle, who declared it was so immoral she would never let the virtuous General anywhere near it. None the less it won the Prix de la Nouvelle Vague and it nearly won the Prix Femina and Prix Goncourt. And it demonstrated the exchange between good and bad, which Vadim had put on the screen in *And God Created Woman* and which he would do again next year in *Le Vice et la Virtu* – without Brigitte. Vadim, orphaned by his father, brought up by his mother and sister, three times a loser now in personal relationships, also said it demonstrated the root strength of women versus men.

In a nutshell *Warrior's Rest* told the story of a young girl with everything going for her who rescues a totally nihilistic man from suicide and matches his depravity with depravity of her own until he can bear it no longer and agrees to make the ultimate sacrifice to the bourgeoisie and marry her. The Italian critic, Ugo Astolfo, wrote about the film:

No thinking person can explain why a country like France seriously accepts Vadim, who has the culture of a platypus, the taste of a Jayne Mansfield and no talent. The film contains enough boredom to last an entire generation. How could even the most innocent viewer believe that Bardot could, as did the mousey, frigid heroine of the book, reach the age of maturity ignorant of carnal pleasure? The scenes are disconnected and silly except when Bardot appears nude. If we had to understand what it was all about from this film, we would remain ignorant for the rest of our lives.

The French, however, always inclined to intellectualize the act of love, adored the film with its scenes of bi-sexual orgies. Indeed the advertising campaign in Britain revolved around the fact that one million Frenchmen could not be wrong. For the English audience it presented problems. 'Brigitte is obliged to act with those comparatively few portions of her anatomy which are not censorable,' wrote Thomas Wiseman in the *Sunday Express*. But a lot of people still sensed that, censorship or no, the passion had gone out of Brigitte, that she had fulfilled her purpose. She had ignited men's imaginations and then dashed them by fleshing out women's desires. Having taken all her clothes off, having exposed women as throbbing, bleeding mounds of flesh, not icons at all, what was she supposed to do next? Having dispensed with God and morality you sacrificed all power to shock. That was why she clung so firmly to the idea of retirement. Jean Cau challenged her that she would be back in the running again immediately if she was offered $100,000 to make a picture – that was Marilyn's price as she went to her death. Brigitte tossed her head and said no, she had been offered $100,000 and she would rather have £50 for doing some little job which made her happy.

From January to April she retired with Sami Frey, only coming out of her seclusion to conclude her divorce – once more the grounds were serious insults between herself and Jacques Charrier. Custody of the baby was finalized in Charrier's favour. 'Brigitte's truth is her solid bourgeois virtues,' wrote the *Le Monde* critic about *Warrior's Rest*. Bourgeois stability was an utter failure on-screen.

13. Dear Brigitte

The period of stability did not last long. In 1963 at the Cannes Film Festival Bardot spotted a South American businessman named Bob Zaguri. 'My heart turned over,' she says. Zaguri was handsome enough, dark, of course – since that was what she liked, and he had the advantage of not being in the front line of the film business. Things looked bad for Sami Frey, 'the only man who could make me vibrate fully as a woman.'

As if to mark the new vibrations Brigitte had also allowed herself to become embroiled in a new contract. If she needed a new direction Jean-Luc Godard, the most avant-garde of the 'new wave' directors, badly needed some commercial credibility. He had in mind a story to be called *Le Mépris* (*Contempt*), which appealed to Brigitte's current thinking: 'A fleeting feeling of the vanity of all things,' Godard described it as. 'All that happens and is of no importance. All this is a space well defined by the *Odyssey*, the sea, the Mediterranean sun.' For those who were not on that wavelength the story, taken from the novel *Il deprezzo* by Alberto Moravia, also bore some similarity to that of Brigitte's marriage to Vadim, who with his compulsive need to interweave art and life was the forerunner of the 'new wave' writer-directors. In *Le Mépris* Paul Javal, an existentialist hack writer accepts a commission from Fritz Lang to rewrite the story of Ulysses, Penelope and her suitors in order to maintain his wife Camille and her affection for him. In fact, dogged by suspicions of her jealousy and infidelity, it is he who is losing affection for her. He decides to quit while the going is relatively good and to kill her off symbolically in a car crash. Godard's cameraman was always convinced that the director was trying to explain something to his own wife, the Danish star Anna Karina. 'It's a sort of letter costing a million dollars,' was his opinion.

Whoever's story it was Brigitte was wild with enthusiasm for this pretentious idea, which seemed to give her the intellectual credibility most actresses crave. '*C'est formidable*. I've joined the "new wave",' she cried. 'Godard was really scared, you know. Me too. We call each other Monsieur Godard and Mademoiselle Bardot.' Godard had actually wanted Frank Sinatra and Kim Novak when he first put the project together with Carlo Ponti and Joe Levine. Ponti wanted his wife, Sophia Loren, and Marcello Mastroianni. Levine for one was delighted when Brigitte's name was mentioned as long as she was willing to do an obligatory nude scene. She was, as usual. 'Those interested in Brigitte Bardot's bottom – in Cinemascope and colour – will find ample reward,' wrote *Esquire*. Levine teamed her with the American actor Jack Palance and waited for the New York critics to enthuse. Bosley Crowther spoke for them all when he wrote in the *New York Times* 'Out of it all comes nothing – or very little that tells you why this wife is so contemptuous of her husband. Maybe he should be contemptuous of her.'

All this did, however, serve to resuscitate Brigitte's public image. Like Penelope/Camille she was juggling suitors when she went off to Capri to make *Le Mépris*. Naturally the photographers showed up every morning and every evening to see whether it would be Zaguri or Frey who appeared with her on her balcony. The scenes were so arranged that Jacques Rozier and Oswaldo Civirani with Godard's connivance were able to shoot two little documentary sequels to *Vie Privée* about the trials of being Brigitte Bardot, called *Paparazzi* and *Tentazioni Proibite*. The 'new wave' was entirely delighted with this Russian–doll–type scenario of the film of the film of the film of the real film of a book of a myth. Meanwhile Brigitte's priorities were to weigh the problem posed by her two men. Zaguri was not an actor and therefore not a competitor, which was a point in his favour, not that Sami had been either for some time now. While Brigitte was working and preserving her, according to her, basically optimistic view of the world, Frey was not working and was brooding and hypersensitive – probably about the fact that he was not working. Sami had been wonderfully attentive at the expense of his own career and this brought its own problems, namely how to respect a man who was simply an escort. Brigitte was caught in the old trap of trying to change reality. The truth was that if you imposed your own will totally on reality it became boring. If you were imposed upon, you were at risk. With Zaguri, who financed everything from cars to films and who seemed to be able to run his empire by remote control Brigitte felt safe. 'He dominates me and I love it. He fills every moment with rich South American laughter. He is a big man. This will last.'

Brigitte was back saying the sort of things that made her Brigitte and when she came to London to make *A Ravishing Idiot* with her second American leading man, Anthony Perkins, she had to pay the price. The Italian *paparazzi* had paved the way by filling the magazines during the summer with their account of the change in Brigitte's love life. Now crowds started to gather outside the Westbury Hotel on the corner of Bond Street where she was staying. It was late October 1963 and it was late afternoon before she dared leave the hotel a couple of hours later than scheduled. By this time the home-going crowds had built up still further in Mayfair and in Flask Walk, Hampstead, where she was due to start shooting. Traffic ground to a halt as her limousine arrived in the narrow street and an impromptu signing session was set up on the pavement. Finally the police arrived and ordered the director to stop shooting. He had had enough anyway and ordered everyone back to the Billancourt Studios in Paris where he decided it would be cheaper to build Flask Walk from scratch than shoot it for real. Moreover the audience would see more of it.

Before she left London Brigitte held a press conference. 'I never thought it could happen,' she said, sipping a glass of her favourite drink, Scotch. 'In Italy, yes, but not London. I have never known anything quite like it before. It was frightening. I can never say the English are unemotional again. But why, why me?' she kept stammering. 'If I go to the theatre I have to slip in at a side entrance. If I go to a restaurant other people stare. The meal is ruined. Yet I have no wish to do an "act" by hiding. It is for that reason that I rarely appear in public. Then of course, if I fail to appear at a gala they accuse me of spoiling the show. That's unfair.' She was back on familiar ground. She wanted to be a woman, not an actress, she said. She liked lots of sleep and all animals, except fish. 'I have two dogs, a spaniel and a cocker spaniel, I have six doves and ten love birds. I even like mice and I tried to save one recently when my cat caught it, but the poor mouse died.' The public were enchanted. 'I know I have something,' Brigitte acknowledged. 'Publicity doesn't account for it. If you have something you will get on by yourself. If not, you will always be unknown.' This time she did a volte-face. True they had miscalculated in England by not taking enough precautions to protect her. Last time, eight years ago, she had been a mere curiosity in *Doctor at Sea*. Now she was a fully-fledged scandal but basically it was when she was *not* working that she was most at risk. At La Madrague that summer the photographers once again climbed her trees and spied on her every movement. On a film set she was protected from these annoyances. And so she agreed to star with Jeanne Moreau in Louis Malle's new film *Viva Maria* which would be shot in Mexico.

For Bardot this was a brazen step. She hated flying, yet she would travel halfway round the world. She couldn't speak English, yet she would agree to go to the premières both in New York and Los Angeles. And she would act with one of the most important names in European theatre. By now she was committed to her career if for no other reason than that she had acquired a taste for the money and the lifestyle that went with it. The penny had dropped during her affair with Zaguri. With him she had already had a little taste of the international high life. For six months he had shown her round his home country. At first she was enchanted. When she and Zaguri were on their own, riding a yacht in Copacobana Bay, everything seemed idyllic. When he took her down to Buzios, the little fishing village where the Jesuit fathers had first landed on Brazilian shores 400 years previously, she had a religious experience. She thought she was in heaven. The couple lived in a fisherman's converted pigeon loft right on the beach. Behind them the lush Brazilian jungle chattered with parrots. In front the sand was kissed by the South Atlantic. They idled around, swimming, skin-diving, and galloping horses through the surf. She danced at the carnival and generally improved Franco–Brazilian relations, which was said to thrill de Gaulle. The two lovers bought an apartment in a fashionable suburb of Rio de Janeiro called The Enchanted Valley. She had done very little that year except make a brief appearance as herself in the American film *Dear Brigitte*. She had the itch to get back to work and when Louis Malle brought his film script down to La Madrague for her thirtieth birthday party she was very interested.

Bardot was riding high at this time and had none of the apprehension of becoming thirty that she had had with earlier birthdays. In fact none of her birthdays on the decade itself have provoked as much distress in her mind as her twenty-fifth, her thirty-fifth or her forty-fifth. As she turned thirty it was the early sixties and her particular lasciviousness was being matched all around, so in some ways she no longer felt on a limb. Zaguri seemed to have found a way of living with her caprices and there were even rumours that she was going to have his baby. She told everyone that she was certainly not planning to get married again. 'What on earth would I do that for? For society? I am against marriage and I don't give a fig for society. They may call me a sinner but I am at peace with myself. Do you really think a woman is better off if she is married and she doesn't dare divorce because of what people will think? She goes through hoops to be with her lover a couple of hours a day and everyone says morality has been upheld. That is sin to me. She should leave her husband and live with her lover in the sun.' Nothing seemed to matter to Brigitte any longer. Other stars like the Beatles had enjoyed unprecedented mob receptions the previous year. Nuclear madness was in the air, brought to a head by the Cuban missile crisis. Any hopes of guidance from the world's leaders seemed to have disappeared in Dallas with President Kennedy's assassination. Another death had rocked Brigitte herself almost as much the year before – Marilyn's. 'She was really like me,' Brigitte realized, it wasn't just a fabrication. 'She wasn't really an actress, more of a personality. She was a pioneer like me because she gave the American cinema a new style. She wanted to be free and freedom is my watchword, it is the one thing that other people can't really forgive me for. Marilyn, like me, was a woman who felt really alone despite all her fame. The difference between us was that I came from a rich and happy family and I had a first husband who supported me. When I think of her I think her problem was not having anyone she could turn to.'

The survivors meanwhile were set to enjoy themselves. As the other guests at La Madrague that day – they included her little sister Mijanou – raised a toast to Brigitte, she seemed particularly happy. She blew out all thirty candles on her cake and Anthony Perkins, who had remained a friend after the making of *A Ravishing Idiot*, remembers her giving a little speech which made everybody laugh. 'The ideal age is the age I am now. At this age one is old enough to know what one is doing and young enough to do it all the same. I am thirty but there are things about me that are still fifteen. I have gone through much in my life and yet I do not feel that I have suffered great tragedies. I love to love and I hate to leave, but I love freely and I leave freely.'

All those French writers who had not explored the myth of womanhood at the time of *And God Created Woman* now seized on this birthday to analyse Balzac's opinion that thirty was the perfect age in a woman's life, when she presented the most desirable combination of beauty, spirituality and intelligence. Marguerite Duras was not sure. 'Something has happened to this woman,' she wrote, having set herself the task of studying in detail the pictures of the world's most photographed woman like a progression of doom.

Certainly her body, though a trifle less well moulded inside her golden skin, still remains superb. But in her face something has frozen. A slight puckering of the mouth and the eyes, which yesterday was not there. Yesterday, facing the world, this face was majestically carefree. Today she keeps a close watch on it. That is the difference – her pose. In other words, fear. Is this the end of a dazzling morning? Of course not – but already the warning songs of evening are here. An evening full of wolves.

Brigitte in her happy frame of mind didn't react but she might well have remarked that Marguerite Duras was one of them, prematurely baying at the carcass of the sex-symbol. The problem of her inordinate beauty was that everyone was on the watch all the time for the moment when the worm would start crawling out of the mouth of the statue of Venus – even Brigitte herself.

Duras did, however, spot the inner loneliness of this crazy perfectionist position. This was her description of Bardot's life aged thirty.

She is basically lonely, absolutely on her own at the head of a team which does not exist. In her private life she is very bored. Above all she likes people who amuse or interest her. For instance, the public jesters of the St-Tropez bars, the lonely, homesick and charming young men from every walk of life. She trails around her various homes, decorated by up-to-date antique dealers, with no idea of how to spend her time. Nature has happily endowed her with a delicious talent for idleness. But this is not enough to kill time. So she invents childish games to shake off her boredom. She receives few visitors. She lives alone with her lover so long as she is in love with him. I am certain that she has never known the end of a love affair, the heartbreaking depression of loneliness and liberty. But she knows that other tragedy of starting afresh right away. Has she ever paused between two romances – got her second wind – has she ever done this? I don't think so. Her will is strong. Nobody has ever broken the toy. Any woman would be the same if someone had irreparably wronged her by loving her too much.

When a man attracts her, Bardot goes straight to him. Nothing stops her. It does not matter if she is in a café, at home or staying with friends. She goes off with him on the spot without a glance at the man she is leaving. In the evening perhaps she will come back, perhaps not. Thus the woman who has never been forsaken does not understand – among many other things – the atrociousness of her behaviour. Although she has left many corpses in her wake she herself remains unharmed. This is what I mean when I say that nothing has ever happened to her yet.

I am sorry that nothing more important has happened to Bardot than to be our idol; that a very strong wind never encountered before has not blown across these last few years, that she has never committed a great and noble mistake. But how can this be averted even if we wished it? One day she will discover that what is happening to her is neither more or less than the fate of all human beings and nothing else.

Any reference to the fabulous feet of clay appealed madly to the public, who still couldn't quite make up its mind who Bardot was. 'All of France is agog,' wrote Marguerite Duras. 'All the French highbrows are on her side. As for the public at large, they are split between the men who are all in love with her and the women, who sometimes accept her.'

What the public did know was that she was earning thousands of francs one way or another for herself and for France. Ralph Thomas and Betty Box, who had been delighted with her performance in *Doctor at Sea*, regretted that they were never able to afford her after that one film. She was now getting £100,000 a film, plus a percentage. It wasn't Elizabeth Taylor's $1 million but it was three times Marilyn's price. She was a tough negotiator and when she was asked to appear in cabaret in Florida she named $1 million as her price. Nothing more was said of it but she didn't want to go anyway. It had all begun the year she earned more in exports than Renault cars. In his memoirs Vadim describes another of the hidden blessings that she brought to French business. When he was dining with Jean Delmore, the chairman of Air-Liquide, years after *And God Created Woman* had been made, Delmore thanked the director for allowing him to build his first liquid oxygen plant in Japan. Columbia, who had made billions of yen with the film in the Far Eastern market, had put the money into liquid oxygen when they discovered they could not take it out of the country. It was ironic, just, and surely not totally coincidental that liquid oxygen had been Louis Bardot's business. Added to all this there was the tourist trade in the South of France, not to mention the fashion business. Brigitte was now the figurehead of the freewheeling sixties – easy money combining with easy morals in hot places. Whatever she wore, whatever she drove, whatever she did made news and made money.

In St-Tropez these were the great influx years. Jeanne Moreau bought her house then, a wonderful hidden stone mansion up in the hills beyond La Madrague surrounded by vineyards, oaks, and truffles, and it was she who found the little medieval hamlet called the Nest of the Night Owl (subject of a Hockney lithograph) for Tony Richardson, who directed her in *Mademoiselle* and *Sailor from Gibraltar*. Huge yachts lined up off the headland or in the tiny harbour where a brilliant master was needed to unravel their anchors each morning when they put out to sea. The Krupp yacht anchored next to the *Christina*, carrying the teenage Alexander Onassis who wanted to meet his favourite film star, who was of course Brigitte. On Tahiti beach film producers like the Hakim brothers roamed looking for topless talent. It was all around, eating lobster and drinking champagne, desperate to find some way of earning enough money to buy some of the smallest bikinis in the world at the most inflated prices. When Pilou died in 1975 he must have thought that his daughter had launched a permanent form of paradise in this world. Even Toty, who drew her last breath in 1978, did not see the end of it. Brigitte was the queen and people came to her, not vice versa. But like all queens she needed tribute for practical reasons. Thus Malle's idea, only briefly sketched out as yet in between rehearsals at the Spoleto Festival, was very well received.

Malle says the project came to him in desperation one day when he was nearing the end of shooting what many people believe to be his best film, *Le Feu Follet*. It was about the suicide of a man who couldn't cope with being thirty years old, oddly enough the same age as Bardot, and although it was based on a book it was also pretty much the story of a close friend of his. Malle thought he was going mad with self-indulgence by the end of shooting and he wanted a light-hearted project with two beautiful women to turn his thoughts around. The identity of the women seemed obvious since he was the only director who had worked with both Moreau and Bardot at the time and worked very successfully with them. Moreau was in *Le Feu Follet*, she had been in several films and Malle had been intimately involved with her. Like Truffaut, who thought she was quite simply the best actress in the world, Malle knew you could coax absolutely any performance out of this brilliant, secretive vessel. He knew Brigitte less well, though a two-month shoot is a crash course in a sort of intimacy and he had seen the power she had to make other people challenge themselves, which made her very strong indeed as an idea. In *Vie Privée* he had seen Marcello Mastroianni, despite all his macho declarations to the contrary, wither before any confrontation with this new form of womanhood, where the body was ripe for domination but the mind refused it. Traditionally two women stars should have had no time for each other, but traditions, particularly those which flattered men's egos like that one, were being thrown over. Malle, who is a highly intelligent, educated man as well as a filmmaker, took a look at future history and saw that women, liberated from the yoke of disillusioned monogamy, were prepared to reverse their polygamous submissive past in favour of a certain toying polyandry. 'I wanted it to be a spoof on westerns like *Vera Cruz* with Gary Cooper and Burt Lancaster. Two women adventurers, Jeanne and Brigitte, instead of two men, the trained actress with the film star, the sophisticated woman with the instinctive child, a cliché of friendship and antagonism set in exotic country. I went to both with just four or five pages of premise and said this is the idea. I want to throw you somewhere in Mexico in the jungle. Both responded very warmly about the idea of working with each other.'

'This is really going to be fun,' predicted Brigitte. 'It is a sort of burlesque comedy with music. I play an Irish anarchist in the 1914–18 war. I blow up bridges because my father is an anarchist. It is a fairly odd sort of story because Jeanne Moreau is a music-hall singer who is looking for a partner and we sing together through wars and revolutions.' She said she loved the idea of starring with Jeanne Moreau. 'Perhaps you might say we are two aspects of the ideal woman. I hardly knew her until the film was proposed, then we dined together, listened to songs together and we hit it off immediately. It is the first time I have accepted to play with another star of the first rank. We will have exactly the same billing and that pleases me – it is such a change.'

Moreau too sounded quite confident. 'Films have never shown the kind of relationship that can exist between two women. Men like to think that women must be constantly jealous of each other, never trusting, never in rapport. That is not true of course and certainly not today. . .' It was one of those projects which appeared unanimously well starred because there was a certain familiarity to it all. Bob Zaguri liked the idea of it being set close to home in central America. Even Olga Horstig, who had packed her first client, Michèle Morgan, off to Vera Cruz in the early fifties to co-star in *Les Orgueilleux* with Gérard Philipe, was soothed by all the connections. Mexico and Mexican crews were familiar territory to both French and American film-makers, who had decided to put up the money.

'Little did I know what was about to happen,' says Malle.

The problems started immediately. 'After three months I sent off a first draft to both actresses,' recalls Malle, 'Then three days later I got a telephone call from both agents, just one hour apart, and they both said the same thing – the other girl's part is better. That was just the beginning. We were all supposed to be close friends but suddenly they wanted a lot of money, probably to assert themselves, then there was American finance so their agents started asking for the moon.' In the end a contract was made reflecting the difference between an actress and a star with Jeanne getting $150,000 and Brigitte $350,000. 'Then Jeanne wanted Pierre Cardin [her boyfriend at the time] to design the costumes but I wanted a friend of mine. In the end Cardin signed but my friend made them. It was a load of compromises. At one point Jeanne and Brigitte got on my nerves so much I decided to abandon them both and make the project in English not French with Sarah Miles playing Jeanne's part and Julie Christie playing Brigitte's. It was twenty years ago and they were both lovely, perfect.'

But the French version was salvaged – the film had after all been written with Moreau and Bardot in mind and there was a good deal of intentional self-caricature in both their parts. 'I knew them both very well,' says Malle, 'So the Brigitte character was all about being impulsive and generous, funny and absurd, irresponsible and scandalous as she was and Jeanne's character was introspective, sensual, more poised, insecure. At the time these two women were huge myths in their own right in France, in Europe, and in America. The whole project was meant to be mythical from A–Z and as a consequence on the first day of shooting we had 120 journalists on set. Everything that happened was reported in *Paris-Match* and of course some things that didn't happen, which then proceeded to happen, so that in the end the girls who were supposed to go into the whole thing in good humour and good grace, who had been fond of each other and curious about working together, ended up not speaking to each other.'

The first thing that happened was that Brigitte arrived two weeks late in Cuernavaca with an entourage that would frighten the Queen of Sheba. Bob Zaguri, who had been put on the payroll, arrived with her of course and they rode around together in a Cadillac put at Brigitte's disposal by the French cultural attaché. There was also a secretary, a hairdresser, two photographers and an Alsatian. Once in Mexico she added to the menagerie. Pretty soon two ducks, a chicken, two St Bernard puppies, two horses, a donkey, and a rabbit were sharing her accommodation in a wing of the house where Louis Malle lived with his fiancée. Moreau, in a house of her own, was waiting for Cardin to join her. But shooting did not go ahead immediately because both girls reported sick. Brigitte had laryngitis. Then Moreau discovered she was allergic to pineapples and started making plans to return to Paris. Brigitte sent her a message at the last minute which dissuaded her.

All the same the very first day the girls got together the trouble started. There were four months to go. Tempers were already short because of the extreme heat and the thin air at such high altitude. Watched by the posse of journalists Brigitte and Moreau, both suffering from stage fright, prepared for their very first scene. Malle takes up the story: 'Moreau had the reputation of being the real professional, the perfectionist, Brigitte the person who hardly read the script, who couldn't care less, didn't know her lines, didn't know what was going on. Well, I soon realized Brigitte wanted to emulate Jeanne because her dialogue was word perfect. Jeanne, meanwhile, hadn't bothered to learn a word because she had assumed Brigitte wouldn't. It was a comedy of

199

errors which took place in several acts.'

The problem, according to Malle, was not getting Brigitte to act but getting her on the set at the same time as Moreau. 'As an actress Brigitte was never close to what Jeanne could accomplish with her extraordinary stage background in the Comédie-Française. Brigitte, invented by Vadim, never bothered to work but she was an incredible natural talent, there were extraordinary moments when she was in a good mood, the problem was to get any continuity into her performance.' Brigitte started off by being very nervous, thinking she had made a big mistake in ever agreeing to turn up at all. 'She was a real pain while Jeanne was very comfortable.'

She was late on any pretext whatsoever, often ill, she was bored by the location and becoming so with Bob Zaguri. She resorted to all sorts of attention-getting devices which included trotting out her impersonation of Charlie Chaplin, which she had learned from Pilou, for the crew who were resigned to whatever they could get on location, and entertaining all the dogs in a Mexican village to dinner. Zaguri sternly reproached her for this tactless behaviour in front of the hungry locals but Brigitte didn't care. She banned him from her bed and took in a stray dog instead. 'She hated to be exposed, she hated to act,' says Malle. 'A number of actresses as opposed to actors have weird neuroses about acting, about being manipulated, exposed, thrown to lions as in Roman days. They have this feeling of being used which is not exactly untrue. This explained why she was so difficult, why she didn't show up. She had the terrible reputation of not being a professional and finally made the right decision which was very brave at the time, to give it up.'

However, it was not quite as simple as that because of those flashes of inspiration when she was in one of her occasional good moods. It took three or four weeks for Jeanne to become quite nervous of Brigitte as an opponent. 'She was quite hostile to *Viva Maria* for a long time in fact. She refused to have anything to do with the publicity and thought she would rehabilitate herself by making a couple of intellectual pictures,' says Malle.

All in all Louis Malle very quickly began to understand what Truffaut meant when he said a director always starts on a film with grandiose ambitions but by the time he is halfway through, all he wants is to finish the film without anyone dying in the attempt. His scriptwriter Jean-Claude Carrière thought there was very little chance of this and went home to work with Buñuel, wishing him luck. Malle sent him a telegram on the last day of shooting simply saying 'I've done it.'

What had he achieved? Though the film didn't turn out as he had hoped – an insane spoof on the children's adventure book with wonderful engravings, dating from the turn of the century, *Le Tour du Monde Illustré*, which he had found in his parents' attic and which Jean-Claude Carrière and Brigitte herself had known and loved as children – he had given a potential nudge to Brigitte's suspect career. 'France had been taking bets for years as to who would be the winner between her and Moreau,' recalls Malle. 'The competition became a point of pride between them, which is what happens when you discover your adversary is better than you thought. I tried very hard in the cutting to make them equal but if anybody Brigitte was the winner. I didn't tell them before but Brigitte had the best part – the easiest, the most extrovert. There is no exception to the unfortunate rule that the active character always commands attention over the passive one. It was quite simple – when the two of them were on-screen you looked at Brigitte.'

Now for the first time Bardot was poised to take Hollywood by storm. 'If I didn't visit America before, it was because I was afraid of the unknown,' Brigitte explains. 'I knew very few Americans, though I liked the ones I had met. I like the way they think big. When I was just starting out European producers and directors treated me like dirt but Robert Wise, who directed me in the Warner Brothers film *Helen of Troy*, made no distinction between American stars and myself. If Warner Brothers hadn't wanted to tie me down for seven years, I would have gone to America – thank God I didn't, seven years later I made *And God Created Woman*.'

Recently she had enjoyed making the cast and crew of the American film *Dear Brigitte* come all the way to Paris if they wanted her to be in their film for five minutes and they included James Stewart. 'I thought he was absolutely extraordinary,' Bardot says. 'He was so kind and considerate and had such professional integrity. I thought he was one of the greatest stars in the world. I met Cary Grant too. He wanted to meet me so I asked him over for a drink. He was very courteous. There was a ridiculous incident because I couldn't speak English properly. He had spilled some whisky on his tie and I offered, in English, to wash it off with water. Only, instead of saying "tie" I said something absolutely awful, which made Cary Grant blush and then collapse with laughter. I blushed too when someone told me what I had said.'

Brigitte also liked American generosity. 'They don't quibble over pennies like they do in France when they make a film. It is an absolute dream.' With those sort of opinions the Americans were prepared to adore her. They stared at Brigitte in the flesh when she turned up in New York for the première of *Viva Maria*. While Moreau sulked, Bardot trouped. Dancing on tiptoe when she walked and stinging with her words like some beautiful boxer, Brigitte wowed the American Press. She seemed to be everything a star should be and they were looking for one in the wake of Marilyn Monroe. 'In thirty years of journalism I have never seen such a dazzling performance as that put up by this thoroughly scared girl on her first visit to the United States,' wrote one writer who watched it all. 'She made tough American newspapermen and women eat out of her paws.' Her three press conferences on the American continent were a particular triumph. 'She fielded often absurd, sometimes insulting questions with aplomb and wit. She drew a number of genuinely appreciative laughs from people who are not easily impressed.'

Where American actresses were using their box-office drawing power to make pretentious political statements, Brigitte stuck to the old-fashioned way of doing things which had always worked best in Hollywood's hey-day. She rode around with her entourage of six – hairdresser, dress designer, business agent, two press agents, and Bob Zaguri – at autograph-signing pace in the glass-topped, bullet-proof limousine which had once belonged to President Eisenhower. She roamed Schwab's Drug Store on Sunset Boulevard where Lana Turner had been discovered while drinking a milk shake. 'I did not come here to talk about politics,' she tossed her head. It was quite plain that she had come to talk about herself.

'How old are you?'
'Thirty – and you?'
'What effect does it have on you being a sex-kitten?'
'None, as long as I have a figure for it.'
'Do you take yourself for a sex-symbol?'
'I take myself at face value and that is enough.'
'What do you think of free love?'

'I don't think when I make love.'

'What sort of woman are you?'

'Want to come away with me for a week?'

'I'd have to ask my wife.'

'That's what I meant – you, me, and your wife.'

'What does Brigitte Bardot really want to be?' asked Vincent Canby of the *New York Times*.

'Myself,' she said.

'What is that?'

'Look!'

And look they did at the girl in the tight-fitting-raspberry-knit dress or the outrageously glamorous fur coats, who said she never expected to grow old for she expected science to find a way of making time stand still especially for her. America called her 'Miss World, Miss Universe, Miss Gemini 6 and 7. Miss Everything'. But they didn't go and see the film.

14. Famous Love Affairs

Gunther Sachs married Brigitte Bardot for a bet. In 1966 he was a very handsome man and although he was German he had just the sort of dark looks that appealed to Brigitte. Hair which was never quite in place, good bones, sensitive lips, and a generally lived-in face despite his relative youth – he was only thirty-two, not even two years older than Brigitte and was definitely not ready for chrysanthemums. He also had a character which appealed to her. His voice suggested it all. At home in four languages he didn't quite belong in any of them. He didn't quite belong anywhere and in that he seemed like Brigitte. He had the reputation of being a playboy to her playgirl. 'However much she might like to do so, Brigitte just doesn't fall for serious men,' says a friend. 'She likes the playboy type and then she wonders why it goes wrong.'

Yet on the face of it Gunther was the most ideal of her three choices of husband as she made them at the time and she saw it straight away. He was rich, richer than she was which made a change, and he knew his way around. He could offer her a flamboyant sort of security which appealed to the good little bourgeoise in her. His mother was a member of the Opel car family. He was heir to a title, albeit a minor and a relatively new one – his full name was Gunther Fritz Sachs von Opel. His father was heir to the engineering fortune built up by his grandfather, who invented the freewheel bicycle. He had been educated at the best European schools and in the best European sports. He was a brilliant shot both with a gun and a club, he drove like the wind and piloted a bobsleigh in the same manner. He was very much a man's man in the tradition of aristocratic families and in the same tradition he courted beautiful women. When he fell in love he treated them well, which appealed to Brigitte, who as soon as she set eyes on him sent for his curriculum vitae. And he loved French women. When he was studying art history and mathematics at

Lausanne University he met a fellow-student called Anne-Marie Fauré, daughter of a French–Algerian politician. Her parents were not much impressed by this potential match, but after much winning and restrained behaviour he managed to turn their resistance to all things German into approval and he married her in 1954. Three years later she had a minor operation and died of completely unexpected complications. She was twenty-five and she left Gunther with a one-year-old son named Rolf.

Already Gunther was no stranger to tragedy. His parents had separated when he was a very small boy and the family was completely torn apart when his father kept the elder son, Ernst Wilhelm, while Gunther stayed with his mother Elinor in Switzerland, his lifestyle funded by the sale of her Opel shares to General Motors. When his father committed suicide Gunther himself seemed to embark on a dramatic courtship of death. He threw himself into both business and pleasure, though with a family income of £250,000 a year the former came in for a little neglect. His best friends were like himself, the children of the super-rich, Prince Aly Khan and the South American Porfirio Rubirosa, who were never out of the gossip columns in the fifties. Both died in car crashes. Gunther on the other hand was a winner. The year after Anne-Marie's death he became the European bobsleigh champion. He was to be seen in all the best resorts where the rich collect at predictable times of the year. He spent Christmas at St Moritz for the opening of the Cresta Run and New Year's Day in Gstaad, drinking *Glühwein* on the Wassengrat. He spent February in the West Indies and his summers in St-Tropez where he had a villa, La Capilla. He had homes in Paris, Munich, Lausanne, London, Gstaad and an estate in Bavaria. By the late fifties he had certainly not escaped the notice of Roger Vadim or any other young film-maker looking for money which wouldn't be missed. In fact his close friends included Serge Marquand, the brother of Christian Marquand who had starred with Brigitte in *And God Created Woman*. Vadim starred him as the Prince in Brigitte's 'come-back' film after her suicide attempt. Basically though, Serge had another source of income. 'Serge has always been Gunther's fool,' says a mutual friend. 'He amused him. He made him laugh. In return Gunther would toss him a big chip to play at the casino. Or he would give him a birthday party. He would never do anything useful for him because he wanted to keep him around.' Thus the two of them played together and romanced together. Serge married a German model, Anka Hahn, a previous companion of Gunther's who had just spent £5,000 on clothes for her wardrobe. Gunther fell in love for the second time with the Swedish model Birgitta Laaf. The two young lovers went off in hiding to Gunther's hunting lodge in Bavaria to plan a wedding as soon as possible.

Once again tragedy struck. In the fairyland setting of southern Germany Birgitta fell victim to a nightmare disease – it was discovered she had a spinal tumour. She lost the use of her legs, she couldn't move at all, and gazed listlessly out of the window at the mountains, the fir trees and the onion domes of the little churches whence no help came. Gunther was practical and supportive. According to friends he carried Birgitta in his arms to various doctors all over Europe. He even took her to Lourdes before he found a surgeon who could help in Heidelberg. The operation was a success and Birgitta made a full recovery. But Gunther did not marry her after all. Over the years many beautiful women had slipped through his fingers by mutual consent, Tina Onassis, ex-Queen Soraya of Persia and Marina Doria, the world water-ski champion, among them. Sachs called women the most divine creatures in the world and naturally he set his sights on the most divine of all. In 1966 Bardot had no competitor. Most of the current sex-symbols were merely imitators of her style. Marilyn was three years dead. Brigitte was the survivor, as was Gunther in his own way. The rest of the world were just their courtiers.

They met in a restaurant in St-Tropez and each had his court around him, yet there was one ambassador who belonged to them both – Roger Vadim. He introduced them. Bardot left her entourage, which included her suitor of three years now, Bob Zaguri, Gunther left his and they ended up in La Capilla alone. The evening was a triumph of timing. Gunther had been coming to St-Tropez for several years, one summer he had even rented a villa next door to hers, and he went on to own the famous boutique Mic-Mac, which became a clothes empire. Lately he had been dabbling in the film business. He had made a documentary on the South Seas and had recently made one about St-Tropez and sold it to an American television company in which he had neglected to star Brigitte and featured instead Prince Rainier of Monaco and Princess Grace. It was high time he made amends. He had even met Brigitte on several occasions. He had shaken hands with her on location of *Vie Privée*. Brigitte had given him a rose to plant in the next-door garden. But as far as their love lives were concerned they had both always been otherwise engaged. Now Gunther had just put his latest love, a German model, Heidi Balzer, on a plane for New York. Brigitte, restless with Bob Zaguri, had already broken out briefly with her middle-aged dentist in Paris, Paul Albou.

That night, as usual in the climate of compulsory pleasure which characterized the sixties, they were both looking for something to do. They found it in the Vieille Fontaine restaurant just outside St-Tropez. That night too the bet was made and taken. Gunther was a gambling man and one of the first things he did was take his entire entourage to Monte Carlo to visit his royal friends and to play at the casino. He also invited Brigitte and installed her in her own suite in the lovely nineteenth-century Hôtel de Paris, overlooking the Grimaldi palace on its rock the other side of the harbour. They listened to guitar music together and visited a fortune teller, who told them they were lucky for each other. That evening Gunther won £30,000 at the tables which he presented to Brigitte. The omens were looking good. Brigitte told her agent Olga Horstig that she had never felt so romanced or been so much in love. She had already found herself entirely enchanted by his way of sending over 100 red roses a day for La Madrague. This was a kindred spirit who didn't do things by halves. When he feared she would tire of the doorstep delivery he hired a helicopter to fly over the garden and drop them right into her lap. It is difficult to forget such grandiose seduction techniques, which never happen to most people in a whole lifetime. While they were lunching in Paris he would suggest dinner in Marbella – just for fun. 'I was completely overcome by the passion Gunther put into seducing me,' she remembers. 'It was out of this world. It stemmed from all that money certainly, but there are lots of people with money who don't find nearly as many amusing things to do with it. When he dropped the roses I spent my entire day looking for them in the undergrowth. They were everywhere, I didn't know what to do with them, it was raining roses. Then one day he arrived by helicopter himself. He threw his suitcases into the sea and then jumped in and came to join me.'

Brigitte reasoned with herself that there could be nothing that he wanted except her. Where she had three properties he had six. Where she had one eight-year-old Rolls-Royce, bought after her very first success, he had any number of brand-new cars. Her boat, the *Jannique*, was child's play compared to his yacht, the *Dracula*, a name which somehow reminded her of Vadim with his life and death preoccupations. Vadim was extremely enthusiastic about this match with a man who was, in a way, 'family'. 'Gunther is perfect for Brigitte,' he kept saying. 'He is a strong man. He is like me. I wish them all the luck in the world.'

With this sort of encouragement soon she was ready to be invited to Sachs's Bavarian hideaway in Rechenau. Again there were thousands of flowers. Brigitte's room was filled with them. They overflowed on to the balcony and beneath it every evening a little group of musicians gathered to play. Gunther had done his homework too. She loved the guitar and so she would be serenaded by it. During the day they lived out a peasant fantasy, dressed in local costume in lederhosen and dirndls. At night they made love in the dense silence among the fir trees, broken only by the occasional torrential shower. One night Gunther put on a firework display for the people as well as his fiancée. There was really no other way for a fairy tale to end but in marriage. 'What else can you give the man who has everything?' says Brigitte.

The evening at Danny Kaye's was not the first time my path had crossed with Brigitte Bardot's. That was in Paris when we both used to go to the nightclub Castel's in the Latin Quarter. We would come into each other's orbit once again in the South of France. But in Hollywood at a supposedly intimate gathering I learned something that I did not know before and even Brigitte, who had a head start in such matters, learned something she didn't know before. Though she had often been alone when she least expected it and surrounded by people when she least needed it, she didn't realize that she was a curiosity even to her closest friends and lovers. This struck her as quite callous. Vadim had ignored her when she wanted attention, Charrier had paid her too much. Now she saw what they had in common – both were trying to find a way of treating her as a wife as distinct from public property They failed, and Charrier put it quite colourfully: 'You can't have for yourself what belongs to the whole of the country, whether it is Brigitte Bardot or Camembert cheese.' Gunther's solution was not even to try to keep her to himself. He took ten people along on the honeymoon including his friend Serge whose brief was to make a film of even the most intimate moments – perhaps to sell to American television where a version of it was indeed shown. Serge and his wife Anka had been there all along, even throughout the final heady days in Bavaria.

The whole thing was a flying circus and it was laid on, wouldn't you know it, by Vadim who had never really relinquished his role as Brigitte Bardot's chief press officer. As with everything they did, Vadim had put his toe in the water first. He was delighted to welcome her to America, for hadn't they always been planning to conquer the world together? With his marriage to Annette Stroyberg and his affair with Catherine Deneuve at an end he had married Jane Fonda in 1965. It was very much an affair of the heart and at first sight they had chosen an unlikely and frivolous place to tie the knot – Las Vegas. Jane was already deeply into politics, though not as deeply as she would be in the future, and one of the first things she had done with Vadim was visit Moscow. Back in the States she involved herself immediately with the black movement and later with the anti-Vietnam demonstrations. It was impossible not to have an opinion on these issues in America in the sixties, a country frightened and disillusioned by Kennedy's death and torn apart by the war. For the first time the entertainment business, which had flexed its muscles during the McCarthy period, solidly queried the meaning of patriotism. Even those entertainers brought up the hard way in the ghettos, like Danny Kaye himself, to love their country right or wrong could not ignore the lack of morale they saw first-hand on the Vietnam battlefield. Entertainers had always offered their public a temporary illusion, but at this period fantasy and real life became inextricably involved in a haze of political idealism and personal pleasure, sustained by hallucinogenic drugs. To alter eternal laws was the creed and nothing else mattered, certainly not marriage, a mere conventional gesture which might or might not endure. So it was in a spirit of spontaneity and disregard for bourgeois convention, as well as of cynicism, that someone like the passionate Fonda and the star-struck Vadim flew to Las Vegas – the capital of American divorce – and stayed for two days at a gambling hotel, the Dunes Palace, to plight their troth.

For Sachs it was the obvious place, a town where money could buy anything. For Brigitte, who was quite simply naïve in such circles, it was colourful, it was fun, it was brash, it was horrible but it was exactly what Europeans expected of America. Continuing his expert courtship Gunther the German bridegroom paid his French bride the sweet compliment of arranging everything, with the aid of his friend Senator Edward Kennedy, whom he had met after Rubirosa's funeral, for 14 July, her country's national holiday, Bastille Day. Fourteen was also one of the numbers that had come up during his winning streak in Monte Carlo. That was the night they had first toyed with the idea of marriage. Gunther had asked his secretary to order Brigitte a wedding present from Cartier's in Paris, a tricolor bracelet, three rings intertwined, one of rubies, one of diamonds, and one of sapphires. They picked it up on their way from Rechenau to the airport in Paris, along with the traditional tight French marriage contract absolving them of any property settlement, prepared by two sets of lawyers. They also picked up two trunks of clothes, not that many for a superstar. Somewhere along the way Brigitte found the time to telephone Bob Zaguri at La Madrague and tell him not to wait up - she was going on a shopping trip.

Brigitte and Gunther stepped off the plane at Los Angeles, Brigitte having travelled under the name of Mme Bordat, an anagram of Bardot, and Gunther as M. Scar. So she was quite surprised to be greeted by the usual posse of reporters and photographers. She had brought her own cameraman, Philippe d'Exéa, with an exclusive contract on the reproduction of the Bardot image, precisely to prevent such a thing. Gunther had brought his favourite stringers from *Paris-Match* and everyone had believed Senator Kennedy who had promised to keep things quiet. Accepting the inevitable they announced their engagement on the tarmac. It had been a ten-hour, tourist-class flight so everyone was feeling a little frayed and things were not over yet. The couple were due to be married just after midnight in Las Vegas, still an hour's flight away. Philippe d'Exéa and Serge Marquand were witnesses and neither the French bride nor the German groom were quite certain what was being said by the American judge, John Mowbray. 'May the road rise to meet you and may the wind be ever at your back,' was one of the things he said, toasting them in champagne after the eight-minute ceremony. There was no wind at all. Even at that time of night it is cruelly hot in the Nevada desert in July. Gunther wore his usual glamorous uniform of the international playboy: black mohair blazer, white flannel trousers, white silk shirt open to the waist, and Gucci shoes without socks, which would become a talking point to be emulated by everyone in those circles to this day. Brigitte wore the briefest of red silk shifts and carried a single red rose. By the time they had finished the wedding breakfast at the Tropicana Hotel it had wilted prophetically.

The circus carried on. Danny Kaye, who was very proud of the fact that he could pilot a commercial transatlantic jet if ever the bottom fell out of the comedy business, was at the controls of the little Lear which carried them all to Los Angeles. There Gunther and Brigitte checked into a bungalow surrounded by hibiscus, bougainvillea, and oleander and the constant chirrup of water sprinklers in the garden of the Beverly Hills Hotel. By this time the entourage had grown. The entire contingent of *Match* correspondents in the United States had to come to pay their respects. They felt they knew Brigitte personally because they had covered her trip to Mexico to make *Viva Maria* as well as its opening in New York and Hollywood. Brigitte, suffering anyway from jetlag, began to feel a little nervous when they didn't stop at the bedroom door but simply came and sat around on the bed. She was quite relieved when it was time for lunch and she could get them all out of there to the table which had been prepared by the swimming pool. She seemed quite dazed during the meal. 'She was wearing a lime green dress and she asked for a pistachio ice-cream. I remember she didn't know what colour it was and was quite amazed when it matched her dress,' one guest remembers. 'That struck me as peculiar at the time. That Brigitte, who was the epitome of fashion, could be quite ignorant about it. She was a curious mixture of cunning and naïveté.'

In the evening she demonstrated this further. If she sat romantically on Gunther's lap throughout, it was in the spirit of determination that at those close quarters none of the escort brigade could get between them. Under her flirtatious manner she was in a very sharp mood and when Gunther and Danny, who was about to be made vice-president of the Lear Company, idly picked up a model of a jet from the coffee table and tried to persuade her to be photographed with him, she said sweetly '*Pas de publicité*', and the jet was put down while they smiled at each other for the cameras.

But the haze was never far away. The speed of the trip, the bewilderment of it all, the recreational pleasures of Los Angeles all took their toll of the honeymoon couple. It was at the height of the drug culture, a time when cocaine was served in a salt cellar on every dining table and kind souls slipped acid into each other's morning tea. After just two days' relaxation Brigitte and Gunther set off for Tahiti, another 5,000 miles away (territory previously pioneered by Vadim in an effort to save his marriage to Stroyberg). There they island-hopped in the inevitable private jet, pursued by the inevitable photographers. Even in these exclusive circles it was the same old story. Dogged by farce Brigitte stepped on a sea-urchin and needed stitches in her foot. The honeymoon was beginning to seem more like an assault course, which included a couple of days in Acapulco on the way home in a hotel run by one of Hedy Lamarr's ex-husbands, where once more Brigitte required medical attention, if only to demonstrate that she was not getting enough of the other sort. The final stretch was a trip back to Germany to introduce Bardot to Gunther's family, including his little boy who was now eleven. This gave Brigitte a nasty jolt, it reminded her of her responsibilities. Back home in France little Nicolas was six and a half. Brigitte did not enjoy the grand society ball which her husband threw for her and the way even her new stepson treated her as a sacred cow rather than family and asked for her autograph. Back in Europe too she was strangely troubled by an open letter from a Dominican priest to the magazine *Vie Catholique Illustrée*. 'May God forgive you for the harm you are doing us,' he wrote.

By the time they arrived back in Paris – the whole trip had taken less than a month – Gunther did not seem to her at all like the man she had married. Several onlookers say that he has never been the same man since. Certainly his hair has whitened dramatically. Just as Charrier had in his way, Sachs now set about showing Brigitte that she could have too much of what she thought she wanted. With Charrier it had been cloying emotion, with Gunther it was appreciative crowds. 'He took ten people along on the wedding trip,' Brigitte recently told the latest man in her life, film-maker Alain Bougrain-Dubourg, when trying to explain why her affairs always seemed to go wrong. 'I had just one old friend, Philippe, and he had ten.'

'Why did you go on with it?' asked Alain.

'Well, if Gunther made a bet with his friends, I made a bet too in a way – with myself. Once I had decided to do it, I had to go through with it. It was like that with all my films too. A sort of wager with myself that I could do them.'

Gunther wanted witnesses to the marriage, a photographic record or else, in true twentieth-century fashion, he couldn't be sure it had happened. Brigitte had started out by laughing about it but by the time she had got back from the honeymoon she realized that once more neither of them was in control. They were never alone. Brigitte, who hates being alone – 'Solitude scares me, it makes me think about love, death, and war. I need distraction from anxious black thoughts' – longed for the spiritual intimacies of a real marriage. Sachs preferred to take 150 guests to Maxim's. What he offered along with the oysters and champagne was Brigitte, the legend he was genuinely proud to have married. He knew no other way of behaving. He says he has never stopped admiring her, that he used to refer to her as woman times woman because she was so much larger than life and that he still treasures the letters she wrote to him testifying to her love. After their divorce he put them in a bank vault in Munich.

To a certain extent Sachs changed his lifestyle for her. 'I stopped going to my office and worked from home. I took to conducting my affairs from home and have done ever since.' At first Brigitte's little acts of defiance, like dining in the best restaurants in Paris barefoot, delighted him because they were part of the legend he had bought. And his generosity delighted her, especially when he bought her a pet cheetah called Princess to celebrate, as he put it, his love of speed and her love of animals. 'Even if you can buy yourself anything you want in the world, it is not the same as when someone else spoils you,' says Brigitte. 'It was as if the world was stopping still.' But behind closed doors these symbolic gestures turned out to be quite hollow. Beneath Gunther's tinsel there was simply more tinsel. Brigitte came to loathe his flat, at 32 avenue de Foch, the same block the Rainiers lived in. She called it the Gunther Hilton and whenever he was away she stayed at her own apartment in the avenue Paul Doumer, in the wrong end of the sixteenth *arrondissement*. She said she had to because Gunther had not given her a front-door key to the avenue Foch. Yet that had been the contract, no mutual property.

Brigitte was bewildered by the venal carousel of the very rich, fooled, according to close friends, by his holiday image as the barefoot boy, resentful when he had to return even briefly to his business dealings. Gunther in turn was bewildered by Brigitte. 'She could be full of tenderness and love one moment, the next minute she was low key, apathetic, useless. Then she switched to wild enthusiasms. She can do anything she wants to do. She is a woman of high intelligence, a superb writer who conveys the intensity of her feelings in beautiful, erotic language. She has amazingly shrewd judgement, a very quick grasp of almost any

213

situation. She is often right but she is also lazy and other influences tend to impair or supersede her judgement. Then she can be quite wrong.'

According to Christine Gouze-Renal, Brigitte was complaining about the emptiness of her marriage only a week after she returned from the honeymoon. 'All those marble bathrooms and footmen in white gloves, she didn't know what to do.' But it wasn't as simple as that. From both Gunther's point of view and Brigitte's it would be convenient if this marriage, this treaty between two grand houses, worked. 'Our view of life, our philosophy, our ethics were the same. We were in total agreement about the things that should or should not be done,' said the bridegroom. These included spontaneity in love-affairs – if genuine passion intervened between a couple it was the duty of the victim to go with it and the spouse to retrieve them from it. Brigitte, however, the actress ever receptive to another identity, the teenager who could never decide what she wanted out of life, believed in sequential passions, the one supplanting the other, while Gunther had the colonial attitude of the entrepreneur. He believed in the idea of game-playing. 'If such a thing happened again – and basically it was what happened with Brigitte – I would sit down and think and work out a strategy.'

This was the line he took when in early September Brigitte went back to work to make a film called *A Coeur Joie* (its English title *Two Weeks in September*), in Scotland. One of the things Brigitte had bequeathed Bob Zaguri when she eloped to Las Vegas was a contract committing them to work together on her next film. Brigitte now chose the story and the director, Serge Bourguignon, won a Hollywood Oscar with his first film *Sundays and Cybele*. She also chose the co-star, Laurent Terzieff, who had auditioned with her for *La Verité*.

A Coeur Joie was an Anglo-French production with Francis Cosne, the producer who had collected her from the St François Clinic, picking up the French 70 per cent, and Zaguri who would be on hand during the shooting, looking after Cosne's interests. This cosy scenario looked unpromising to Gunther, who was too aware of his own image to be hanging around his wife in the claustrophobia of her particular pond. Part of his philosophy, anyway, was that lovers should be able to be parted for just about three weeks at a time without needing to ask any questions after. For Brigitte, the perfectionist, this was the way things went wrong and, as if to prove her point, she seemed determined to make them go wrong.

It was an uneasy film set, full of huge egos and yawning lacks of confidence. Bourguignon, who felt he had made a painfully inadequate second film in Hollywood, kept boasting he could control Bardot, yet she was frequently absent from the set. Whenever she spoke of the plot of the film it smacked loud of an allegory about her marriage with Sachs. She was a cover-girl living in Paris with her lover and when that affair became banal she ran away to Scotland with another. During the escapade a wedding dress is torn from her body in a moment of heavy symbolism. 'Love is the greatest illusion,' she would say. 'At the instant you seem to share the whole world with someone else you are in fact completely alone . . . love is the supreme expression of egotism. The point is to dare and not be sorry whatever happens.'

Gunther, guilty at this stage only of being himself, did indeed come and see her in Scotland but he brought with him his golf clubs which infuriated her. He could not see why – the best thing about Scotland after its whisky was its golf, was it not? She had already forbidden him to shoot in the hunting lodge at Rechenau. For Brigitte the best thing about any place was herself. As usual she took a sledge-hammer to crack a nut. When the cast and crew moved to London she fell into bed in the most public way possible with her English co-star, Mike Sarne, and refused to emerge for several days even to come to the studio. It was a silly, short liaison, the fancy of an ambitious young boy just starting out for an older, careless woman. Mike Sarne theorized at length about her magnificence, comparing her to Mae West, whom he subsequently directed in Gore Vidal's film *Myra Breckinridge*. For Brigitte the affair served a much less ethereal purpose, which was to free her from the bondage she envisaged if she allowed herself to buy Gunther's sophisticated philosophy.

By the time the two of them were reunited again in Paris after he had made his annual appearance at the Munich Beer Festival, she was armed against him by the mere fact that she had tasted pleasure elsewhere. This time his apartment looked even colder than it had before. 'It was a magnificent apartment but there was nothing of me in it. It had been furnished by an interior decorator which made it completely impersonal.

'My apartment is my own work. I live surrounded by books and I have read them all. His library is much more beautiful but

215

you can't read the books. I was really shocked when I found that our!' The yards of leather-bound books were blank between the covers. Still she moved back in with him. In the daytime she went to her own territory at the studios and she resented leaving him asleep. His image thrived late at night in cosmopolitan restaurants with the people she hated. When he tried to bridge the gap by suggesting making a film together about themselves she turned him down on the grounds that he wasn't a professional. Neither of them was willing to give an inch.

Privately Gunther's little coterie were now taking bets with each other as to how long the marriage would last, but just as they descended upon each other to collect their winnings the couple would appear together once more, apparently deliriously happy just to be man and wife. They were together in Rome in March 1967 when Brigitte went to make the Edgar Allan Poe story *Histoires Extraordinaires* opposite Alain Delon. Brigitte's part, appropriately enough about a gambler, was to be directed by Louis Malle who had not had enough of her yet. Another was to be directed by Vadim starring Jane Fonda. Gunther was pleased to find his old playmate but Brigitte, who has always confessed to being wildly and irrationally jealous, was apprehensive about meeting his new wife. Interviewed for her thirtieth birthday by her old friend Françoise Sagan, Brigitte could not believe it when Françoise had claimed she had never felt jealous nor had any reason to be. Now Brigitte was sitting opposite Jane Fonda at dinner in Rome, a girl who based herself on her subconsciously, unconsciously, and right out in the open, in fact in every way since she had married her ex-husband. Brigitte didn't want Vadim herself but she had never been very pleased to come up against his new wives, starting with the pregnant Annette all those years back in Torremolinos. She knew exactly what Vadim thought of her and Jane, he had compared them often enough even in public and it sounded very much like a compliment to himself: he told Henri Gris in *Ciné Revue*:

> The big difference between Brigitte and Jane is that Brigitte is not a professional. She got where she is because she wanted to be a dancer. She only agreed to be an actress because it is impossible for a dancer to be married. Dancers work all day and all night and in between they travel. Brigitte didn't want that and she only agreed to make films because she wanted to be

famous . . . she became an actress by accident, whereas Jane set out to be one. But Jane is no less a woman. Bardot is a girl with petty problems. What shall I give my dog to eat today? What should I do with this armchair? Shall I go to the flea-market or not? They are all little, tiny domestic dilemmas. Whether or not to go to the beach and sunbathe. Jane doesn't have that sort of useless problem. She doesn't try to make choices between things that don't exist.

Jane and Vadim would be together for a while yet, in fact next year on Brigitte's thirty-fourth birthday Jane would give him another daughter, Vanessa, named after Vanessa Redgrave whom she admired for her political involvement.

Against all odds Brigitte actually liked Jane, except on occasions when she was feeling unaccountably insecure about her looks. And Jane, who finds it easy to like other girls, took a shine to Brigitte, throwing open to her the old farmhouse at St Ouen about twenty-five miles from Paris, which she had bought in the early days with Vadim to house the religious triptychs she had started collecting out of their mutual passion for art. Later Brigitte would just arrive on the doorstep if she felt like it and Jane enjoyed fixing her up with men to amuse her. Seeing Jane and Vadim together Brigitte realized that they were not much happier than she and Gunther. They too had married their fantasies rather than reality. Vadim's obsession with the virility of America, Fonda's fascination with old-world culture. What they really had in common were things in museums. Their paths had converged like rays of light, only to splay out again quite irreconcilably at the stage when Fonda cut off the hair she now wore like Brigitte's and became, like Brigitte, a caricature of herself.

Gunther and Brigitte were together in Paris for the first anniversary of their wedding when Gunther threw a big party in Maxim's. At the same time he opened a string of new boutiques making Brigitte, who always likes to see her own efforts putting money in her own bank account, slightly nervous that she was being exploited for publicity reasons. They were together in Munich, where he opened an art gallery, and they were together that summer in St-Tropez, when she bent over backwards once more to become the perfect countess by inviting both his son Rolf and little Nicolas down for a summer holiday together. Nicolas seems to have been surprised by his mother's looks, as if he hadn't seen her for a long time, telling her that she was very beautiful. She saw nothing wrong in that.

Then, just when it looked as if they were doing fine, Gunther was the one to get it wrong. One day he invited a young model down to La Madrague to join the houseparty. 'I was hoping to develop a new style of marriage,' he said. 'But it misfired.' Brigitte behaved in such a macho way that Gunther sometimes felt he could not be blamed for defending himself. This time, surely, it was the end, the friends said, but no, Philippe d'Exéa took the blame and pretended the extra girl had been invited for him. The marriage survived the New Year of 1968 when Brigitte arrived in Gstaad to join her husband and stepson once she had completed her traditional New Year's Eve television show in Paris. She was the centre of attention following the show because one of her outfits, an extremely short and transparent skirt made from the tricolor, had been banned. The rest of the show, including a sketch in which she pretended to be Shirley Temple, went down well. She was just getting nervous about the prospect of meeting the Shah of Persia at his Suvretta chalet in St-Moritz when she was recalled to St-Tropez. Raoul Levy had died by his own hand.

Raoul and Brigitte had had their differences but with his suicide at the age of forty-five, part of her own past also died. Apart from anything else it brought back her own brush with death seven years previously. Gunther, who had lost the real playmates of his youth, understood why she dissolved into such a black mood over this curious little opportunist Levy who had emptied a shotgun into his stomach when one of Sachs's own Mic-Mac shop assistants had refused to open her door to him in the middle of the night. But despair was not the way out. You didn't have to pay your dues yet, this was what being rich was all about. Sachs was offering Brigitte, in return for just a little discretion, the best of both worlds. He was offering her security and all the pleasures of the flesh, eating, drinking, carousing, changed consciousness in every imaginable way, the company of beautiful people, the adornment of clothes and jewellery, the fun of fast cars, planes, and boats straight off the drawing board, beautiful houses with beautiful contents, and, if animals were what she liked, then animals she should have with the best pedigrees and the finest lines. Brigitte insisted on strays.

Raoul had not been happy with what had happened to the image of women, in part due to his production of *And God Created*

Woman. It had been a long time since he had advised Brigitte to
take the windfall of fame seriously, to keep her clothes on and
learn to act. Now his last thoughts about her appeared in *Playboy*'s
'History of Sex in the Cinema' as a sort of epitaph to him and a
warning to her. 'The demystification of the stars, due to too much
publicity about their private lives, is ruining the box office,' he
wrote. 'There is no longer any mystery about Bardot. The public
knows too many intimate things about her life. Bardot sells
newspapers and magazines, but she does not sell tickets.' The
article in which those particular words appeared described her as a
'kiss and tell' wife, which is to say that she disdained to hide her
quicksilver changing of lovers from either her husband or the
public.

This was the crux of the problem in the Sachs marriage. The sex
life of two partners, both with macho attitudes, was becoming a
war unto the death. A man was supposed to do these things, felt
Gunther, who was a traditionalist at heart, not a woman, not in
public, and certainly not his wife. When Brigitte made a record
with Serge Gainsbourg, Gunther flatly put his foot down and
refused to let it be released. The record, with which everyone is
now familiar, was 'Je T'Aime, Moi Non Plus', re-recorded later
by Serge and his lover Jane Birkin. When Brigitte made it in 1968
Gunther said it sounded quite simply as if they were actually
making love in a recording studio.

He was not quite so protective of his image when it was
announced that Brigitte's next leading man in films was to be Sean
Connery and he let her go to Almeria to make the film *Shalako*
alone, saying he would visit her. Brigitte said it was going to be
made in Mexico but Gunther said that was far too far to fly to a
film set, so the production moved to Spain. He did indeed visit
briefly. But when he was not there the European newspapers were
full of pictures of Gunther escorting beautiful girls to all the usual
European watering places. The reports drove Brigitte into a
frenzy of bad behaviour, which included leaking her own
thoughts on Sachsy, as she called him, to the newspapers.
'Gunther has certainly not given me what men are supposed to
give women,' she said, 'tenderness. So I've started noticing that
other men look at me with tenderness in their eyes. Why should I
go on suffering? In my life it's all minute by minute. If something
doesn't work I have the capacity of suffering the hottest torment,
then erasing it and starting anew. Maybe that is what keeps me as

if I were still eighteen. I could get married fifty times, almost every time I fall in love.'

As she left Paris for Almeria in January French teenagers voted her their most popular pin-up and she concluded it was because she lived like them. 'They like me because they sense I will never settle down, that, like them I am completely available,' she said. On *Shalako* she was determined to show it. 'She seemed obsessed with the idea that she was ageless,' said Kenneth Green, publicity manager of the film, who had coined the idea of the Pekinese profile when he first met her on *Doctor at Sea*. 'A perennial teenager who wanted to show that she could go on dancing, singing, and whooping it up all night.' She asked the producer, Euan Lloyd, to install a powerful stereo in her suite on the top floor of the new Hotel Aguadulce (built like all new hotels with particularly thin partitions) with speakers in every room including the bathrooms. She wanted to give parties every night to anyone who would come – waiters, the local bigwigs, the poor off the street, or technicians from the film. 'She had no fixed rules about whom she befriended,' says the producer. 'If a shoeshine boy had something she liked, he was her friend.'

For all that the picture had seemed well aspected. Euan Lloyd had started with the idea of making a western with Henry Fonda and Senta Berger. Then Fonda backed out and the much more profitable Sean Connery stepped in. Then Lloyd decided to replace Berger with Bardot. He told Connery so on the telephone at three o'clock in the morning. 'Bloody marvellous!' the actor responded. Brigitte Bardot thought so too and summoned Lloyd to St-Tropez the moment she read the script. Olga Horstig concluded the usual financial deal for $350,000 and 15 per cent. But Bardot wouldn't sign the contract. When Euan Lloyd bumped into James Bond producer Harry Saltzman at the Byblos Hotel in St-Tropez, he thought he knew the reason why. Saltzman, who had lost his James Bond to Lloyd, now wanted to poach Bardot for his next Bond girl. Bardot was in fact offered a Bond film but she said no – unless she could play James Bond himself of course. Failing that, all she actually wanted to do before she signed for *Shalako* was meet Sean Connery. But she wouldn't come to London to do it, she had to meet him in France.

Lloyd anticipated no end of ego problems over this on the Sinatra–Bardot lines. 'If she thinks I am going over to France to be given the once-over, she can forget it,' was Connery's immediate reaction. Much to Lloyd's surprise both Connery and Bardot agreed on his compromise, a meeting in the northern seaside town of Deauville, and what is more they liked each other. Gunther Sachs gave a fancy dress ball for fifty friends to celebrate the event and the mayor of Deauville, in an attempt to draw custom away from St-Tropez, donated two neighbouring plots of land to the married couple on condition that they built houses there. Everybody was absolutely thrilled with each other until they arrived in Spain with Brigitte at the head of a convoy of forty-seven press vehicles. 'Someone has to tell this lady this is going to be a serious film, not a bloody circus,' said Connery.

Circus it was all the same. When Sachs visited he took one look at Almeria, declared it 'ugly, dirty and too hot', and left. Bardot consoled herself with the usual stray dog, which she bathed and perfumed in her suite and fed on pâté de foie gras, whereupon it died. For a whole day she sat glazed and grief-stricken, refusing to eat or drink. A journalist, who had been refused an audience with her, took to following her round on his hands and knees barking. Brigitte had him thrown off the set. Suddenly she found herself wildly attracted to Stephen Boyd whom she had not been able to stand when making the 1957 Vadim picture in Spain. When this was reported by the Press Brigitte threw a mammoth fit of temperament and rushed off to St-Moritz to see her husband. When she returned the parties began. Brigitte did not start work until ten in the morning – she had that written into her contract – but others started at six and tempers were becoming short. While she did the minimum amount of work on the set she posed for the maximum number of press photographs. She knew exactly what the photographers wanted. She messed her hair, hitched her skirts and patted the horses, although several people thought she didn't really like horses. And through it all she talked about Gunther. She seemed obsessed with him. 'Love is the most important thing in my life,' she said, 'but it's not top of Gunther's list. He likes going out, parties, friends. He is beautiful, seductive and all the women want him. But that means there must be a contest between us. He doesn't want to change his life for me and I don't want to change mine for him.'

When the film was over – she left behind a reputation for flamboyance second to few actresses – she took a plane and joined Gunther in Rome, taking her kid sister with her as arbiter. Mijanou had always got on well with Gunther, who wanted to star her husband in a film with Brigitte. Frayed tempers were frayed even further by the constant presence of the *paparazzi* who wanted to know the exact state of play between the Count and Countess Sachs. Gunther punched cameramen and snatched cameras but still the pictures appeared. Bardot returned to St-Tropez. 'Don't mention that man to me!' she fumed whenever her husband's name came up in conversation.

She consoled herself in public and in private with Luigi Rizzi, a rich Italian ship-owner's son, who at twenty-three had gone into the nightclub business. Luigi and she lounged around La Madrague, doing a little boat building and a lot of kissing. Then they set off to Sardinia to the Aga Khan's holiday resort. On the way they stopped off at Genoa to meet 'Gigi's' mother. Did this mean they were planning a wedding? The Press carried pictures of the carryings on. It also carried pictures of Gunther Sachs on the nudist beach on Sylt in the North Sea with a model friend and jetting from New York to Rio de Janeiro with a coterie of girls to open some new boutiques. Brigitte kicked 'Gigi' out and took a plane to Munich for the German opening of *Shalako* but this time something was different. Gunther, who had always spent time with her when they found themselves in the same city, simply did not turn up. He didn't turn up at the Hamburg opening either, even though Brigitte spent her thirty-fourth birthday lingering in one of his favourite nightclubs. She went to each different opening with a different escort. In Paris and London it was Patrick Gilles, a garage owner's son from St-Etienne, a boy ten years younger than herself. 'Every year I am getting younger,' she boasted.

The freneticism of this period actually put years on her face and figure. Friends suspected it was not so much that she was burning herself out as that she was furious at having played for high stakes with Gunther and, once again, lost. They should, Brigitte thought, have been able to come to some arrangement. He should have found her so desirable that he stopped her from running around, humiliating him and herself in the process. If love had been his priority, as it was hers, it should have worked out.

That winter, frustrated by the lack of success of *Shalako* in the United States – it was never released in France – and by the failure of her marriage, Brigitte escaped to the Bahamas with Gilles, renting a bungalow on Naked Island, riding in the surf with him as she had with Zaguri and even playing golf with him, which some people saw as a cry of anguish for Sachsy, who was being quite offhand in Europe. 'I don't even know whether I am divorced from her or not,' he declared. He had instructed his Swiss lawyers to sue for divorce and they came up with the grounds that Brigitte had 'abused the idea of marriage and left home premeditatedly.' Gunther was now inseparable from one of the girls who had accompanied him on the Mic-Mac tour, a Swedish model called Mirja Larsson whom he would finally marry. He had moved on. He was one of those men who subscribed to the belief that there is always another woman waiting to fill the gap in a man's life. He simply could not live with the idol of France, but he was sufficiently traditional never to be discourteous when talking about her. 'I've heard it said that Brigitte Bardot is a dumb woman who somehow has the knack of seeming clever in interviews. I compare her to great creative women like Coco Chanel. This – her extremely high intelligence – is her most unknown aspect. It shows up in her writing, which is outstanding both in style and content. In fact she should have been a writer first and a dancer second. Acting is only her third choice of profession. It also shows in her conversation, which can be brilliant when she's feeling that way, with all the crackling repartee of the French intelligentsia. But she can also sit in a corner and say nothing all evening. She is moody with the same commitment and force as when she is active.'

Sachs did not mind about Gilles. He did not mind any amount of stuntmen or garage hands, he wouldn't have minded anyone if she had simply known how to play things down and have her cake and eat it, which was the way of the rich. What he did not want was to be cuckolded by any rival in the eyes of the world and to have her infidelity thrown in his face. There was one man who thought himself king of Hollywood and Brigitte had been 'mated' with him by kind friends in exactly the same way as she had been mated with Sachs, king of the European pleasure circuits.

Sachs and Bardot had first been introduced by Vadim. Vadim's wife was now determined to introduce Bardot to Warren Beatty at the farmhouse in St Ouen to which Brigitte kept running every time her husband was out of town. Jane Fonda became quite worried about Brigitte. Ever since she had made *Masculin/Féminin* for Jean-Luc Godard in the winter of 1965 following *Viva Maria*, she had become a virtual recluse with her animals unless entertainment was laid on for her. Gunther was one performance, Warren was another.

Jane Fonda prepared the meeting carefully, says Fred Lawrence Guiles. She had known Warren since they had both worked for the director Joshua Logan and when he came to Paris she was determined to lure him out to the country where the prize would be Brigitte. Fonda asked her old boyfriend Sandy Whitelaw, who was working in the French capital, to drive him out for dinner which she had spent all day preparing. She showed him lovingly round the house and her art collection while Bardot arrived in time for the meal. While everyone was eating Jane actually wondered whether Warren already knew Brigitte – and knew her well. He complimented Jane on the meal but, looking at Bardot meaningfully, then said he knew something which tasted even better. Vadim, who was very drunk, then made the vulgar comment: 'In that area Jane is not quite in Brigitte's class.' Jane was beside herself with fury, Brigitte was far from displeased. She had been paid a compliment, she liked vulgarity and she could console herself that there were holes in everyone's marriage. There were holes in her own whenever the cinema was mentioned. Gunther didn't like to think of the three of them, Vadim, Brigitte, and Fonda tittering about private jokes in their profession together at St Ouen.

Bardot persisted. In early 1969 she made *Les Femmes* with Gilles as her on-screen lover. She made the film for only 80,000 francs, less than half her normal fee. Again it seemed to mirror life. It was about a woman who falls in love with a Don Juan and leaves him before their love is played out. 'I would do exactly the same in real life,' she said. 'I would leave with good grace, even at the very summit of our love, before love began to tarnish. This is the only victory one can have in love, knowing when to quit. It is a principle I have followed all my life.'

She was still seeing Warren from time to time and she was with him, hiding in a corner of the Cafetière restaurant in Paris in dark glasses and headscarf, when her third divorce was announced. But she had come to realize that fame forced men and women to pass each other like ships in the night. Many people's marriages fail because they have too little of everything going for them. Sachsy and Bardot or Mamou – he never called her by her Christian name – had too much.

15. Masculine and Feminine

Brigitte Bardot was divorced from Gunther Sachs on 2 September 1969 at Filisur, the little Swiss town with the highest airport in Europe (only big enough to take private planes) just down the slopes from St-Moritz. She was about to be thirty-five. She was totally free. She had been moulded in marriage, duped, and disillusioned and finally she had fought her corner and, somewhat reluctantly, discovered herself. The seventies, which were just about to begin, were the era of women's liberation and here she was on their doorstep, a liberated woman. She made a few more films and then she realized she didn't want to do that any more than she wanted to be married. 'Films take up your time and energy,' she said. 'They imprison you and force you to be on the go all the time. I am a woman who has undoubtedly made a success of her career but certainly not of her private life. Let's say that because of that I am someone who is incomplete. That is why I don't want to work any more.'

But had she made a success of her career? Her last films started to explore the aptitude for comedy she had shown as a young girl but once more she refused to stick with anything and work at it. The first seventies' film was *L'Ours et la Poupée*, ('The Bear and the Doll'), an American-financed, supposedly sophisticated European comedy destined, in the minds of the writers, for Catherine Deneuve and Alain Delon. Deneuve and Delon said no as soon as they saw the script. Bardot said yes immediately. Her co-star was to be the son of her old friends, Daniel Gélin and Danièle Delorme, in whose apartment she had first been tutored in acting by Roger Vadim more than twenty years previously. The boy had been six when his parents stood witness to her wedding to Vadim, now he was twenty-four, more or less the same age as her current lover Patrick Gilles. It is a curious time in the life of a woman when a boy she has known as a child becomes a potential lover.

225

Perhaps for the first time she feels what it might mean to be a man in a traditional position towards a woman, which is that both of guardian and predator. Bardot at thirty-six could still look in the mirror and know that on a good day she could pass for ten years younger. She has also always loved to work with people who are known to her. Such familiarities reassured her, but according to the critics they should not have done. Vincent Canby in the *New York Times* described the result as: 'a witless romantic fable about two perfectly mismatched lovers . . . Charm is the ingredient that is in singularly short supply . . . largely, I suspect, because Miss Bardot, once a sex-kitten, is now approaching middle age with all the grace of a seasoned predator.' Cruel words indeed, for charm had always been Miss Bardot's long suit even in the opinion of her harshest critics.

On the other hand the idea of the predator did not turn off all the women in the audience. They were simply delighted to see the magnificent tigress turn the tables on the menfolk and illustrate that the bond between older women and the younger man, which had always been acceptable in the salon or the brothel, was now acceptable in wider social circles. Felicia in the film was a married woman, well, she had been twice in the past – the film opens with her second divorce – she was not a whore, neither was she an intellectual, she was middle of the road, middle class, surrounded by an array of creature comforts to make an advertising man's mouth water. Brigitte herself says she liked the film and that it was an improvement on the past. She declared she would be paying more attention to her scripts in the future.

The next script had originally been written for two amateur actresses but Bardot thought she saw it in the makings of a second *Viva Maria*. *Les Novices* was about one of the great French fantasies which had dogged Brigitte's career, the sexlessness of sex and the interchangeable nature of good and evil. Vadim's two published books illustrate this interchange. The Devil and the Angel in their titles both refer to their author. The story featured a nun and a prostitute with Annie Girardot repeating the Jeanne Moreau role of older mentor to Brigitte both in life and in art. Brigitte came to love Annie and to depend on her while Annie tucked her into bed and made sure she got ten hours' sleep each night. Alas Annie's tart had more heart than the film itself and frankly no one was convinced by the broad and clumsy attempts to break through the screen and lasso the audience into the brothel by means of

Bardot is always particularly charming on television
(*Rex Features Ltd*)

Reunited with Charrier and fourteen-year-old Nicolas in 1974
(John Hillelson Agency Ltd/Andanson/Sygma)

Un certain âge – Brigitte celebrates her birthday with Laurent Vergez, Françoise Sagan, and other friends the same year
(John Hillelson Agency Ltd/Wherle/Sygma)

Proud Papa Pilou
*(John Hillelson Agency Ltd/
M. Valentin/Sygma)*

Brigitte buries Pilou in 1975, with sister Mijanou, niece Camille, and mother
Anne-Marie, outside the church where she married Vadim
(Rex Features Ltd)

A calm relationship with sculptor
Miroslav Brozek
(*Rex Features Ltd*)

Cornered and campaigning – to
save the seals, 1976
(*Rex Features Ltd*)

Brigitte, happiest now protecting
wildlife. The Brigitte Bardot Wildlife
Foundation was set up in 1976
(*Keystone Press Agency Ltd*)

Airlift to the Newfoundland ice-floes,
1977
(*John Hillelson Agency Ltd/
L. de Raemy/Sygma*)

Happiness is the sound of chomping setters at Bazoches
(*John Hillelson Agency Ltd/L. de Raemy/Sygma*)

United by animal causes – Brigitte and Alain Bougrain-Dubourg
(John Hillelson Agency Ltd/L. de Raemy/Sygma)

Peace at La Madrague
(John Hillelson Agency/Jicky Dussart/Sygma)

sniggering winks and swaggers to camera. Brigitte was looking for something really good, the age-old cry of the middle-aged actress, and for a while it looked as if luck was on her side when Visconti decided she was absolutely perfect for Odette, the woman who, despite his usual sexual preferences, managed to drive Proust crazy, or at least his creation, Swann. Visconti, who shared Proust's preferences, was nevertheless fascinated by a perfect example of the female species, by the sheer mounds of flesh which crop up in unfamiliar places. It was Bardot's bosom which decided him on this casting. Vadim too was still trying to bring Brigitte over to Hollywood, but Bardot in France was talking up a storm of a career rather than acting in one.

Both those projects fell through, liberating her, however, for *Boulevard du Rhum*, which gave the French – it was only shown in France – a flash of what they like best, gangsterism rather than Bardot. Brigitte loved everything about it which Gene Mosko-witz in *American Variety* hated. It was camp, picturesque, naïve, a parody of a parody and she came out of it the handsome thirty-six-year-old woman she was rather than a would-be sex-kitten. She was stuck in the Sinatra trap, the inevitable one which audiences and critics alike prepare for the superstars they have loved in their youth because they don't want them to get old because they themselves don't want to get old. At this point the star has to show that he or she is wedded to the business, not just the master or mistress of it – not the perfect challenge for the fickle Bardot. She did not want to mourn for the years, neither did she want anyone else mourning. She had learned early on in life that if she could not have something, she could still make fun of it.

Fully-fledged satire was the idea behind *The Legend of Frenchie King*, otherwise known as 'The Oil Girls' (*Les Pétroleuses*). Most people assumed it was a satire on the western genre, but it was actually of the opposite sex, something which Bardot, like every other woman, had been warming up to for a little while. At the end of the film the Oil King himself says 'The West ain't no place for a man.' Bardot, in leather hat or wielding a gun, terrorizes the town, leaping on her horse and fist-fighting Claudia Cardinale to the point where the director, Christian-Jacque, said, 'I was in a cold sweat all over. They set to with such a will that I was afraid to have an invalid on my hands.' But it was also a satire on Bardot herself, just as her whole career had been, with the sort of internal jokes in which the movie business specializes. For example the

227

Mexican town in the picture was given the name Bougival Junction, after the little riverside spot near the Bardot home in Louveciennes where Louis XIV's great waterwheel was still attracting summer visitors right until the end of the sixties.

Les Pétroleuses didn't win any awards. Claudia and Brigitte did not really get on. While Claudia talked about her son, Brigitte refused to talk about hers. (Jeanne Moreau had a son too but she had not let that come between them.) But whereas Jeanne Moreau had a sort of modest demeanour which Brigitte had no need to fear, Claudia had a generous physical presence, *and* she was five years younger than Bardot. The two actresses parked their Rolls-Royces side by side in the hot sun for no other reason than to show that they had Rolls-Royces. Brigitte had bought hers in 1958. It was now thirteen years old and the good housekeeper in her resented it. A couple of years previously a garage had taken her to court because for three months she had refused to pay nearly £1,000 for the repairs they had carried out. She claimed they had exceeded their brief: '£400 for removing a few dents and £600 for overhauling the engine is exorbitant – even for a Rolls.' The court disagreed and made her pay. She was out to get rid of it but meanwhile she made it work for her on the set of *Les Pétroleuses*. In her heyday it had been her one traditionally starry showbusiness acquisition and her appearances in it were worthy of anything Hollywood could have imagined in the thirties. Bardot liked to be driven around in her Rolls together with her stand-in, her secretary, and her publicist, by a black chauffeur called Ibe, dressed in a white Mao Tse-tung suit and wearing dark glasses. She had bought him four identical suits costing £70 apiece from the St-Tropez boutique, Mayfair. Ibe was an actor-dancer who came from the Ivory Coast, whom she had hired the year she married Sachs. He raised a few eyebrows when she was making *Shalako*. That was when she had had the Rolls sprayed white. Claudia's was simply grey. Bardot herself commented on the pecking order of the two actresses. 'CC comes after BB *naturellement*.'

Christian-Jacque, who like most men loves rivalry between women, was delighted with the film but again the reviews were dismal, this time in France as well as America. 'BB, who looks like a cat thrown in a bath of cold water each time one asks her to do a few movements, proves once again that her knowledge is of the most limited,' wrote Jean-Loup Passek in *Cinéma 72*. 'She, who could have become our Judy Holliday, is from now on simply a pair of initials over which the moneylenders are still fighting in the temple. How much longer can this go on?' There in the end was the message of hope and condemnation. Judy Holliday was dead. True she had lasted till the age of forty-three but she had been inviolate under the sod for more than six years now. How to go on was the question.

When in doubt Brigitte had called on Vadim for more than twenty-six years now. It was ten years since they had made a film together and that was *Warrior's Rest*. But when she put her flat in the avenue Paul Doumer on the market, he read the signs correctly. Brigitte was thrashing around wondering what to do next, and as usual when she wanted to make a new start she turned to interior decorating. This time she turned her back on almost everything she had collected over fifteen years at Paul Doumer. She put the flat and its contents on the market for £100,000 – the price of a film just four years back. 'It was suffocating me,' she said. 'So much happened to me there. There were too many memories. I could not breathe there. I did not want to be reminded of the past all the time – so much past.' Instead she bought a splendid new penthouse in the avenue de Lannes, right next to the Bois de Boulogne, and furnished it in a frankly vulgar way with a round sunken bath topped by a huge mirror and a queen-size bed straddled by a tent. She could operate the television, the stereo, and the light switches from her bedside and look down out of the window at passers-by. It was more like something out of a Hollywood film, or indeed Hollywood reality, than the cosy clutter Brigitte had always managed to achieve in the past without her interior decorator, and it gave Vadim, by now divorced from Fonda but still based in Malibu, an idea. In Hollywood such an apartment would be the province of a man, indeed I have seen numerous bachelor versions of it and so has Vadim. If Brigitte could live in that impersonal way surrounded by the functional trappings of the hardened suitor, Vadim realized that it meant Don Juan, the legendary seducer, was in 1973 a woman not a man – was of course Brigitte herself. This idea provided the basis for her penultimate film.

Her private life supported Vadim's thesis. She moved into the new apartment with Patrick Gilles but she had hesitated often enough about this liaison, having one fling after another before, during, and after. Though Marguerite Duras had reproached her on her thirtieth birthday for flaunting her sex drive, luring a succession of poor, silly boys into La Madrague and putting their suitcases outside the door in the morning, it was actually in her late thirties that this became true. Most of the boys were just that, boys, ardent in their attentions or their ability to nightclub into the early hours but without much more claim to fame. Some of their names are barely familiar: Eric Salmon, Christopher Lance, Christopher Weddow, an English tourist to whom she gave house-room for three weeks before his mother called him home. Some like Luigi Rizzi, or Jean-Noel Grinda the tennis star, are more glamorous but they didn't last much longer. Only one, Warren Beatty, is a household name.

The King of Hollywood and the Queen of the Riviera saw each other from time to time into the seventies often in the company of Jane Fonda who had left Vadim now and was accompanied in France by Donald Sutherland, though her real love-affair seemed to be with left-wing politics. Otherwise Brigitte was devouring men with the menopausal freneticism of a predatory male. 'In roles and also in private life she would have lovers the way men would have lovers in those years, but for a woman to have those affairs and to be guiltless about being a sexual butterfly and fooling around, always in the newspapers, an object of scandal in France, that was considered avant-garde,' says a close friend. 'I think she was not maybe rationalizing it but she knew exactly what she wanted and she was not even trying to hide her life and that was what was new. A lot of women behaved the way she did before but for a woman with such a public image to be so honest about her life was shocking at the time, would be today – I don't think things have changed that much.'

Jacques Renevant, who used to help run the fashionable Left Bank discotheque, Chez Castel, where Brigitte and I used to dance the night away, describes exactly how she set about seducing men. 'I was her boyfriend for eight days,' he recalls happily pointing out that it was a different era for everyone and he is now very pleased to be married and settled down. She started off with the advantage of being BB, of course, and that very fact launched an electric current into the air at Castel's or wherever she was on any given night that Renevant says he has never seen emanate from any other star. The night she set her sights on him was completely typical. She was thirty-six, it was 1970, she was allowed to get away with anything.

'One day Patrick Gilles called me up and asked me if I would play tennis with him. I went to avenue Paul Doumer to pick him up and Brigitte was there. She noticed I was wearing a chain with a Scorpio sign and asked me when my birthday was. Then on my birthday she called me at Castel's to invite me to the birthday party of one of her other friends.' Renevant says she was always the one to make the running and the only one who ever broke that rule was Gunther Sachs.

Even after her relationship with Jacques Renevant was finished she had her photographer, Philippe d'Exéa, call him to tell him to get ready to go to Tahiti with her and that she already had the plane tickets. Jacques didn't go but he saw her from time to time all the same. Once he picked her up to take her to a party a friend was giving especially for her. Brigitte was watching the Euro-vision song contest with some hangers-on and she fancied an unknown German singer. She immediately lost interest in the party and asked one of her friends to telephone Germany and find out the singer's name. As soon as she had decided on someone across a crowded room or restaurant she would make whatever enquiries necessary to trace where the man could be found at home. Then one day the telephone would ring for him and she would ask him to meet her. 'I am Brigitte Bardot. I want to meet you,' is the straightforward way in which she put it.

The request was never turned down. Brigitte and the man would meet at first on neutral territory, probably for an innocent lunch. Afterwards the man, who had been very apprehensive, was likely to come away with a sense of disappointment because no proposition had been made. Brigitte would behave for all the world like an attentive, caring, kind friend, as if the two of them had known each other all their lives, and it would cross the man's mind that he, of all the men she had ever met, was the only one who would step away from the friendship without having made it into an affair. She could behave like a 'fleur bleue', a shrinking violet, is how Renevant puts it. Men found this very exciting and some of them have not recovered from what would happen next.

For three or four days Brigitte would prove herself the best platonic friend a man had ever had. They would eat lunch and dinner together, they would go dancing and out on the town, they would giggle and laugh, she would adopt his interests, she would do anything she needed to ensnare him. It was wonderful. Then one night the inevitable happened apparently by mutual consent.

It was a brilliant natural ploy, reinstating the man's predatory instincts and protecting Brigitte's modest supposedly feminine ones, which had been violated by the first overture. After that the couple had to be inseparable for as long as it lasted.

'I had to follow her even on to the set of the film she was making, 'The Bear and the Doll',' says Renevant. 'I had to be there even when they were doing her make-up or dressing her and she always asked my advice which made me feel very important. She came to Castel's every night. But she didn't like to go out and as a rule she only did so when she had quarrelled with the man in her life.' Every single man was dominated by the myth of her fame. They had all seen her films and on-screen and off her physical presence was so strong that it didn't matter if she had nothing else to contribute. Jacques' week with Bardot was a marvellous interlude, he says, and then one day it was over. To him it meant exactly what it had been and no more. But less sophisticated lovers, realizing that she never acknowledges the past and has apparently forgotten their cherished adventure, even their identity, suffered a terrible psychological emasculation which they carry with them for ever like jilted girls.

One lover says the myth was so strong that it often negated the actual physical experience of making love to her. It was like being asked to perform for the Queen, such a terrifying challenge that Brigitte's sexual reputation could go against her sexual interests. Then, even while you were making love to the star, you were savouring the experience on an analytical level, trying to fix into your brain for some inexplicable reason the exact nature of her most intimate features, trying to understand why the person you were holding in your arms was Brigitte Bardot. The *frisson* was most of all in the head. It worked because she was dangerous, about to leave you or be snatched from you. Her volatility, her lasciviousness, her vulgarity, her physical arrogance, her habit of treating you as a pupil she could initiate into some sexual trick she had learned heaven knows where, her easy tendency to boredom, exaggerated her hold over a man more than the feel of her skin – grainy from the sun – the rough whip of her hair, the controlled movements of the dancer. It was in all a shocking rather than sensual experience. When you began to enjoy her as a woman the affair was almost over.

Though Patrick Gilles moved into the boulevard de Lannes, the tented bed was soon occupied by another, Christian Kalt, whom

Bardot had met when he served her a drink in Meribel. Kalt was a gadfly of the resorts who sometimes taught skiing and generally paid his way with his athletic and strangely feminine-looking freckled good looks. He willingly followed Bardot to St-Tropez when she beckoned and they made a pretty couple for a while. Kalt, Gilles and the rest were paralleled in Vadim's film by Paul, Pierre, and Prévost, a priest, a politician and a millionaire, not to mention a Spanish guitarist who slashes his wrists after the act of love, all driven to distraction by Jeanne/Bardot. In real life Kalt couldn't bear it any longer and walked out during filming. Vadim produced a young medical student to calm her, which, as someone on set remarked, was for all the world like sticking a dummy in her mouth. There was something fearfully undignified about the situations she kept getting herself into, which had nothing to do with the sexual revolution described by libbers. She still maintained a belief in the potential longevity of pathetically unequal relationships. Don Juan, the real thing, pushed by nature to unbutton his codpiece wherever pleasure beckoned merely to add to his list, was not really taken in by the vision of eternal love, but Brigitte was. Vadim thought perhaps that eternal love, or at least eternal camaraderie, could only be achieved between members of the same sex, people who thought alike, if then. If she could really shed her sexual inhibitions, really become like a man and toy with a woman, then she might be free.

Always on hand to liberate her through a mixture of fiction and fact, Vadim set to to invent a film script with the Prix Goncourt-winning novelist, Jean Cau, who had been fascinated by her indeterminate gender ever since he interviewed her for *L'Express* on the occasion of her first 'retirement' from the cinema in 1963. Cau went overboard on that occasion saying: 'I explained [to Bardot] that – whether one was called Stalin, Napoleon, de Gaulle or Bardot – it was almost the same thing from a certain point of view. You climb step by step to the heights of fame. As you rise the air becomes rarefied, the vision gets blurred, you feel giddy and when you are there on top of the pyramid you are alone. Isn't this true?'

'Oh yes, that's the terrible thing,' Bardot answered, '. . . I have been given everything but I cannot make use of the gifts.' Cau wrote: 'If I were dealing with a child, I should say I had before me a headstrong little boy. At half-time in our interview Brigitte Bardot is a boy-woman.' By the time she was thirty-five, he was writing in *Match* and had decided she was 'a stuntwoman of life, love and morality'. The stunt that he would write for her in *Don Juan* was a bedroom scene with Jane Birkin, who had made history by appearing full frontal in a 'serious' film, the cult sixties hit *Blow Up*. Brigitte and she had something in common in that they had both been close friends of Serge Gainsbourg. Faced with a self-confessed non-actress Vadim always saw such off-screen connections as promising, but he failed to bring any intended eroticism to the screen, possibly because Brigitte is simply not turned on by girls, which even he was forced to acknowledge. 'If one woman in the world is not bi-sexual it is Brigitte. She never could stand that. She is not at all sexually interested in girls.' Her list of adventures remained erotic only in an intellectual sense, and borrowing the symbolism of the original Don Juan, Vadim had her pay for her unprincipled seductions in the flames.

Like the phoenix Brigitte rose again to take part in one more film, a suitably mythical venture, the quest of a medieval youth for perfect love with a bit of sex along the way. Brigitte was cast as the courtesan Arabelle, her character based on that of the liberated queen Eleanor of Aquitaine who didn't wait for the 1970s to marry three husbands, followed one of them to war and picked up several lovers along the way. Brigitte, co-starring with a cast of doves, puppets, and the young man Colinot, played by Francis Huster with sticking plaster over his private parts so that he would not be embarrassed in bed, was enchanting. In comparison with another hard-living French actress, Natalie Delon, who was also in the film, and with the ingenue Muriel Catala, who was being called the new Bébé, she felt old. One day on the set somewhere near Biarritz she took a look at herself in the mirror in her trailer in medieval costume topped by a particularly ridiculous hat, and she announced that this time she was really giving up films. She was thirty-nine and the studios struck her as a pretty stupid place to be for a grown-up. A French opinion poll put her fifteenth in a list of eighteen top box-office draws, with Alain Delon heading the list and commanding £250,000 a film, while her price had dropped to £50,000.

Bardot was convinced the cinema was making her older than she need be. More than any disillusionment, sadness, and tears, she was convinced that the lashings of make-up had contributed to her first wrinkle at the age of thirty, and now at thirty-nine, a particularly vulnerable age for most women, she did not want the camera to preserve her shortcomings for posterity. If Brigitte has always been vainer than most women, perhaps it is because for at least twenty years of her life she was more beautiful than most. She is quite frank about this. 'People asked me to undress because I was beautiful and being beautiful and young I was happy to do so. I think it is disgusting for the old and the ugly to reveal themselves with all their bulges and shortcomings as they do every summer in St-Tropez.'

Vadim thought retirement was inevitable. 'I don't see how she can continue to act if she doesn't want to change,' he said. 'If she accepts to mature the way Elizabeth Taylor has done, sure, why not? But Brigitte cannot go on playing Bardot the way she was five or ten years ago. There comes a moment when it doesn't work any more. I hope for her sake she is not going to make any more movies.'

Louis Malle on the other hand thought her decision to retire was an act of extraordinary courage. It is not easy to break even the bad habits of twenty years. Other directors simply wouldn't believe it and one of the first things the French did on hearing the news was to invite sixteen of them to say how they would use Bardot in a movie if they were given the opportunity. Some extremely varied talents responded. Hitchcock said he would cast her as a 'jokey' princess. He thought she was naturally aristocratic. Antonioni saw her as a Renaissance character with something ethereal and poignant about the features. Renoir saw her as one of his father's paintings, springing off the canvas. Vittorio de Sica said she could play any woman at all of any nationality. Preminger added the rider that the woman would have to be in love and Fellini said that if she didn't exist we would have to invent her: 'Her figure aside, the most striking thing about her is her range of facial expressions. She could play ten characters in the same film.'

Other directors thought she would come back if offered the right project, after all she had been talking about retiring since the age of eighteen. Robert Muller, Billie Whitelaw's husband, wanted to star her in a musical version of Emile Zola's *Nana* on the London stage. A French producer wanted to make the life of the American singer Neil Diamond with her playing opposite Jean-Paul Belmondo.

'A quick study', 'a natural talent', 'a brilliant instinct' – all these characteristics told Brigitte herself the time was right to bow out. She had said often enough that it was obscene for a sex-symbol to

235

be playing a mother of five or even a grandmother. Audiences might have differed with her about that, but there could be no doubt that in the early seventies the cinema as a medium was undergoing a change and myths were being buried. Bardot, who was used to being a myth, wanted not to be buried alive but preserved in aspic, or at least celluloid. Apart from anything else she didn't like what was happening to the movie business and hadn't done so for a long time. She was beginning to sound almost like Raoul Levy when she talked about nostalgia for the mystery of sex. 'I think it calls for considerable talent to make good erotic films. It's not enough for the people who make them to live in a country where there are no sexual taboos and where you are allowed to portray physical love on the screen. I don't think the Swedes are necessarily good at sex films just because they take the mystery out of sex. Sex needs a little mystery. Liberty, yes, but mystery too.' Everybody was trying to make erotic films now, she said, they were as fashionable as they had been prohibited in her day. People went too far, but perhaps some balance would come out of it all which would throw some light on the tortured love lives of human beings. Brigitte admitted that her contribution to this whole scenario hadn't been as spontaneous as was made out. She had thought and thought and thought about what she was doing and then adopted a way of life which seemed inevitable at the time. But at the end of it all she was still a prude, still shy and still afraid. 'I decided to free myself from my upbringing but one never does. One never really gets rid of one's background or education; one only gets over it. I don't regret any of the things that remain from my background. They come in very useful.'

Perhaps because she was so thoroughly middle class there wasn't a film that came out in 1973 for which she could find a good word and she thought *Last Tango in Paris* was frankly disgusting. Pornography apart, for the next decade, with occasional exceptions, television would be the great entertainment medium and Bardot shrewdly never gave up her television connections which she uses to this day, broadcasting live from a series of animal shelters. But in film circles at the moment not a single voice can be found to predict that she will ever again be bankable in France. The words the French film business uses are cruel and final. She is some sort of dinosaur who would be completely out of place in the three current financial vogues on the

Champs-Élysées. One ambitious woman producer, who has completed a 40-million franc film with such international names as Catherine Deneuve and Simone Signoret, outlines these specifically in reverse order: the classic love and adventure story so recently *démodé*; science fiction; and the sort of basic chauvinistic comedy which Brigitte started in, these days set in some Club Méditerrané, and which will eventually be outdated.

In Hollywood the old studio heads, to whom the razzmatazz of showbiz was first nature, were all dead or dying. Harry Cohn, head of Columbia, dead at only sixty-seven in the year of Bardot's first scandalous success, was the exception to a bunch of extraordinarily long-lived talents. Samuel Goldwyn ninety-two, Adolph Zukor one hundred and three, Jack Warner, who had run the studio that offered her her first contract after Cannes, eighty-six. The audiences they knew were dying with them, the success of small-budget starless movies like *Easy Rider* and the exorbitant demands of the trade unions, which meant that every film had to be a blockbuster success, combined to pull the rug from under the feet of the old film business. Vadim shot one of the last old-style movies on the MGM lot, *Pretty Maids All in a Row*, with 3,000 employees at a cost of $3½ million when a quarter of that sum should have been sufficient. Most of the lots were given over to television and the new middle-class Hollywood restructured itself rather tamely on the whole to churn out middle-class junk for the small screen.

Bardot had never taken Hollywood by storm, even *Shalako* with James Bond star Sean Connery had done nothing compared to home-grown westerns. Now she had lost her opportunity. In the early seventies Vadim was divorced from Fonda and in that cliquy town, where the Fondas were royalty, it was quite enough for him to lose his power base. He shuttled back to France to make his next movie *Don Juan* and again to make *La Fille Assassinée* with Sirpa Lane, which would take his fascination with de Sade to the limit, and to make his most recent movie in which his own son by Catherine Deneuve starred. In between times Vadim stayed put on the beach at Santa Monica, Hollywood, where he still lives, but he found it increasingly difficult to talk a new project off the ground. Nowadays he supplements his income as often as not by reading scripts, not writing them, for such studios as are left. Brigitte figured that it was no use for an ageing Continental sex-symbol to rely on him.

There was another curious factor lurking in the brains of the West Coast at the time. Hollywood could not make up its mind which sex Bardot was – literally. The rumour was rife that Brigitte Bardot was a man! It must have crept into their minds when Mike Sarne, one of her lovers, decided to direct Gore Vidal's trans-sexual story *Myra Breckinridge* with Mae West and Raquel Welch. Sarne had fallen in the most unreal way for Brigitte. From the moment he set eyes on her she could do absolutely no wrong. 'She was unquestionably The Star,' he wrote in an essay called *The Definition of Stardom*. 'All others . . . were merely present to fill out the background. The director, I soon discovered, was her abject creature to be dangled and tormented, teased and twirled about her slender fingers . . . Her appearance affected me more strongly than I can logically understand . . . the fan knows his idol. He has been privy to her silent thoughts. He is one with her in the cerebral love-making that takes place in the darkened cinema . . . she is Bardot . . . compare it if you will to meeting Mickey Mouse . . . she is a tramp. A tramp like Charlie Chaplin, not Marilyn Monroe.' Sarne spotted the curious ambivalence of sexuality and indeed that of stars in general. He was so taken by her that her gender hardly seemed to matter. She was a fallen angel and everyone knows angels have no gender. She was a doll with a plastic gusset instead of private parts. Plastic gusset, plastic surgery – certain Californians, who as a race expect anyone over the age of thirty to have submitted to some improvements at the hand of the surgeon, found it quite believable that she had started out life as a man and had been rearranged during any one of her hospitalizations.

Although the French knew every last detail about her life, by the time these details had crossed the Atlantic and a continent beyond there were no facts at all to speak of. They knew simply that she had been a scandal and, twice denounced by the Catholic Church, once after *And God Created Woman*, once when she had upped and married Gunther Sachs when she was supposed to be going shopping, that she was still a scandal. That the Sachses had never really lived together in the same apartment added fuel to the rumour. People who believed it could tell *Time* magazine why she had not added her name to the list of French celebrities who had had abortions. She had had no abortions because she had never been pregnant. Nicolas Charrier? Most people did not even know of his existence and those who had heard of it had seen no evidence of this child, whisked away into purdah the minute he was born. Even his father had been photographed holding a baby who wasn't his. And where were the pictures of Brigitte awaiting his arrival? She had lived behind closed doors because she dared not go out, she had said, but what was the real reason for her faint-heartedness?

The rumour in California as she made films called *Masculin-Féminin*, and *Don Juan* in 1973, was that she had been created from male flesh. It explained her too perfect figure, the generous eyes, lips and bosom, those of the cartoon girl, the slim thighs, hips, the erect stance and the long legs – that of a classical youth. It explained the magnificent lion's mane of hair, flourishing because of masculine hormones, despite any amount of abuse from the sea and the salt water. It explained her inexplicable psychology, her predatory whims, the succession of helpless young boys, her coterie of older women and men like Allain Carré with a chip on their shoulder because they didn't quite fit in. It explained why Visconti had been so taken with her of all women. It explained the rumours of strange homosexual initiation rites in the woods in St-Tropez.

Europe, which never could have evolved a theory like this, thinking it too literal, would have loved it. Gender bending and other mysteries, even before Boy George, were chic in artistic circles. At least one cabaret artist during these late Bardot years, Amanda Lear cashed in on the suggestion, supported by Salvador Dali, that she had had a sex change somewhere in her past.

Hollywood was different, however. Hollywood hated such things. Hollywood was outrageous in its way, but it was also strangely virgin. You didn't have to be Brigitte Bardot herself to get spat at by middle-aged housewives in shopping malls for wearing a mini-skirt in the sixties and early seventies or for not pinning back your hair and discarding your bra if you were obviously physically attractive. The women who made these judgements wore earrings the size of a diamond mine, they dressed in emerald green and purple from top to toe, they wore fluffy pink swansdown slippers to the supermarket and they dressed their poodles to match themselves. Hollywood for the most part was vulgar, at its most adventurous it was acid-damaged and hippy-silly, decked out in ethnic 'head' gear and feeding hash Brownies à la Alice B. Toklas to infant children, but it was not prurient. The French could write at length about cinema as art but as perpetrated in the original Dream Factory it was mass entertainment, and the masses were not prurient either. With the huge rising costs of cinema they simply did not want to take a gamble on what they began to suspect might be Roger Vadim's biggest con of all on a public hungry for entertainment, passing a man off as a woman, and more than that, making him into the biggest female sex-symbol of all time.

That was the rumour going around and the only people who toyed with the idea of employing Bardot in America in those last years were the hotel managements in Las Vegas, which simply did not comply with the ordinary rules of New World society. Like Victorian fairground entertainment, where Mae West had cut her teeth in the ring with her bare-knuckle boxer father Battling Jack West, Las Vegas enjoys freak shows. Vadim's old studio, MGM, put out an offer of £200,000 for Bardot to appear in cabaret in the New Year of 1974 for ten performances at their new hotel complex. There were even rumours that she might finally be united with Sinatra but he refused to appear and so did she. She was too afraid of the stage and of what any appearance might unleash. Bardot was utterly shocking to the American mentality, a case of the decadent older generation shocking the new milk-and-corn-fed, junk-culture youth who liked all their input pre-digested like babyfood rather than challenging to the system like strong meat and wine. Their darling woman was Marilyn, who simply never had that unisex quality of Dietrich with her upper-crust Prussian background or Bardot with her race-horse thighs. 'A magnificent animal' was the verdict of many people who have had contact with Bardot – not a magnificent woman. There was no element of the courtesan playing a cat and mouse game with men which both sexes understood because they had evolved it together. Malle, who had worked with them both, said Jeanne Moreau liked to think of herself as the perfect nineteenth-century odalisque, the quiet, secretive female who could never quite be understood and yet who in return understood all men's appetites: 'Always playing with innuendos. Sexually very exciting because of the twilight zones. Brigitte was much more immediate, all out. Brigitte the great sex-symbol was this extraordinary animal but Jeanne was the erotic one.' That image Moreau had of herself turned a nation on, where Bardot, once they had satisfied themselves, turned them off. There was something of the teenage hockey player about Bardot; too blatant and too physical, a

240

completely uncerebral force which demanded to be pleasured like a man, even masturbated. She made other people redundant.

The Americans retaliated by inventing Dolly Parton with a bosom like two inflatable balloons which reminded a nation of bottle-fed boys of their very first female fantasy, of drowning in a glut of mother's milk. They invented Fonda, the female sergeant major, who needed ranks of other people to fall in step behind her.

They were both in their ways concerned, altruistic human beings, different to Bardot with her 'Public opinion, my arse,' and her statements of retirement from the human race as well as the film business. 'I hate humanity. I am allergic to it. Men are beasts and even beasts do not behave that badly.

'If I could do anything about the way people behave towards each other, I would, but since I can't I'll stick to the animals.'

16. Babette goes to War

Brigitte grew up with animals. Her very first nursery companions were her cat, Crocus, and caged birds. Her mother had her poodle and as soon as Brigitte had a home of her own she too had a dog to go with it, Clown, the cocker spaniel. Clown in turn fathered Gin, her sister's black spaniel by the family bitch Youki. Pilou was devoted to the spaniels and would take them out for walks after a long day at the factory. Brigitte took Clown everywhere with her. He was allowed on the set while she was filming, he had a walk-on role in *And God Created Woman* and he had to get used to all the different rented houses. When Brigitte first got him as a puppy she had to go up and down three flights of stairs whenever he needed to go out. So it was only when she bought La Madrague that she could really indulge her love of animals without being a slave to them. Even there there was not much land for non-domesticated animals, for anything much bigger than a rabbit. They had to wait until she bought Bazoches shortly after the birth of Nicolas. She filled the farm with goats, sheep, horses and donkeys and that was where she went when she really wanted to retire from life. She went there after her divorce from Sachs to play with her current favourites, a donkey called Cornichoo and a red setter called Patapon. She treated her animals as near as possible as human beings. Mauricette Marcey, her housekeeper for several years, tells the story of Brigitte arriving in the kitchen one day and announcing that the hens seemed bored. 'They need a cock!' was her diagnosis and off she went to market to find an imposing specimen. Madame Marcey was very embarrassed by her mistress's overt attitude to sex and was not too pleased to find guests like Michèle Morgan sunning themselves stark naked in the garden, where they wanted waiting on hand and foot. Brigitte worked her overtime, she claimed, and she finally fell out with her mistress over money, not nudity or animals.

242

Not so the mayor of Bazoches who decided to eliminate whichever predators were poaching the wildlife in the area by laying baits of poisoned meat and positioning snares. Brigitte accused him of murdering ten of her dogs. 'I spent whole weekends in the forest calling for them.' Eight of them were never seen again, one was fatally wounded in a trap and another poisoned. The fate of these animals seemed particularly cruel to her because she had saved them once from the local pound. A friend had telephoned saying they were about to be put down and Brigitte had jumped into her Rolls-Royce and loaded it up with fifteen strays behind the partition and ten cats in front. All were transformed into pets whatever their past history of usefulness or misuse. She added to them on the spur of the moment whenever she came across an animal she thought was being abused. Once in a Paris park she offered a man cash on the spot for an old donkey that had outlived its working days pulling a children's cart and in 1972 she stopped a man on a country road near St-Tropez and bought the lamb he was leading to the slaughterhouse.

Brigitte identified with these animals because she felt misused herself. She felt exploited by the cameras and tormented by the public. She felt the cameras were guns with their telescopic sights and the people who wielded them were like Victorian collectors who wanted to get the most magnificent specimen of a particular species into a museum – in her case the museum of the printed page – to stifle her in mid-movement however undignified or unrepresentative, to stuff her for posterity into some library of photojournalism where she made money for them on account of all the other voyeurs who didn't even have to enter the jungle of the media business to examine everything about her. Fans pondered her measurements intimately and fondled her in their dreams. Instead of an eight-foot gorilla or a condor with a six-foot wingspan or the head of a magnificent moose they had a Brigitte Bardot with a 38-inch bust, a nice little 20-inch waist, long slim legs and a most unusual multi-coloured mane. It made her react with the same fear as the cornered wild beast. 'I simply sense whenever I am being photographed,' she says, 'That is why I understand what it is to be a wild animal caught in the telescopic sights of the hunter. The photographers didn't want to kill me but they did kill something in me. They focus on you from far away and they steal something of your soul.'

In Rome, making *Vie Privée*, it had been a gloriously hot

summer yet she, the one who was the focus of all the stress and strain of picture-making, was the one person who could never relax in it. Her friend, the producer Christine Gouze-Renal, used to go for picnics by one of the marvellous deep volcanic lakes in the Roman countryside. They all abandoned their clothes and went swimming, but Brigitte had to stay at home. Then one day she decided to disguise herself as a little old woman with a hat, spectacles, and a stick. She went to the lake unseen, took off her disguise and threw herself in. 'It was wonderful for five minutes,' she says, 'Then a boatload of photographers came. They behaved abominably as usual. One of them actually put his foot down on my chest to photograph me lying on the shore.' Louis Malle, who watched all this, found it quite fascinating. He says she encouraged these reactions just as a frightened beast attracts the hunter or a squealing woman encourages the rapist. 'She would never leave the apartment in the avenue Paul Doumer without wearing a hat and sunglasses and then people would automatically turn and stare and become aggressive towards her. I used to try and make her go out to the cinema without taking all these precautions and indeed I succeeded. When she left BB behind things were a lot easier.' But she didn't necessarily like that either.

The opening shots of the film were shot in Geneva in a shopping mall. Gregor von Rizzi, one of Louis Malle's friends, had read the script and told the director that he had taken the hounding of the star to ridiculous limits. Such exchanges would simply not occur between the public and one of their stars. 'Then suddenly a very well dressed woman stepped out of the crowd, a Vuitton sort of a woman wearing a fur coat, the last person you would think would do a thing like this. She spat at Brigitte. Brigitte tried to hit her and there was quite a scuffle. Gregor, who was holding Brigitte's arm, said he would never have believed it if he had not seen it.'

The Americans witnessed it when she went to the New York première of *Viva Maria*. She was mobbed by the crowd, hit in one eye and blinded by the photographers' flashbulbs. Two doctors had to tend her, though both, uncharacteristically of Americans, waived payment because of her identity. Gunther had seen it at the Cannes Film Festival at a time when they were not even getting on very well, when he wondered why she would not go out on the town every night to the most popular restaurant, where they would be sure to be found by everyone who wanted to look. He suddenly felt an overwhelming sympathy for the woman he had married. He was used to crowds, he was even used to cameras, he was used to being recognized and to seeing his name in the papers, but it was nothing to the madness which surrounded her. With all his sophistication Gunther felt horribly claustrophobic as the ravening mob who leered and lurched outside the elegant Carlton Hotel in Cannes surged towards his bride, looking for all the world as if they were going to tear her apart to see what every bit of her felt like, to eat her alive to see what she tasted like. The hotel had to hire bouncers to stop them careering down the corridors and into the boudoirs of the objects of their desire. Outside they fluttered up and down the windows of the Rolls-Royces and tugged at the door handles. When Gunther and Brigitte arrived at the Palais du Festival near the harbour it looked as if she would have the breath squeezed out of her between the crowds outside and the photographers inside on the steps of the palace, who were reduced to holding their cameras up above their heads in the hope that the lens would somehow find their idol. 'Please don't crush her for me,' Gunther pleaded. She had told him it would be like this but he had not been able to imagine it when Charles Debray, president of the Festival, kept telephoning him to try to persuade her to make an appearance for the first time in ten years at France's number one showbusiness event. He had taken Debray's part and finally she had agreed in the careless spirit of a bet that characterized the Sachs's relationship with each other.

Once, when she was simply going out for a quiet dinner at the harbour in St-Tropez, she had to escape into a little boat with someone she hardly knew who volunteered to row her to safety. They both half expected the crowd to dive into the water or leapfrog across the other boats till they reached her and the man rowed as fast as he could to escape his worst imaginings and hers. 'When I heard this story,' said Gunther, 'I began to understand why she hated going out.'

Once her home was filled by animals there was no reason to leave it. She was no longer afraid of demons once she heard the heavy breathing of her setters and, indeed, those demons, which were ones of emptiness, were cast out by the day to day business her animals imposed upon her, without demanding anything the way that children do. As in everything she was given to overdoing things. Gunther counted fourteen dogs and eight cats when they were together, though he couldn't be sure about the cats because they were always having kittens. Brigitte took the adult animals everywhere with her. When she went to Meribel for winter sports the dogs trotted along behind her in the snow. She also treated her lovers as cuddly toys or security blankets, unable to sleep unless one was in her bed. By the time she got to Laurent Vergez she used to take his pullover to bed with her if he was not there.

Laurent was the boy she was in love with when she first retired from the scene, the one who had been introduced to her by Vadim, who still understood her tastes though he was beginning to despair of them. 'Always living with young boys, always between two love affairs, scared she will lose one and not have another to take his place. It was sort of charming when she was young, this way to be frightened by people, to need slaves around her, to refuse to quit the childish universe she was in. I understood the reason she was like that. It's different when you are thirty-five, thirty-eight, forty . . . It is a good way to become petrified. To turn to stone.' Vergez, an actor turned photographer, immobilized her in the nude in celluloid once more and the pictures appeared in *Playboy* billed as Bardot in her fortieth birthday suit. It was the start of a cult of photographing older women. Joan Collins also celebrated her fortieth birthday, if we all got our mathematics right at the time, by appearing as a nude centrefold. This celebration of the older body was a way of everyone who had invented the youth cult and killed God now attaining eternal life.

As if to prove there were no limitations imposed by the advancing years Bardot's love life hurried on apace. The twenty-nine-year-old Vergez did not survive long into her forty-first year. That winter on her annual skiing trip to Meribel she met the local sculptor Miroslav Brozek. He too had been an actor under the pseudonym of Jean Blaise, but he was a lot more successful in his new career. Brigitte, who has always been an amateur artist as well as a model – she sat for Vadim and he sat for her – went to see Brozek's new exhibition at his studio. 'She looked into my eyes in a way that said more than words,' the young Czech reported. 'At once we were in love.' Brigitte gave him a nickname, Mercu, which was a hopeful sign. 'I also gave him my passion for animals.' Miroslav found them preferable to human competition. Each morning in the chalet started by taking them for a walk. They included Nini, Monche, Thenne, Macho and Pichnon.

Though hardly as great a success as her, Miroslav too survived the huge gamble of the cinema and forged a satisfactory new life for himself away from its compulsive thrills and spills, and this gave her genuine hope for the relationship which she started to invest with all sorts of philosophical qualities. 'I have become deeper, more still,' she told everyone. 'We are very secret and savage together.' With Mercu she stopped running around and appearing with the international hot-mob at disastrous functions like Mick Jagger's St-Tropez wedding to Bianca. She began to understand that a relationship needs hard work. 'I used to think the easy thing was to live with the same person all your life, now I realize that is the difficult one,' she says.

She also tried very hard to shed her image as the original seductress of an infinite number of toy-boys by boosting him, at least in words, as her lord and master. 'He is fantastically talented. Now I just adore to be like his wife. I am available to him. I stay with him. If he needs me I am there.' At one point it even seemed as if she might be pregnant by Brozek.

The new stability was very important to Brigitte because all through 1975 she knew she was losing one of her most important roots, her father Pilou. He was seventy-nine on 8 May but there was not much cause for celebration that year because his health had been getting steadily worse for some time. Brigitte, who had not always seen eye to eye with him, became very much the dutiful daughter in his last months, often visiting him in hospital with her mother, who clung on to a white poodle for comfort. His courage took him through the summer but he died, like a lot of old people with the hopeless prospect of winter ahead, on 5 November. Brigitte buried him in the Marine cemetery in St-Tropez next to her grandparents in a white tomb covered with geraniums and oleander. It was as good a place as any to be buried in the rich red earth of Provence under the kind sun with the soothing sound of the Mediterranean only a few feet away, but that didn't make it any easier to accept. Brigitte, who had given up her career when she saw the inevitable signs of mortality on film, was now obsessed by the idea that death is the only real pornography. As early as 1961 after her suicide attempt she had started to adopt old people to try to give them a new lease of life. One old lady, Suzanne Penière, sent her her engagement ring for her animal causes when she thought she was dying of cancer of the throat. Brigitte went to visit her at Christmas, taking a television set and a Christmas tree. 'She fainted she was so surprised but she got better, she lasted for years. She chose me as her granddaughter and I chose her as my grandmother.' When she died at the age of eighty-four in 1981 Brigitte buried her next to her parents in St-Tropez.

She was not alone in seeing the reaper as the ultimate rapist, but the thought struck her as so horrible that her eyes still well with tears and she starts to stammer whenever it crosses her mind. He is indiscriminate in his potential to corrupt, unlike Vadim's hero, the usually abused Donatien de Sade, who at least needed to be fond of his victims in order to enjoy their demise. Violation, corruption, disfigurement are harder on the complete narcissist than anyone else. 'Death is terrible,' she says now. 'The only thing you can do nothing at all about. It is our punishment and I am sure we deserve it.' She became suddenly disgusted by the human race with its poor prognosis for survival. Whatever she had believed in the past she knew first hand now that she was no more omnipotent than anyone else. With all her money and her fame she had not been able to save her beloved grandmother, who died in 1970, or Pilou and she would not be able to save her mother either, for although Toty was only sixty-three, she suspected rightly that her death would not be long in coming. 'You make all this effort to look after yourself,' she says, 'You take care of your body, of your face, just to end up . . . nothing, decomposed.' It was just like a love affair: you invested so much hope and so much of yourself in it only for it to lose all its vigour at best. She couldn't get away from the thought of death and indeed from her usual first reaction when anything seems inevitable – to forestall it. Those were the tactics she used with lovers, to go to the rupture, to embrace it willingly before it crushed you and she began to understand what she would never have been able to put into words when she cut her wrists in the summer of 1960, fifteen years before – that if death insisted on being the final lover, she would take him by force and surprise if necessary rather than the other way round.

She began to think about death every day rather than love. 'If other people thought about it more they would be better,' she says. 'They would be less wicked and less selfish. They all think they are immortal, that they will live for a thousand years. It is not true, I could die tomorrow. That's why I never make plans.'

That winter a new sort of Brigitte was born, out of the old one it is true, for you can still hear the same petulance in the words, the same confusion over her personal worth. But now she realized she despaired of the human race she stopped trying to charm it and she acquired a sort of vicious eloquence, which in other circles might be that of the hellfire and brimstone preacher. Brigitte touched the headstone on Pilou's grave – 'when I love people I touch them, when I can't touch them, why not touch the stone?' – blew him a hopeless kiss and decided to devote herself to animal causes. In May 1976, which would have seen Pilou's eightieth birthday, she created the Brigitte Bardot Wildlife Foundation.

As early as 1962, when she had only just recovered her stability from her suicide attempt, she had started a crusade on French television to introduce the humane killer into the country's slaughterhouses. Brigitte in gingham with a little girl's headband and a charm bracelet, looking like a vulnerable teenager with tears in her eyes, alternately wielding a stun gun and kneading her knuckles on her lap, spat out her description of how animals' throats were cut in French abattoirs as opposed to the infinitely better system in England and Denmark. 'They like to eat meat in those countries too,' she wailed, 'but they don't torture the animals to do so.' Despite her sentimental attitude to animals she has never been a vegetarian and indeed to some people seems to have a bizarre fascination with their suffering which prompts her to describe in graphic detail some of the intolerable things that happen to them at the hands of human beings.

On this occasion the approach worked. The humane killer was introduced into French slaughterhouses and the law which was passed has been known colloquially as the BB law ever since.

Twelve years later she turned to the cause of baby seals. She had seen pictures of the annual cull on French television and in 1976 she made plans to go to Newfoundland to confront the hunters – 'hunters is too good a word for them, why not butchers?' – in full view of the world's press and television cameras. She was convinced that the butchers would fade away in her presence and that the whole episode would make a very good documentary for French television. She enlisted help from Jacques Cousteau himself, from a polar explorer Paul-Emile Victor, from the environmentalist Philippe Cottereau and from the Swiss ecologist Franz Weber. But she only got as far as the departure lounge at London Airport where she broke down in tears behind her dark glasses. Miroslav blamed it on a fever and took her back to Paris to appeal to the Canadian government through more bureaucratic channels. There she got as far as the Norwegian Embassy, where she joined a public demonstration against the killings. She also helped make a television film on the subject, which riveted public interest – Bardot has always been very good on television – and led to an offer to make more social documentaries, preferably on animal subjects. This in turn led to the meeting with a new love, the French David Attenborough, Alain Bougrain-Dubourg. It also led directly to the setting up of the BB Wildlife Foundation.

The press conference to launch it was a presage of disaster. Although arrangements had been made to beam it by satellite to the United States to win American funds for the cause, Brigitte collapsed in tears and rushed for the door when she saw how many people had responded to her invitation 'to drink a cup of champagne with Brigitte' at a fashionable restaurant in the Bois de Boulogne. At one point she managed to stammer her message of doom across: 'The planet is in a state of war and unless there is action by its inhabitants, irreversible accidents will put the survival of the species at risk.' To avoid this happening the Foundation had multiple grand aims. It would sponsor a crusade against animal abuse in schools and cinemas and via the media. It was against experimenting on animals, abandoning them, exploiting them or using them for profit. It would limit the hours they had to work and ensure they had sufficient food and rest. It would promote ecological research and act as an information exchange.

The French, who like each other so little, and who are possibly more devoted to their animals than the English are supposed to be, took this message to heart, but the Brigitte Bardot Wildlife Foundation ended in farce. After only three months she called for help from her new lawyer Maître Gilles Dreyfus. The Foundation had been overwhelmed with response and Brigitte felt daunted by the administrative tasks ahead. Volunteer staff were replaced by paid professionals which made her worry just how much money would be left for the animals. In September 1976 she wrote a letter to all her supporters: 'The complexity and the multiplicity of problems concerning the defence of animals and the abundant show of generosity by French people who have responded to my cry of alarm have meant paradoxically that the Brigitte Bardot Foundation ceases to exist.' Gilles Dreyfus added: 'Miss Bardot fulfilled her obligations, but she obviously could not be expected to spend twenty-four hours a day working for the Foundation. That is not her job. As a beautiful woman she is not prepared to enter the Holy Order of Animals.'

Many French people now asked themselves exactly what was

her job. Environmentalist Philippe Cottereau, who had arranged for Columbia Broadcasting in the United States to donate $½ million to her Foundation if she would allow herself to be photographed in an American wildlife park, was furious with her when she refused even that. 'She certainly loves animals. The only problem is,' he said unkindly, 'she is not prepared to lift a finger personally to help them. She is just a wealthy lady who prefers to play cards in her villa in St-Tropez.' Other people, who had heard rumours that she was planning to turn over one-third of her income to the Foundation, were confused when no such figure appeared to be forthcoming. She seemed to set herself up as an image; she invoked people's imaginations, she emptied people's pockets in cinema queues, in record shops, in newsagents, or into the coffers of Greenpeace. She was inextricably involved with the human race, and her new passion for animals, yet her passions were not always carried through.

Franz Weber and Miroslav Brozek finally accompanied her to Newfoundland in time for the next year's cull in April 1977. The seal cause seemed somehow made for her and pictures of Bébé Bardot prone on the ice smothering a Bébé Phoque with kisses were eagerly snapped up all over the world. She released a record of herself singing a little song which went something like this: 'The sky is lighter with my dogs at my heels. . . why ever kill the baby seals?' The proceeds were to go to Greenpeace. The sight of BB returning from her triumphant trip to Newfoundland with her lover and a baby seal called Chou Chou – after her character in *The Bride is much too Beautiful* – to add to her menagerie at La Madrague provoked a somewhat sceptical response, and Chou Chou went to live in the Seaworld at Antibes. Rumours from Canada failed to convince her public that she had really done any good for the cause at all. The trip had vacillated between ostentation and, once again, farce. Armed with a battle cry 'At the present rate of killings the last of the seals will be finished by 1985', Bardot had hired a private jet to join the International Fund for Animal Welfare supporters on the ice-floes of north-east Newfoundland. But she lingered so long over talks about setting up a fake-fur fashion house and over a meal that the helicopter with fund officials took off on the last stage without her. Then, rather than go on to the front like another actress, Yvette Mimieux, who was equally appalled at the seals' fate, she called a press conference in the relative luxury of the village of Blanc Sablon. The French public recognized Brigitte's principal skill as talking up a good campaign. 'The ice was red. I saw it from the plane, streaked with red for miles and miles and strewn with tiny carcases. They kill them with iron hooks, you know, little two-week-old seals, defenceless little balls of fur and life and love. They skin them on the spot and you can see the little heart still beating in the bloody mass that remains. And later the blood congeals and you remember the stench all your life.' It is arguable that she was less successful in doing anything to stop the slaughter. It would probably have made no difference had she thrown her body between the hook and the hunted as other people did. But her public may have felt frustrated by the news of the closure of the Foundation after just one brief summer.

Bardot was very hurt by the attitude of the French Press, who seemed to think this trip to the frozen wastes, beautifully kitted out as Anouk of the North, must have been a publicity stunt. Franz Weber tried very hard to dissuade them. 'Since she dislikes long travel and fears flying, going to Canada with me was an act of courage for her,' he said. 'We reached the tundra in a small plane. The ice and the blood of the seals frightened her badly. And it was dangerous: she had one nasty slip. She couldn't have faced ice, helicopters and the press conference – because her very greatest fear may be of journalists – without great determination to fight to the end. Brigitte Bardot is wonderfully steadfast. She is wonderful in general – a fantastic, complete person.'

'It was horrible,' says Brigitte of the trip. 'I'd been used to travelling in incredible luxury: first class tickets and suites in the best hotels. And suddenly I found myself in the cold, in this rickety plane, being insulted when I landed and nobody taking me seriously. I was refused meals by the Canadians and thrown out of the only inn in the village.' She accused the public of insensitivity and they accused her of the same thing.

Professional people still recognized that her name was a draw, among them Alain Bougrain-Dubourg, a television producer for Antenne 2, and the Council of Europe who, inspired by the letters she had written with Franz Weber to world leaders like Giscard D'Estaing and Jimmy Carter on the subject of ecology, invited her to attend their debate on seal hunting early in 1978. Brigitte was welcomed by the council president, Professor Karl Czernetz, who said: 'I believe it is not out of place for a parliamentary assembly to salute someone who, like Madame Bardot, interests herself in this cause.' She was touched when Frau Magda Hubinek from Austria commended her first-hand investigations and a Dutch member, M. Cornelisson, told the Assembly it was largely due to her that public opinion had burned against the annual seal massacre. However, the Belgian member, Claude Dejardin, thought her presence in the public gallery was turning the debate into a circus. 'I hope there will be as many delegates and members of the public present when we discuss human rights,' he said.

To the animal-loving public her squabbles with other animal lovers seemed bizarre. While talking about dogs found in labs with their vocal chords cut so they could not cry out in pain, elephants burned to death in menageries, rabbits with their eyes destroyed by cosmetics, while rolling around these atrocities in her beautiful mouth, she put her lawyer on to Paul-Emile Victor's Environment Group asking to be repaid the rent she had provided for an office and the salaries of the office workers. She also asked for symbolic one-franc damages to be paid to the Foundation for 'injury' to its image. The Foundation had raised £7,500 but had spent double that on labour, stationery and postage. 'Perhaps I would have done more good if I had bought 25,000 tins of dog food and distributed them to strays.'

Brigitte in her retirement seemed to reach for her lawyer at every available point. After a prolonged period of holidaymaking with Miroslav in the South of France and the French Alps she turned her attention to the disfigurement of St-Tropez and slapped an injunction on the mayor. He had conceived plans to expand the little resort upwards as well as outwards in the form of a tower block designed by one of France's leading architects. Brigitte would have none of it. If the scheme took place she said she would personally quit the village which for so long had given her protection, charm and freedom, and live instead on a tropical island. Mayor and council were tempted to take notice of this threat, considering the financial ramifications of her presence. But all the same there were certain indications that Brigitte would never leave this place. Her house, La Madrague, had been almost constantly on the market since she had married Gunther Sachs but no appropriate offer had been made – or taken up. Her first attempt to sell it came just a year after the ceremony when the hordes of sightseers became too much for her in July. The asking price was £180,000. Three years later she refused £200,000 for it and by the time she had retired she had put the asking price up to a quarter of a million. In spring 1977, when she was occupied with the seals, the asking price had leapt to £350,000.

It was the same in Paris. No one ever seemed to take over a Bardot apartment. When she moved she simply added to her list of properties, buying a particularly grand one in the rue du Bac with enough space for a helicopter pad on the balcony.

La Madrague remained in the family. The estate in St-Tropez went ahead and Brigitte stayed, even building herself another house, La Garrigue, in the woods. From there she set about persuading the mayor to ban nude bathing on her local beach, Le Virol.

The law has been her hobby for some while, a way of defending herself from the problems of being Bébé in whom everyone wanted a share. As we have seen with the garagiste, she did not like paying bills unnecessarily. In a rare moment of criticism, Jacques Charrier even claimed she would not give a dinner party in the sixties, without charging the guests £2 a head. In 1968, the year before the Rolls-Royce incident, a painter named Gilberto Severi filed a suit in Milan for payment for a painting of Gunther Sachs as Adam and Brigitte Bardot as Eve which he claimed had been commissioned by them.

Then there were the libel suits. In the early sixties she won a significant lawsuit against the *paparazzi* in St-Tropez about the right of an actress to have some private life. Over the years it has inspired all sorts of people from Alain Delon to Catherine Deneuve to set lawyers on anyone exposing any fact that was not strictly professional. Deneuve appeared to take this to ridiculous extremes recently when she wrote to French newspapers threatening to sue anyone who exploited her relationship with her son, Christian Plemianikoff, in connection with his new film career with Roger Vadim. She didn't mention he was Vadim's son, too. Bardot was never far behind. 'My client is not like General de Gaulle,' said her lawyer in 1965, 'she has not made a gift of her person to the nation.' Over the years Brigitte invoked this statement again and again, though the cases were often resolved with the nominal award of one franc's damages in her favour, and an acknowledgement in whichever publication had breached her privacy.

In 1967 she and Gunther filed a suit against the Italian magazine *Playmen* for publishing photographs of the couple sunbathing by their private pool on the Appian Way, her topless and him nude.

In 1969 she filed a claim for £8,500 damages against the weekly newspaper *ICI* for saying she had had a skin operation. Robert Badinter, her then lawyer, argued that any adverse reference to her looks constituted a threat to her earnings. In 1983 she won £2,000 from the satirical magazine *Hari Kari* which dared to show her as an old witch with a single tooth, and 1979 had seen a huge legal battle, which she won, against Paul Raymond over nude pictures taken on her fortieth birthday. He published them in one of his magazines, having bought them for £3,000 from a reputable source. Raymond and his editor, Roger Baker, paid £10,000 to Bardot after they had been seen by nearly a million readers world-wide. Their defence was that these were posed pictures showing Brigitte in the nude or wearing black boots or lace panties, – they were probably from the set taken by Laurent Vergez – and it was obvious that Brigitte knew what she was doing.

The whole incident seemed to be a curious dry run for a lawsuit which she then launched against a French publishing house concerning the latest Bardot book in France – which is frankly a combination of a fanzine and a photo album. The author, who specializes in this sort of thing, described it as an homage to Madame Bardot, whom she had always admired. Madame Bardot apparently reciprocated the admiration and she wrote and told her so, but Madame Bardot's advisors, who immediately slapped an injunction on the book when it appeared on the stands, did not. The ball was set rolling by Olga Horstig who made polite contact with the publisher, claiming to be a little offended because he had not thought to send Brigitte some copies of the book – including three autographed ones for Olga, Brigitte herself, and her friend Alain Bougrain-Dubourg. Within an hour of delivery of these copies, and before they could possibly have been read, Gilles Dreyfus had one in his possession and was preparing a suit against the publisher for violation of Brigitte's private life and her rights to those pictures which were not film stills. The case was heard in the Magistrates Court in December 1983 and the magistrates assessed around £4,000 in damages, while maintaining that very little harm had been done to Madame Bardot. The book was certainly not removed from the bookshops and several lawyers tried to encourage the publisher to go to a higher court where they were sure the outcome of the case would be reversed. British newspapers were tempted to act on this advice when they were successfully sued over articles and photographs which appeared in their first editions on sale in France just after Bardot's forty-ninth birthday. Once again the damages were relatively small and, on balance, it was judged better to pay them and to keep French news, particularly that concerning Brigitte Bardot, back for the later editions which do not cross the Channel and remain out of reach of French jurisdiction. The French have learned by experience not to comment on these foreign verdicts.

Bardot has gone for big targets and small ones in law, knowing that the latter usually fade away or pay up. When Linda Yellin, the film-maker who made *Playing for Time* with Vanessa Redgrave and the story of Charles and Diana (for American television), proposed to make a biographical film of Bardot to coincide with her fiftieth birthday, Bardot issued a statement to the effect that she would sue anyone who did such a thing without her permission. CBS Broadcasting are going ahead and making the film.

Her agent Olga Horstig and her lawyer Gilles Dreyfus want to encourage the idea that she will win the case that they are preparing which would virtually copyright any mention of her name in France, but other lawyers are sceptical. Rita Hayworth's daughter, who tried the same thing in the United States to protect the reputation of her mother, was not successful and Frank Sinatra, with a similar case against his latest American biographer, has so far received only one reaction to it – that she intends to publish and not be damned. Success in this case would lead to a form of censorship where the Press was the poodle or PR representative of any personality it wanted to discuss. As it is, the litigious nature of Bardot's advisors has already made the French public very sceptical about their most famous star. A woman who traded on her public identity, who became a considerable property owner and investor as a result of this, can hardly now turn on her fans, teasing them with her public position as animal spokesman or star of documentaries about herself – like Bougrain-Dubourg's *Telle Qu'Elle*, from which she stands to benefit, meanwhile censoring all other comment.

Fans of hers were disappointed when she resorted to the law to get her sister out of her flat in St Germain, and this suit was finally dropped at Brigitte's request. Mijanou today lives very much under her elder sister's thumb though they are 1,000 miles apart. She lives in their grandmother's house at Louveciennes where she has built a little studio in the garden – visits by appointment – to show her rather limited range of home-made do-it-yourself double-decker space-saving rustic furniture which has featured in *Elle* magazine as very suitable for the typical cramped Paris apartment. At forty-five Mijanou enjoys gardening as much as anything, but she is as sharp as a button, permanently in contact with her sister and very protective of her.

The thing Brigitte fears above all is an erosion of her financial position as one of France's wealthier self-made women. From time to time, therefore, she has allowed herself to be lured out of retirement by the advertising profession. In 1974 she made a tourist board film for £20,000. 'This is the first commercial I have ever made and I would only do it for France and for the president Giscard,' she said. She earned £100,000 after a year of negotiations from a thirty-second television commercial costing £500,000 altogether, set in a reproduction of the drawing room of La Madrague to advertise a men's perfume, Zendiq, produced by Goya, having first assured herself it was free from animal extracts. She worked with a passion at this for twelve hours at a stretch, greatly impressing the Goya representative with her terpsichorean ad libs and the British television audience who jammed the station switchboards asking when the commercial would next run; though Mary Kenny sceptically wondered whether this was to the advantage of the product which women would buy their men, since Bardot was famous for her allure not her consistency. In 1984 Bardot started to make television commercials for an American telephone company.

She started a range of beauty and fashion products called La Madrague modelled on Sachs's Mic-Mac. The clothes label is discontinued but she still has the cosmetics and her own brand of sunglasses. She has made ads for Karting and, horror of horrors, for Blackglama mink, causing the public to regard the life of a woman who can rail at the same time against killing animals 'to make fur coats for rich cunts' as a series of suspicious contradictions. The photograph of her in a mink coat was actually taken some years ago by her lover of the time, Jean-Loup Sieff, the only picture in the history of the famous 'What Becomes a Legend Most?' campaign not to be taken by Richard Avedon and Bill King who, between them, had focussed on Lillian Hellman, Rudolf Nureyev, Lauren Bacall, Lena Horne, Luciano Pavarotti, Marlene Dietrich and almost everyone else in becoming fur coats. Peter Rogers, who masterminded the campaign, was not pleased with the shot which he said made the wayward Bardot beauty look like a well-groomed Jane Fonda. What's more there was altogether too much animal skin in the photo and too little human. He changed his mind when she joined the French Animal Protection Society and spiteful French shopkeepers found they could boost their mink sales by sticking her picture right in the middle of the window.

Misunderstandings over her animal interests keep cropping up. One respected French cancer research scientist, Professor Henri Sarles, won £210 in a lawsuit against her for libelling him over his work. She called him a 'hangman' and a 'torturer'. A judge, Michael Saucer, subsequently commented; 'She criticizes others for experiments on animals, yet she is a partner in a cosmetics firm which uses rabbits. She would do better looking after battered children.' In 1982 she claimed she rescued three Dobermann dogs from a building site in St-Tropez. Builder Jean Vella, who claimed he was using them as guard dogs, disagreed and sued her for theft. Only this year there was the tactless affair of the ivory bracelet which she sent to Canada's Animal Protection League in Quebec just after the country had signed an international treaty banning the import of ivory. The Canadians turned the gesture against her by considering a prosecution if she did not have a permit to export the bracelet. Even as she was drafting caricature letters, 'Brigitte sends you a big kiss', to Bill Travers, her old friend from acting days, offering her enthusiastic services for Zoo-check, his London-based campaign against the cruelty of zoos, it was noted that her setter Nini drowned in her swimming pool because he could not climb out. Moreover, when one potential biographer offered her a share of royalties for any animal cause she cared to name, he received a very curt reply from Olga Horstig saying quite pointedly, 'Brigitte isn't interested in all the animals in the world. She has her own and that is enough.'

Brigitte reached for her lawyer again when her mother died at the beginning of August 1978 in the American Hospital in Paris after an emergency operation for a stomach tumour. This time she accused 'unnamed people of failing to assist an endangered person'. Nothing would bring Anne-Marie back and it was difficult for Brigitte, the eternal child, to realize she was now the biggest one around, older than her sister, her lover, her son, his father. She was very proud of Nicolas, who was now eighteen and attended his grandmother's memorial service in Paris with her on

10 September. She retired back to La Madrague with Miroslav. The affair had now lasted six years but it did not survive her forty-sixth birthday when she claimed he just jetted to America without telling her. Well, she had done that before him. This time she did not seem too upset, the reason being that her activities with French television had brought another young man into her circle, a producer called Alain Bougrain-Dubourg.

17. The Truth

The 1980s dawned well for Brigitte. For the first time since her days with Vadim she had the company of a man with a viable destiny of his own who seemed to want genuinely to try and fit in with her.

Brigitte rationalized that she had learned a lot from her experiences. Where she had thought it was a piece of cowardice to stay with the same man all your life, as her mother had done, she now realized the cowardice was *not* to. On the contrary: two people had to take their courage in both hands and not dodge the issues, live life as it turned up but with the underlying belief that they were a couple no one and nothing could shake. She told all this to Alain Bougrain-Dubourg. She decided to stop worrying that there was something better round the corner.

In this she was aided somewhat by a delicious second teenage which comes over a woman in her forties. If before she has nothing to lose because she has no experience to fill her with fear, once past the magic milestone she has enough experience of society to release her from her responsibilities. In today's climate of middle-aged health and beauty she also still has her looks. A forty-year-old woman can become a raver or a recluse and the rest of the world shrugs its shoulders.

Contrary to all the expectations she had had when he had been born, Brigitte felt younger now she had a grown-up son, not older. She had become closer to him after he reached the age of fifteen and treated him like a brother. He was no problem. He had not turned to drugs or drink or dropped out of life like so many of the sons of stars. He might annoy her by potting at cats with his shotgun in his spare time, but his image was that of a gentleman and despite his provocative bloodline he had not cheapened his life in any way. He was a diligent student at Dauphine University in Paris, though not keen. He did not paint the town red or spend money Brigitte in retirement could ill-afford. Though he didn't pursue Brigitte's bourgeois ambition, like Catherine Deneuve's, that her son should become a lawyer, he was willing to work for his living and was signed up for a while by Pierre Cardin to model his 'Martian' sporting clothes range for men – the black leather jackets and trousers which Cardin likes to wear himself. He also asked him to compose the music for the fashion show to launch the line. Nicolas's start in life was strangely echoing Bardot's own. One of his Platonic companions was his cousin Camille. When he found a Norwegian girlfriend and saw less of his mother she was even a little sad.

If ten years ago Brigitte had thought herself free without a career and without a husband, now she was really free, without a public image and without a mother and father either. She could choose exactly who she wanted to be and no man had to measure up to Pilou, or be chosen precisely because he could never compete.

If she no longer had the figure she boasted thirty years ago when she made *And God Created Woman* – the 36-inch self-supporting bust, the 20-inch waist and tight 34-inch hips – if she was no longer still 8 stone 9 pounds in weight, her beautiful fawn's eyes which changed from brown to hazel to green according to her mood had acquired the sort of sadness which the public respected in Marilyn Monroe's. Brigitte had acquired depth with age and an appreciation of real priorities and if her dislikes had remained constant over the years – for nothing more than coffee, cakes, jewels, and a healthy mistrust for the age in which she was born – why they were not sins. Moreover, her likes had not changed either and they were the core of her personality and they had given her confidence over the years.

Above all she liked music: jazz and Bach and Smetana and Albinoni, anything with a strong rhythm like the insistence of sex. She liked Erik Satie, the surrealist composer who wrote music for typewriters – a legacy from Vadim's tutelage. She loved string instruments and the record she kept playing over and over again to herself over the years was not a pop song like the one which had been ruined by a jealous technician in Pinewood but Bach's *Concerto for Two Violins*. She loved to laugh: Jerry Lewis was her favourite comedian, and that she had in common with most of the rest of France. She no longer went to the cinema – its new stars didn't make her dream. She loved to drink wine and had almost given up whisky, and though she was confident now that all the animals at the modernized La Villette slaughterhouse in Paris were killed with her stun gun she no longer liked to eat Charolais beef. Marguerite Yourcenar, who asked to meet her at La Madrague, put their mutual objection to meat-eating in strong words. 'I don't want to digest agony.'

Brigitte still liked men but she had learned a thing or two about them. She no longer always threw jealous scenes when something called them away from her bedside. In the old days she could lose several pounds a day grieving over a misplaced word. Thinking about her first notions of marriage it hardly seemed conceivable at fifty that she could have expected it all to be lying around reading women's magazines and romantic novels and eating chocolates, that she and Vadim had made a pact 'to make each other's breakfast on alternate days and bring it to the bed, to sleep in the sun all day long, to love it all' all of the time, especially those moments when he told her she was the only woman in the world. It hardly seemed conceivable that she should have been so self-destructive that she insisted on eating her chocolates even though they made her bilious and sick and dizzy, or that she could have waited all day in silence for him to come home, 'my eyes dry, my throat dry and my heart dried up', because she was overcome with suspicion and jealousy. She could remember sobbing hysterically when he came in and explained there was nothing to worry about, even running a fever until she found out the whole truth, but she couldn't remember how it felt any more to be that insecure. Little things like that had eroded all her relationships, all stemming from a lack of confidence in herself, even though she had been brought up to know that you don't ask personal questions of men about their past largely for fear of finding out the answers. 'Men consider it useless, childish and somewhat ludicrous and women worry about it.' All the troubles of this woman, who was a byword for sex off- and on-screen, had come from her personal relationships with men, from self-doubt she could not even act sex on-screen without disintegrating with terror in front of the camera, preferring to play her romantic scenes to a piece of camera tape not a human being. She was the biggest star, says Vadim now, because she was so insecure she would never stop trying to draw attention to herself.

Now, more than halfway into her forties, she felt grown-up at last and able to look reality in the face. It was a marvellous bonus

that Alain Bougrain-Dubourg seemed to understand her mixture
of fabulous courage and niggling practicality. They had met in
1977 in dramatic conditions on the ice-floe where the director was
filming and Brigitte was taking part in her campaign to save the
baby seals, and they took up the cause together. 'We are extremely
complementary,' he says. 'I sometimes have the knowledge of
animal affairs which she doesn't but she has the sensitivity and the
popularity. My relationship with her is my own affair but let me
say it is the most beautiful thing that can happen to a man. People
say she only took up the animal cause because she wanted
popularity but that is obviously not true because she never goes
out of her way to seek it for herself rather than the animals. People
also say she wants to make money out of animals but there is not a
single day goes by when she doesn't send money to some animal
cause, saving the whales or to a dogs' home perhaps. She spends a
lot of money she has earned on them rather than blowing money
like other people do. It's not that she is stingy – another thing
people say – she's not a wastrel. She doesn't have a chauffeur, she
says herself she hasn't bought a dress for ten years, she is not the
sort of person who blows 10 or 20,000 francs in a single evening at
Régine's.'

To most people who saw them together it was obvious that
Alain Bougrain-Dubourg was genuinely fond of Brigitte and was
not trying to advance his career by making the television film
about her life. The idea to do a biographical film about her had
been in the air in France for a long time and stunning sums had
been offered for her co-operation, according to Alain. After he
and Brigitte had worked together on animal programmes for
some time on Antenne 2 the proposition was brought to a head by
an offer from another channel. Brigitte asked Alain to make the
film instead, but he was reluctant to do so until he met a producer
in Monte Carlo whom Brigitte respected and who would understand her coy approach to cinema-making. Sometimes when they
were working together Brigitte simply didn't feel like it, so Alain,
who had to do something with the crew, started to shoot her
dogs. Brigitte rushed to help. 'Take care, you are in shot!' he
would warn. This sense of humour helped.

'At first she didn't want to do it,' says Alain, 'and even when
she agreed it was always a delicate operation. We used the very
minimum of technicians, sound equipment, lights and so on so as
not to upset her. We had no make-up people, no hairdressers, no

script. She was capable of marvellous improvizations, taking out her guitar and giving a street party for the people of St-Tropez. She never knew the questions I was going to ask her and some of them were undoubtedly embarrassing for her, but it was a way of closing the book. This was to be the truth about Bardot, rather than the appearance, with all her faults which are particularly her impulsiveness – she is a difficult character – her tendency to curl up in her shell, her great fragility despite her undoubted talent and potential. That is a great weakness. But she trusted me. She only came into the cutting room once. She didn't even want to see the film until the day before it was shown on French television. That day, just before Christmas two years ago, there was a standing ovation in the screening room. They were not applauding the film, they were applauding the woman because she had survived.' Brigitte's eyes filled with tears. She wept.

The film was shown as a three-part series first in France and then in England and it was finally sold to Home Box Office, the American cable television company. It was not greatly admired anywhere but, like a Milanese art exhibition in 1983 where a thousand images of Bardot were solicited from European painters and sold, it showed that Brigitte still had curiosity value. The week after the French showing 10,000 letters poured in to La Madrague. Most of them were from working men and women. Once in front of the cameras Brigitte had felt the adrenalin flowing again and she had tried to take control. When she thought certain scenes were no good Alain decided she was always right when he screened the rushes to himself. The career she had never wanted had become a matter of habit.

Looking back Brigitte began to wonder what would have happened to her if her mother had not been a stage mother and if she had not met Vadim. She started to try and put it on paper herself, but application and, indeed, memory were not her virtues and the proposed autobiography meanders on. From time to time she rings Vadim to ask him the name of a town where they stayed or a date. He says his memory is no better and he can rarely help her.

Though the public may have felt manipulated by her she decided she had been every inch as manipulated by almost everyone she had ever come in contact with. At this late stage in life she wanted to stand for herself, to be in charge of an entire enterprise from beginning to end, and that in an environment she found agreeable. So she began to work as hard as she was able for her boutique in St-Tropez which she called La Madrague. These last seasons in France have seen a great nostalgia for the heyday of the cinema with boutiques springing up in every holiday resort selling James Dean posters, Marilyn Monroe ashtrays and Kleig table lights. Bardot's memorabilia are concentrated on her own brand new shop in the Place de l'Ormeau in St-Tropez. Brigitte has gone into commerce just like her mother. Her businesswomen friends, Christine Gouze-Renal and Olga Horstig, her stand-in and her make-up girl from the past lend their support and some of the proceeds are offered to the animals.

Brigitte feels justified. She learned things in a hard school – the film business – in which winners want to be the biggest winners of all time and losers are on the junk-heap, finished, unbankable, played out. All through her life she had been at odds with its gambling spirit. Her bourgeois background did not encourage flamboyant gestures. BB is much more like the church mouse, a mouse being her favourite animal, who hives away what she has. But what attracted her to the profession and what she did have in common with it, was the way in which film people created their own universe in which they obeyed their own rules, not those of that other world where people get up at the same time every day of the year and go to the same job, bring up sane children and save for their old age. A film cast and crew live fantasy. They dream it up, find money to finance their dream, people the dream with perfect personalities, orchestrate the perfect outcome. A film, no matter how it finishes on the screen, starts out its life with the most ambitious, luxurious ideals. Bardot was determined to make her own environment and it would, in essence, be a domestic one, the idyll she had foregone for Vadim.

It is a delicate balance she has to maintain with the local people, robust sorts whose lives have never been excited or marred by lack of common sense and who sometimes resent her for the flair she has for having her own way. They accuse her of being aggressive in parking her car any which way, of bossing the delivery men around, and of not being able to decide whether she is a star or not. She plays a peekaboo game with them, of the elderly ingenue – now you see me, now you don't, who am I, please tell me. . . . 'I have never been a doll,' she says. 'No one has ever brought out my depths.' Her companion now is as likely as not to be the local hairdresser, a Platonic friend. 'I might be older than her boyfriends and fiancés but I last longer. Why? Because I make a very good seafood salad and I make her laugh.'

'Prince Charming?' she says. 'I wouldn't recognize him now, except from behind – on the way out! Men don't want to be responsible for women any more, but if two people live together they have to be responsible for each other. Women went too far in trying to get rid of them in the name of women's liberation. Now they are on their own – even if they are young and pretty they are still on their own. And yet woman was created to make a man's life more agreeable, not to work all day and rush home to defrost something to eat in front of the television. Woman was created to arrange flowers, to cook a good meal and keep a beautiful house.'

18. Warrior's Rest

You approach Brigitte's house in the South of France through big double coach doors and a tunnel of eucalyptus, pink oleander, and thick undergrowth. You will find her there in the autumn and spring. In the summer she will be in Bazoches, in the winter in Paris or in the Alps, though she doesn't ski as much as she used to. She will come down the path at La Madrague to meet you wearing shorts and a T-shirt – no bra, and according to her no plastic surgery, – or jeans and boots if it is cold. Her hair will be loose down to her waist or scooped up very informally and tied under a gypsy scarf. She will probably be smoking an American cigarette and if she is pleased to see you she will offer you a drink quicker than anybody you have ever known. Then she will put some music on the stereo. It may be gypsy songs or it may be Bach. If it is cold there will be a log fire in the huge fireplace. A sombrero from Mexico and a poncho from her travels in South America hang over the banister of a little gallery reached by a ladder which overlooks the room. It is a room which still recalls the sixties. There are monstera plants, modern sculptures and log baskets and the furniture is an odd mixture of rustic and white vinyl. There will always be roses in the vases on the glass coffee table and by the white sofa – pink roses. Wherever she goes Brigitte will be trailed by her dogs. In her bedroom the baskets are lined up in rows. You might chat idly on the blue flowered counterpane among her stuffed animals or sit in a wicker chair and entertain her with stories while she takes a bath in the big mirrored bathroom with its twin handbasins for lovers' use. If you are lucky she will ask you to stay in the tiny house which she calls Microbus, which she has built for guests. More rustic than the main house, you reach it down some whitewashed steps. It has wooden furniture, orange and red check upholstery. It is marvellously cool in the summer heat and it is virtually self-contained. Brigitte is always rearranging both houses. 'I have loved Madrague and hated it,' she says.

Instead of turning her back on her memories as in the avenue Paul Doumer, in the South of France she embraces them, she even indulges them, writing her memoirs, looking at photographs and visiting her pet cemetery at the bottom of the garden and talking to the graves. 'I choose to live alone in retreat, hardly seeing anybody,' she says. 'I'm not sad or bitter about it. I can't say I never did anything with my life – on the contrary I did it all and I saw it all. And since I have seen everything I can choose the best. The best is to be alone, or nearly alone with my animals. My dearest wish is that other people realize how much animals suffer. They are not selfish, they are not hypocritical, they need love and attention, they need protecting. I like human beings who like animals, not those who think they are objects to eat or beat or sacrifice.'

Alain Bougrain-Dubourg is just such a person and still keeps in touch with her, spending half an hour on the telephone at a time from Paris. Younger than Brigitte, he is by no means ready for chrysanthemums but he would have felt like it had he agreed to retire prematurely to the South of France rather than pursue his own career in Paris. Brigitte preferred a retired lifestyle even when she was in her teens. She likes to sit looking out over the Mediterranean thinking – about nothing, which is something she has tried to learn from her animals. 'I practise thinking about nothing just listening to the sound of the waves.' She likes to eat, sleep, entertain and be entertained. She shares the locals' aversion to work and their indolence born of the heat of the sun. When celebrities come to the South of France they no longer look her up as one of the obligatory sights, when she crosses the Channel no magazine editors bother her to team her with Lichfield or Bailey, the ex-husband of Deneuve who she loved for his Cockney spirit. No one offers to introduce her to Boy George as they did to John Lennon. No great artists offer to paint her and she lives in regret that when she met Picasso she didn't ask him to pick up his brush. She has retired from more than the screen and she lives in a part hippy world, part local kitsch.

'I have found out that friendship is quite as important as love and it isn't any easier than love. I have very few old friends. What happens is that you share things for a while and then you move on. You can have "affairs" of friendship just like love-affairs.' Just as with lovers she doesn't commit herself to any duty. You will be there and she will and if it suits you both you will have a good time.

In the morning you might go shopping in her Minimoke – the Paris-registered number is 2134 SI 75. You might feed her sixty cats. You may go out in her little rowing boat and take the dogs swimming, or accompany her along the shoreline for a walk. You may go up to La Garrigue for an alfresco meal under the eaves of the modern house in the middle of a pine forest. Brigitte will play the barrel-organ she bought in a bric-à-brac shop, or the guitar, she may dance after a meal, served on oilcloth with wine in re-cycled mustard glasses, she has even learned to be a modest cook.

During the day you will sunbathe or read or eat chocolates. Brigitte may add a page to her book and she will always read and write letters. She gets very gratifying letters from women now they think they have nothing more to fear from her. They also write bewildered letters. What does it all mean? Was it worthwhile? Where does anyone go from here?

Jane Fonda thought that Bardot both pre-dated Women's Lib and symbolized it. Others thought quite the opposite. A British newspaper, which thought her the worthwhile subject of a leader in 1963 two days after she arrived in London to shoot *A Ravishing Idiot* with Tony Perkins, concluded she had set back the women's movement by several decades. They compared her with Marlene Dietrich who by coincidence was also in the British capital at the time. She was magnificently aloof and, receiving me in her dressing room at the Queen's Theatre in the full glare of consider-able wattage, illustrated that it is not light that women of a certain age should fear, like Blanche Dubois, but shadow.

Both Bardot and Dietrich were that unusual phenomenon, the well-born entertainment star. But Dietrich, the writer claimed, was a vamp: 'In her roles she drew men down to destruction.' In her private life she treated anyone who clashed with her with contempt and they included Adolf Hitler. 'She put the women of the West into trousers. She commanded, and men could do nothing but obey.' In contrast he said that Bardot had thrown all the ambitions of militant women away. 'She is even the creation of men. She seems almost intent on leading a female migration back to the harem. Men like to think they are the centre, purpose and sole object of women's activities and existence. Bardot flatters that belief.'

This was a prescient thing to say in 1963. Bardot had by then established her pattern of taking in whom she fancied and chucking them out when she liked. Lots of women, those who cut their fringes like her, grew their hair down their backs, allowing it to become wild and sun-streaked and baked their limbs through and through on the nearest beach, those pioneers of the Pill and of promiscuity, even those intellectuals like Simone de Beauvoir who could see no good reason other than male-ordered habit why women should not behave like men, regarded her as a scion of freedom.

Bardot herself agrees more with the leader-writer. 'To me, being blonde meant living my life for men, being a sex-symbol all of the time, a symbol of carefree, young France. I enjoyed it, but the blonde hair blinded men to the real person underneath. I'm taken more seriously now, and sexually, I please myself more, I ask much more from men – in part because of my new identity and because times have changed. But men still want old-fashioned girlfriends, so blondes are popular all over again. Before I was one of the few top blondes; now there are so many imitations. It is flattering but I have outgrown it.'

The strange outcome of the sexual revolution was that it put a pressure on women that many of them could not cope with, as Vadim had foreseen. They gave all their cards away, and I do not mean in the old-fashioned sense of sacrificing their virginity. That was a symbol. They unveiled the essential mystery of the individual which makes any one person more interesting to another than a bleeding heart or an open book and drew to themselves only weak men who were content to be crutches or lap dogs soothing away what they were apt to call nature's wound, the imposition of menstruation. Women became revolting through their demands for sympathy and their strident insistence that only the sisterhood knew what was right and what was wrong for the world.

Today it is difficult to think of one female star who provokes the imagination rather than the political conscience, never mind a star of the magnitude of Brigitte Bardot. Pornography is not just the vulgar display of pudenda. It is easy gratification in many areas. Nearly everyone in the West today lives like a star. They have easy sex, fast food, ready drugs, available travel. These things are not wrong in themselves but the expectation of them, which dulls their appreciation, is. When the theatre and the cinema became political weapons real life became the arena for bigger and better dreams, and nightmares. Football games are played more keenly by the fans than by the players, the most exciting television series is the daily news, the most rewarding photograph is the real representation of birth or death or copulation. Life, if we are not careful, could be one great snuff movie, the veritable Apocalypse Now. Full exposure can be as alien to truth as censorship and people who care passionately about things, from Mary Whitehouse to striking miners breaking TV lenses, have struck the first blow at the impertinent camera as public enemy number one. Money and the television are our two scourges, says Brigitte.

Bardot is not fond of modern life. She hates the vulgarity she sees all around her in St-Tropez, 'a horizontal Galeries Lafayette, a holiday camp'. She says she loathes promiscuity and she doesn't like the new fashions which don't flatter women, 'clown pants – no doubt they are very comfortable, but you have to suffer to be beautiful.' She is more in favour of artifice than you would think.

Bardot's generation was the cross-over one in the exchange between fact and fiction. With the aid of government money, yet with a lack of earning power, they have switched the realities which directed the fantasies of earlier generations. Now there is a generation of actors who act in street clothes without sets, often because of financial constraint, and private citizens who wear full theatrical make-up on the streets. Nowadays boys want to look like girls and the girls want to look like boys. It is easier to think of men as sex-symbols rather than women and many of them beg some sexual or theatrical question: Boy George in ringlets, Richard Gere as the American gigolo, Liberace riddled with rhinestone, who still packs Radio City Music Hall with middle-aged women, Mick Jagger in full make-up and slashed décolleté. These are the entertainers and the vamps while the women – even Bardot sometimes – go to war. 'When you do it, you don't do it with a smile on your face, you go to war to win, as I do for the animals.' Her generation of women is the one whose role models were their fathers not their mothers.

Brigitte Bardot's hero was her father, Pilou. It was his assumption that she could and would be a star in everything she chose to do. She never thought that women were in any way disadvantaged by their sex. She never thought they should keep themselves apart. To most people of her class and generation sex was the great act of collaboration with woman's natural enemy – man. It could only be performed once a treaty had been drawn up. Bardot is never subtle, never circumspect and she never was. She is no respecter of convention. She never learned to be tactful as a spoiled child. She will flirt with absolutely anybody who can do her a good turn. Whatever passes between them, she doesn't feel she owes them anything. In this respect she is completely amoral. One casual lover of hers remembers how they both went out to dinner one night to the restaurant owned by the local mayor. Bardot told her friend that the object was to spend money – she also told him to pick up the cheque. She wanted a road to be made up near her house and since this was entirely in the gift of the town council she was determined to flatter the mayor. After dinner he came to sit with them at the table. 'She flirted outrageously all because of this dirt-track leading up to her property,' her boyfriend says, adding that he had no cause to be jealous considering the off-on arrangement between Bardot and himself, a married man. Brigitte got her road.

Not to conform to sexual expectations and not to do so publicly was a revolutionary attitude at the time. Lots of people jumped on to that bandwagon but though imitation may be the sincerest form of flattery, it means that the original model must change the rules. Bardot pulled the veil down again as she went into retirement. Pilou would have liked a daughter to behave that way.

Bardot is obsessed with how to make the transition from sex-object to solid citizen. 'It is terrible, obscene to think one will one day look like an old map of France,' she says. 'It is extremely difficult for a woman to grow old. It is very difficult to say to oneself one was beautiful or one was passable and that one day one will be covered in wrinkles.'

'I cannot imagine myself at sixty,' she was saying at thirty-five, the age when a woman first starts taking seriously the idea that she will be. 'I am Brigitte Bardot, and that Brigitte Bardot, the one I see in the magazines and the newspapers, the one who is up on the movie screen, that Brigitte Bardot will never be sixty. Don't you agree?'

That Brigitte haunts her and in these days of modern technology she has more than her memory to rely upon. As well as her films Bardot has all her family snaps and her father's films but she is about as keen on running them as she is on looking in the mirror at noon. In fact she looks good, though that chameleon face described by Fellini tends more to resemble Mae West, Jeanne

Moreau, or Simone Signoret than Jane Fonda, Marilyn Monroe, or Raquel Welch. She is active but she is not young and that thought is a millstone to someone who can vividly recall her days as a little dancer on the cusp of life when she didn't appear to have a body at all – a totally free spirit. The indignity of sharing a common fate is overwhelming. Where is the comfort in knowing her waist will thicken because the waist of every middle-aged woman thickens? There are no compromises to be made with the rest of mankind, its feet of clay and thighs of cellulite, she simply wills it not to be true and when even her will is seen to be powerless as Canute, she does not always take it philosophically.

Joe Mankiewicz, the American director, believes that the transition is especially difficult for the actress. Here he is putting some words into the mouth of his creation Margo Channing in the Oscar-winning film *All About Eve*: ' "I'm forty and maybe a bit more – I have had a highly successful and gratifying public identity which, since age four, has also functioned as my private identity, but which is not me – and when that public identity, that alias, ceases to exist, which will be any day now, I just don't know what the hell will be there in its place - and I love a man who, in turn, can love only the identity which I am about to lose because he has never known any other as me." This is a very special problem, believe me. Indigenous to the female of the theatre folk.'

That was exactly Brigitte's position when she retired from the cinema in her fortieth year. She had been a stage child since she could stand up and she was in love with Laurent Vergez who had been pulled in by Vadim to get a famous and insecure actress through a sticky patch. He loved the actress but he left the woman. She discovered that you could become just as insecure away from the limelight.

Superstars adjust very poorly to life without it and lately the medical profession has found a chemical reason for this. Professor Ivor Hill of the University of Cambridge Clinical School claims that excitement releases morphine-like substances into the body creating as genuine a problem of addiction as heroin. Everyone who has come into contact with human beings on the wave of great personal success knows how provocative they can be when they are high like this, daring other people to object to their wildest utterances and behaviour in a constant search for stimulation. Brigitte certainly knew this. Jumping from man to man, packing their bags and putting them outside the front door of La

Madrague, she broke down social barriers and wrote new rules which were copied by the man in the street. But the man in the street is resilient and cautious compared to the star who is left only with withdrawal symptoms. At this point there is only one overdose left, for the chance of a shot of fame is passed. The super-opiate, the final endomorphine beckons – death – the ultimate tranquillizer. If it will not come naturally, it must be summoned. If it is not summoned by an outraged public, pro-voked and then abandoned by the star himself, if no John Hinckley will do this work, you must turn the gun upon yourself. In many ways it is an unhealthy life Bardot leads, obsessed with ugliness and planning her interment next to her parents.

Her first suicide attempt occurred when she was only eighteen. Her second on her twenty-sixth birthday. Then she seems to have called a truce with herself till her birthday last year when the same thing happened. She organized a birthday celebration at her favourite restaurant, Chez Palmyre, for around a dozen friends. She ordered her favourite food, lobster and paella, and was expecting her boyfriend, Alain Bougrain-Dubourg, to take the plane down from Paris in time for the meal. She was childishly excited. Alain didn't turn up. Brigitte started drinking and one way or another she ended up in the Mediterranean. She was found by a neighbour and the story was in the world's Press the next day. They were expecting it just as they will be expecting it on every successive birthday. Vadim went to her side to discover that there was nothing really very dramatic wrong. 'It is always the little things that get to her.'

'Sex and death', those are the twin pillars of Brigitte Bardot's horoscope according to astrologer Russell T. Grant. There can scarcely be a woman alive who has not at some time looked for an excuse from the occult and Bardot certainly fits into that category. She will recite the characteristics of a Libra at the drop of a hat. Grant asked me to give him the birth date, time and place, and the sex of my subject but not to reveal her identity. Though he also claims to be psychic I was quite surprised at the apparently accurate character analysis his reading provided. 'This is the chart of an extremely beautiful woman,' he said, 'but also a very unstable one. Her destiny is not to be able to hold on to any relationship. She desperately wants the relationship and then she has to kill it. She has to go through the agony as well as the ecstasy. She'll choose any excuse to find fault with a man once this mood sets in. It's a sign which is constantly waiting for the white knight to ride in but even if he does the passion cools all of a sudden. This particular person, with Mars squaring the ascendant, looks like a man-eater. She's captivating, enchanting, she likes to wear baby blues and baby pinks, she looks all milk and honey. But she's a prick-teaser. She's a torrid, randy, sexy, amazingly orgasmic woman who nevertheless has a hatred of men. Her father might have been austere, Victorian, remote, there was some difficulty in her relationship with him and a very feeble relationship with the mother, almost as if she dictated the relationship with her rather than vice versa. Anyway the result is this person could outdo Henry VIII in terms of marriages, not all of them legitimized. I see whirlwind three-day affairs after which she does not know how to get out of the situation without hurting somebody. Reality is not enough. She wants to create a world which doesn't exist. She has to kill someone, so to speak, in order to recreate herself. So, she'll go overboard with passion one minute – and then go off and buy a dog.

'I'm serious – with Jupiter in the first house there is an adoration of animals. It goes deeper than mere love, this girl could be the Mother Teresa of the animal world, a nurse, a martyr even. There's a terrible fear of pain and hurt to other creatures. Animals could even take the place of men, but men are very important.'

I asked Russell what sort of profession he envisaged for our subject. 'Fashion, some sort of trendsetter,' was his immediate reply. Then music, then film or theatre. It would have to be glamorous. 'But with the Sun in the twelfth house this person longs to be famous, coupled with a fear of fame. This is the most furtive of signs. It tends to shun or run away from anything too public. I call it the Queen Victoria syndrome – a need to escape from reality. It's a typical fag-hag sign too. If she hasn't got a homosexual man in her life it won't be long before she has, and he moves in with her.

'The immediate future doesn't look easy for her. I see big emotional problems for a couple of years, a nervous breakdown even, with Uranus attacking the moon. She seems to have lost somebody very important to her – a man or a mother-figure. She has been unstable in the past, full of self-inflicted neuroses, failures, attempted suicides. There looks like an abortion along the way to me, or two or three, because childbirth was anathema to her. She probably had one baby – in wedlock or out – just to try it but the child would not be treated as a child, more like a brother or sister.

'She needs a lot of laughter. Then as soon as she has laughed she will go into a morbid mood. She's volatile, obsessive. She should stay right away from drink, narcotics, intoxicants. She must curb this frenetic path through some sort of creative endeavour like writing, which is different from creative outlets in the past. She must get away from her morbid fears even if it means regular trips to the psychiatrist. She could end up with a close lesbian relationship if she would allow herself to do so, but in the end it is men, men and always younger men. They must be pretty. She doesn't want to get old and her attitude is: "If I have to go, I'll damn well go looking beautiful." '

Grant ended up by saying: 'This is a very fated sign and the people this particular chart most brings to mind are Judy Garland and Marilyn Monroe. These people are like the Phoenix, something has to die all through their lives for there to be a rebirth out of the ashes. It could end up in the worst possible way. This person has already opted out of society – she could opt out of the world.'

Christine Gouze-Renal thought that Bardot had exorcized the instability with that first suicide attempt on which *Vie Privée* was based. 'She will age magnificently now the big crisis is over,' she said. 'Her strength had to come from within, as it did. The deepest despairs of her youth are over. She has come out of the shadows, out of the valley . . . '

Roger Vadim, who knows her as well as anyone, thinks she is suspended in time. He bet a lot of money that she would have to retire for good and so far he has held on to it. 'It is difficult for a child to conceive an artificial world which obeys her laws and gravitates around her. She is now over forty and she has not stepped out of that world. At fifteen she was a young girl who seemed to be ahead of her time. In rebellion against her parents' morality and milieu, endowed with an innate instinct for love, an aware and lucid mind and a fine sense of humour, she was very much an infant prodigy. But Mozart never grew up.'

There is a lot of the child in every artist, which accounts for his raw and energetic vision, but his consolation in the grown-up world is his art. Brigitte does not have this consolation while she refuses to take any talent she might have to its logical ends. She never performs without being driven, which is a legacy of her

276

comfortable bourgeois background. Let drive people call this lazy, the comfortable middle classes are biddable on account of their overwhelming desire to please and conform. When this clashes with a bit of natural spirit the attempt to reconcile the two is a form of curse. For a long time Vadim has thought all her nervousness and reluctance to prove herself stems from her clash with her background. It is to re-create childhood that she has surrounded herself with animals, and even old people. She is in mourning for a childhood that may not pass yet will not stay. 'She was a little anarchist, now she has become as bourgeois as her parents,' he says. 'She will only make another picture if she needs the money and if someone comes up with a script about a girl who falls in love with a seal.'

Other people think the past ten years have been spent adapting to the final inevitability that her looks will fade and that she will find consolation in her talent. One of these is Louis Malle. Though *Vie Privée* takes the ultimate pessimistic view of the penalties of fame, Malle believes things don't have to be so. 'If she can make the transition in her mind to playing different parts she could be one of the great French comediennes,' he told me, 'a rival to Danielle Darrieux with a similar sort of career. She was a sex-symbol in the thirties, then she went away for a while and came back as a great success in comedy. Brigitte has the same talent. She is quite as good as Danielle Darrieux. She could play anything she wants to – she only has to want to do it.'

Jeanne Moreau, a colleague and neighbour, is not the only person to say Bardot won't return to the screen. Moreau speaks very tenderly of Bardot, like a woman of the world who knows how very difficult these things are to other women and would not dare criticize the way those women handle them. 'Scarcely six years separate Brigitte from Jeanne Moreau,' observed Marguerite Duras. 'But they are an abyss. One day Jeanne took her age in her hands, studied it carefully and told it: "Let's make a deal. I shall become less and less young – that's only fair. But you must never again catch me unawares." '

Last year on a visit to St-Tropez, I also visited Moreau in the house which she had bought in the South of France, persuaded by Brigitte. She was the girl who could do absolutely anything on-screen according to François Truffaut. There she was, the real Moreau, with that curious little girl's walk, her little hands turned out to balance her among the grass and acorns underfoot. She

277

wore a slide in her hair, a simple dress and no make-up and, at the age of fifty-five she looked like a little girl still, on whose face life, like a skilful make-up man, might still paint any picture it wanted. As we talked Moreau looked alternately like herself, like Simone Signoret, like Bette Davis, like Brigitte Bardot even. She was waiting for a part and she had no idea what it might be. Meanwhile there was the beautiful shuttered, flagstoned house with its grounds and its swimming pool to keep up. Its vineyards lay unworked since the death of her father. She rationalized that it was the end of an era and time to move on.

Moreau and Brigitte are two actresses caught in the same dilemma. They decided to approach it in different ways but in truth the end result was the same. They both had to grow old in a very different climate from Sarah Bernhardt, who could play Hamlet at eighty at a distance under gas-light. Bardot and Moreau were not only combating the close-up camera but also the terrible compulsion of the century for a new story before the old one had even died. The avarice of the media is the hallmark of post-war times. When the post-war baby boom threw up a host of young adults in the affluent sixties they directed themselves in one way or another towards the media to make their living. These were the children of peace and privilege who had had more leisure time than ever before to read books and to watch movies and to make music. Most of them thought they could make books, movies and music and invent governments just as good as the ones that had educated them, but their assumption produced a strange form of endoscopic art – the art of navel-watching. With experience not of life but only of art itself, thousands of young men and women wrote about writing or painted about painting or made music about music, concentrating on form rather than content, the new rather than the tried. They had the techniques all right but they had never done their apprenticeship in the life-class. The media has become Don Juan violating territory which used to be sacred and virgin. Experience only relegates people to the scrapheap.

The relaxed attitude to morality fostered by Brigitte in her youth should have provided a break for the older generation. In her mother's day it was simply unthinkable for a middle-class woman with an honest position in society to let down her hair and wear it unkempt and dyed blonde. She would not have gone barefoot in a restaurant or worn a bikini on the beach. Her defence against age would have been to dress and behave in a seemly fashion which would encourage the respect, not the advances, of younger men. Now there is no such defence against age. Fifty is younger than it used to be because the people who invented the youth movement are now fifty. They are jogging, wearing combed cotton and painted on freckles – Bardot's invention with the help of Christian Kalt – but in inventing it they consigned themselves to the old people's home. Moreau, the magnificent actress, had to act out her redundancy, become a parody of herself, a woman in a film of narcissistic men in order to finance someone else's improbable project, Fassbinder's last film *Querelle*, yet there was an internal logic to her accepting the part, the logic of *la Ronde*. She had known Genet for a long time, Fassbinder adored *Viva Maria*, he saw it eight times, and saw Brigitte and her as the forerunner of the Baader-Meinhof girls. Moreau staked her hopes on Fassbinder who let her down by dying. Bardot has not so much compassion for other people as to invite them to do that to her.

In her more positive moods Brigitte says 'I do believe every age has its pleasures and that each stage of life brings something different. I am not the same person I was at twenty and I expect that as I get older and older I won't be the same person I am now. It is either that or Death. And as I have no wish to die I'll just have to accept growing old and I just think it is a good thing that these things happen slowly so one can get used to one's new face. When it comes down to it a face is a book, it is the story of a life and the people in it. There are laughter lines and lines of tears, lines of bitterness and sadness. I had my first wrinkle a long time ago, around the age of thirty. Now I have quite a lot of them and if you knew how to read my face you would have a field-day.'

Bardot, a creation of the media, not of her own desperation to escape mediocrity like Marilyn Monroe, should have a core which remains untouched. She has family and therefore an investment in the future, and as a major legend of our time she is well set up and well connected. Vadim says there will be no more stars of his creation or of anyone else's. We live in a world where there is too much bureaucracy, dominated too much by politicians for anyone to make an effective, individual, glamorous stand. Bardot was the last. The memories of influential people are short and cruel when one of their number appears to fall by the wayside, but Bardot always managed to encourage curiosity about her fate even when she decided to retire from the public gaze. If she really needed to summon help she could begin in the highest places. Some Common Market Politicians are even now trying to persuade her to sing for them. Her lawyer, M. Robert Badinter, is now French Minister of Justice. Her former best friend, Christine Gouze-Renal, became the President's sister-in-law.

There are two predictions for the future. One, offered by a friend, is that one final boyfriend will replace Alain Bougrain-Dubourg. This will be the man who undertakes to ghost the memoirs she has been writing for the past five years. He too will leave her when the job is done and that will be the final blow.

The other, altogether preferable, is offered by Louis Malle. In some ways he says Bardot's life has been pathetic in the past. Where Moreau has had thousands of experiences, has loved both men and women from all walks of life and crossed all social barriers and she has her memories and experiences to help her age, so Bardot has been blinkered and afraid. 'She has spent her life with male bimbos,' he says, 'but I have no doubt that she will make a come-back on-screen, that she will be good and that this will be her revenge.'

Filmography

Translations are given in brackets, English and American titles in italics.

1952   Le Trou Normand (The Pub in Normandy), *Crazy for Love* – director Jean Boyer

1952   Manina, La Fille Sans Voile (Manina, the Girl Without a Veil), *The Lighthouse Keeper's Daughter, The Girl in the Bikini* – director Willy Rozier

1952   Les Dents Longues (Long in the Tooth) – director Daniel Gelin

1953   Le Portrait de son Père (The Image of his Father) – director André Berthómieu

1953   *Act of Love* – director Anatole Litvak

1953   Si Versaille M'Était Conte (If Versaille Could Talk) – director Sacha Guitry

1954   Tradita (Betrayal), *Night of Love* – director Mario Bonnard

1954   *Helen of Troy* – director Robert Wise

1954   Le Fils de Caroline Chérie (Son of Dear Caroline) – director Jean Devaivre

1955   Futures Vedettes (Futures Stars), *Sweet Sixteen* – director Marc Allegret

1955   *Doctor at Sea* – director Ralph Thomas

1955   Les Grandes Manouevres (Grand Manoeuvres), *Summer Manoeuvres* – director René Clair

1955   La Lumière d'en Face, *The Light Across the Street* – director Georges Lacombe

1955   Cette Sacrée Gamine (That Goddam' Girl), *Mam'zelle Pigalle* – director Michel Boisrond

1956   Mio Figlio Nerone (My Son Nero) – director Stefano Vanzina

1956   En Effeuillant la Marguerite (Plucking the Daisy), *Mam'zelle Striptease, Please Mr Balzac* – director Marc Allegret

1956   Et Dieu Créa La Femme, *And God Created Woman, And Woman was Created* – director Roger Vadim

1956   La Mariée est Trop Belle (The Bride is Too Beautiful), *The Bride is much too Beautiful* – director Pierre Gaspard-Huit

1957   Une Parisienne (A Parisian Girl) – director Michel Boisrond

1957   Les Bijoutiers du Clair de Lune (The Moonlight Jewellers), *Heaven Fell that Night* – director Roger Vadim

1957   En Cas de Malheur (In Case of Adversity), *Love is my Profession* – director Claude Autant-Lara

1958   La Femme et le Pantin (The Woman and the Puppet), *A Woman Like Satan, The Female* – director Julien Duvivier

1959   Babette s'en va-t-en Guerre, *Babette goes to War* – director Christian-Jacque

1959   Voulez-vous Danser Avec Moi (Will You Dance with Me), *Come Dance with Me* – director Michel Boisrond

1960   L'Affaire d'Une Nuit, *It Happened at Night* – director Henri Verneuil

1960   La Vérité, *The Truth* – director Henri-Georges Clouzot

1961   La Bride sur le Cou (Loose Reins), *Please Not Now, Only For Love* – director Roger Vadim

1961   Les Amours Célèbres (Famous Love-Affairs) – director Michel Boisrond

1961   Vie Privée (Private Life), *A Very Private Affair* – director Louis Malle

1962   Le Repos du Guerrier, *Warrior's Rest, Love on a Pillow* – director Roger Vadim

1963   Le Mépris, *Contempt, A Ghost at Noon* – director Jean-Luc Godard

1963   Paparazzi – director Jacques Rozier

1963   Tentazioni Proibite (Forbidden Temptations) – director F. Oswaldo Civirani

1963   Une Ravissante Idiote, *A Ravishing Idiot, Adorable Idiot, Bewitching Scatterbrain* – director Edouard Molinaro

1964   Marie Soleil – director Antoine Bourseiller

1965   *Dear Brigitte* – director Henry Koster

1965   *Viva Maria* – director Louis Malle

1965   Masculin-Féminin, *Masculine and Feminine* – director Jean-Luc Godard

1966   A Coeur Joie (Glad at Heart), *Two Weeks in September* – director Serge Bourguignon

1967   Histoires Extraordinaires (Extraordinary Tales), *Tales of Mystery and Imagination, Spirits of the Dead* – director Louis Malle

1968   *Shalako* – director Edward Dmytryk

1969   Les Femmes (The Women) – director Jean Aurel

1970   L'Ours et la Poupée (The Bear and the Doll) – director Michel Deville

1970   Les Novices, *The Novices* – director Guy Casaril

1970   Boulevard du Rhum – director Robert Enrico

1970   Les Pétroleuses (The Oil Girls), *The Legend of Frenchie King* – director Christian-Jacque

1973   Don Juan 1973, Si Don Juan Était Une Femme, *If Don Juan were a Woman* – director Roger Vadim

1973   L'Histoire très Bonne et très Joyeuse de Colinot Trousse-Chemise (The Good and Happy Tale of Colinot Lifter-of-Skirts) – director Nina Companeez

Select Bibliography

Aronson, Steven M.L., *Hype*, William Morrow, New York, 1983

Beauvoir, Simone de, *Brigitte Bardot and the Lolita Syndrome*, Weidenfeld & Nicolson, 1960

  Must We Burn Sade?, John Calder, 1962

Camus, Albert, *L'Étranger*, Gallimard, 1944

Caron, Leslie, *Vengeance*, Weidenfeld & Nicolson, 1983

Colette, *Minna*, Ollendorf, 1904

Crawley, Tony, *Bébé: the Films of Brigitte Bardot*, Citadel, New York and LSP Books, 1975

Dalton, David, *James Dean, The Mutant King*, Plexus, 1974

Evans, Peter, *Bardot*, Frewin, 1972

Frischauer, Willi, *Bardot: an Intimate Biography*, Michael Joseph, 1978

Guiles, Fred Lawrence, *Jane Fonda: the Actress in Her Time*, Michael Joseph, 1981

Haining, Peter, *Bardot*, W.H. Allen, 1983

Hayman, Ronald, *De Sade: a Critical Biography*, Constable, 1978

Johnson, Paul, *A History of the Modern World*, Weidenfeld & Nicolson, 1983

Mailer, Norman, *Marilyn: a Biography*, Grosset & Dunlap, New York and Hodder & Stoughton, 1973

Mankiewicz, J., *More About All About Eve*, Random House, New York, 1972

Montserrat, Joelle, *Brigitte Bardot*, Éditions PAC, 1984

Morgan, Michèle, *With Those Eyes*, W.H. Allen, 1978

Parturier, Françoise, *Les Hauts de Ramatuelle*, Michel Albin, 1983

Richardson, Joanna, *Colette*, Methuen, 1983

Sagan, Françoise, *Bonjour Tristesse*, John Murray, 1955 and Penguin, 1958

  Réponses, Jean-Jacques Pauvert, 1974 and Ram Publishing Company, 1979

Sarde, Michèle, *Colette: Free and Fettered*, Stock, Paris, 1978 and
    Michael Joseph, 1981
Ségur, Comtesse de, *Les Malheurs de Sophie*, Hachette, Paris, 1974
Signoret, Simone, *Nostalgia Isn't What it Used to be*, Weidenfeld &
    Nicolson, 1978
Tomkins, Calvin, *Living Well is the Best Revenge*, André Deutsch,
    1972
Vadim, Roger, *Memoirs of the Devil*, Hutchinson, 1976
    The Hungry Angel, Sidgwick & Jackson, 1984
Zeldin, Theodore, *The French*, Collins, 1983

Among the many magazines and newspapers also consulted the
following proved particularly helpful: *Paris-Match, Cahiers du
Cinéma, Cinémonde, Ciné Revue, L'Express, Le Figaro, Le Monde,
Variety, Playboy, New York Times, Sunday Express, Daily Express,
Daily Mail, Evening Standard, Daily Mirror, Guardian, Sunday
Times* and *The Times*

Index

286